POLITICALLY ERECT

Paddy Kelly

POLITICALLY ERECT

A FICTION4ALL PAPERBACK

© Copyright 2018
Paddy Kelly

The right of Paddy Kelly to be identified as author of this work has been asserted by him in accordance with the Copyright, Designs and Patents Act 1988

All Rights Reserved

No reproduction, copy or transmission of the publication may be made without written permission. No paragraph of this publication may be reproduced, copied or transmitted save with the written permission of the publisher, or in accordance.with the provisions of the Copyright Act 1956 (as amended).

Any person who does any unauthorised act in relation to this publication may be liable to criminal prosecution and civil claims for damages.

ISBN 978-1-78695-184-7

Cover Designed by:
Paddy Kelly

Edited by:
Katherine Mary Kennedy, B.A.

This Edition Published 2018
Fiction4All
www.fiction4all.com

Paddy Kelly

Acknowledgments

There are so many to thank for making this story possible, it is difficult to know where to begin. Listed below are but a few of the plethora who have contributed so much. As it would be impossible to rank one above the other and the order of listing in no way indicates the importance of each contributor.

First and foremost heart felt thanks to the hundreds of court judges who gave so many minor or first time young offenders the choice of prison, where they would be housed with murderers, thieves and rapists or enlistment in the U.S. Army where they could learn from professionals.

To the U.S. Ambassador in Saigon who, in the Spring of '75, so nobly wanted everyone to stay and greet the oncoming Communist hordes as brothers-in-arms despite the fact they wanted to disembowel us in public and feed our entrails to the fish in the South China Sea.

And to the thousands of officers and enlisted men who, like those of the first Gulf Training Exercise and the current contrived Gulf War, despite never having been anywhere near the Persian Gulf, awarded themselves thousands and thousands of decorations and awards. Such men and women of the United States armed forces, much like Teddy's mythical charge up San Juan Hill, have followed in a fine tradition.

Lastly, I would like to personally thank Petty Officer First Class, 'Omon'a-tell-you-what-boy!'

Politically Erect

Stump for submitting the wrong personnel file to my Commanding Officer when attempting to bring me to Captain's Mast nd put me in the brig for the treasonous crime of not swabbing the deck to his satisfaction, which thus caused the case against me to be dismissed. Just like that guy named William Jefferson Clinton he done Arkansas proud, boy.

However, time spent in the Navy, regardless of how much, is never wasted, particularly when you're eighteen years old. The phrase that sticks in my mind is the one a crusty old chief petty officer gave us while we were standing bald-headed, in full uniform in the blazing 100 dgree heat of Camp Nimitz in San Diego just after they issued us our 1,000 pounds or so of gear.

"You get out of it what you put into it!" Is what he told us. He was right. Plain and simple. Like marriage. Only without the kids. The drinking and the fighting and the . . . Sorrry! I digress.

The Navy taught me and reinforced a value system which, thanks mostly to those who oppose meritocricy and fight to establish the ridiculous standard of equality of outcome, is taking something of a beating in the contempoary U.S. In the military, particularly during war time, there can be no substitute for meritocracy. The best man for the job is the only credo. Okay, to what's left of you feminists out there – the best **man or woman** for the job.

Regarding *Politically Erect*, as I always remind my students, art must be evaluated in the context of the times in which it was created. To judge a work in the context of modern times ten, twenty or one hundred years after its creation is disingenuous, damaging to the experience you seek and dilutes the potential educational or entertainment value one might garner from it. This story is set in the first half of the Seventies, a time which was definitly a time far removed from an era marked by mobile phones, a war on books and a period where we can peek back over 14 billion light years through space and into the past.

Politically Erect

Paddy Kelly

To my eternal Muse:

**Natasha Feordarova Kavolchuck.
Murdered by her husband at the age of
28 years old.**

Only the good die young.

R.I.P.

Politically Erect

ALSO FOR THE THOUSANDS WHO, DURING THE WAR IN VIET NAM, THROUGH INCOMPETENT LEADERSHIP, PAID THE ULTIMATE PRICE.

Paddy Kelly

INTRODUCTION

This is one of the books that I've waited years to write, primarily because I didn't know I was going to be a writer and I was too busy for the better part of the first fifty years globe hopping, enjoying life, being too self-absorbed to forge a long-term relationship in marriage and just generally going around making a pain-in-the-ass of myself. Now I have the next fifty years to focus on writing and then I can retire and enjoy my older years.

The concpet came to me while managing the emergency room of the Mayport Naval Dispensary in Mayport Florida outside of Jacksonville back during the war.

CHRIST! That makes me sound old. I'm talkin' like Archie Bunker old. (Look him up).

One primary characteristic used to define courage is the ability to act in the face of mortal danger despite one's fear.

A secondary characteristic I believe, is the ability to joke in the face of extreme adversity, whether motivated by defiance or fear. The old 1960's poster of the little mouse flipping off the attacking eagle who is brandishing his talons as he swoops in to gobble up the helpless little mouse never fails to garner a smile.

I clearly remember Icelanders cracking jokes as they stood by and watched the Eldfell volcano's firey rise form the earth consuming their cars, homes and livelyhoods back in '73 or the dozen German civilians from the local village who pulled up lawn chairs and ripped open some beers as they sat and cracked jokes with the poor German parachutists trapped in 250 foot high beech trees waiting to fall to their deaths because

Politically Erect

the fire brigade couldn't get a ladder truck in through the trees. We, (my Special Ops team and I), rigged climbing harnesses, climbed up and rescued them. Needless to say we drank for free all night long in the village.

Joking is certainly a way of dealing with nerves.

The point is self-preservation is a strong instinct and no man can be blamed for not taking action which would indanger his life.

Unless he signed on for that job.

So it was some of the greatest experiencs of my life to have worked with guys who, despite some of them dying or being injured, pushed on spewing snide remarks which seemed to become more clever as the danger increased.

So to men like Tony and Ron, RIP guys. It was great working with you.

Technically this is a work of fiction however all the stories and anecdotes are factual and each chapter is preceeded by a snatch of gratfittii I collected during the Viet Nam conflict. I mean War. No wait . . . I mean Police Action. Yeah, that's it – Police Action. Gosh darn those wily politicians! They got a proper lable for everything. I guess that's what happens when you let lawyers become politicians then they figure out a way to start running the show.

Enjoy the read!

- P. Kelly

Paddy Kelly

CHAPTER ONE

In the Summer of 1971 there were only three ways out of the soul crushing, abject poverty of the Jersey City shit hole of a slum they called The Duncan Avenue Federal Housing Projects: prison, the military or the likely end to both, death. A leftover relic from Lyndon Johnson's failed attempt at the establishment of the Great Society, "Da Projekts" were touted as "affordable housing for the poor." In reality they were a place where people grew old before their time as they gradually came to grips with the fact that this was probably their last stop on the way down before they, along with millions of other Americans, fell off the property ladder altogether into the bottomless depths of the 'Less Fortunate' as they were euphemistically branded.

Located in the ass end of one of the most decrepit residential neighborhoods in one of the most run down, industrial centers on the Eastern Seaboard, it was no coincidence that the nine, thirteen storied buildings on Duncan Avenue were built from plans rejected by the Federal Prison system.

In reality it was a way to keep all the immigrant, unemployed and minority scum away from Da Decent Folk and out of the game altogether.

On the other hand, the average death rate of about one to two people per day in the Projects probably scared the shit out of the surrounding property owners and to some extent contributed to life in that shit hole and the life style that Billy Chance grew up in but at that young age came to regard as a constant adventure.

With the spontaneous eruptions of gang fights, a sporadic police presence and the occasional crazy walking through the streets shooting at anything that

Politically Erect

moved, Billy, with an Irish Father and a Sicilian mother, along with his friends, all of which were black, saw life as something out of a Marvel comic book.

Jersey City held numerous distinctions as a city, to include having several of its mayors and their staff investigated and arrested by the Feds for everything from Grand Larceny to forged citizenship, accessories to murder and serving as the primary operating grounds for most of The Mafia's trucking and shipping crimes.

Not coincidentally the William L. Dickinson High School, (Billy's Alma mater), had the honor of being the first and only U.S. high school to be investigated, taken over and closed down by the Federal Department of Education, a cabinet level office which came about by laws largely founded on the evolution of what Dickinson had become and the numerous prosecutions following its closure.

The criminal charges? As they say in medical parlance
when bacteria are detected in an infection, TNTC. Too Numerous To Count.

Apparently topping the popularity chart of illicit activity was teachers buying drugs from students, gang violence and teachers selling drugs to students. Teachers engaging in frequent sexual activity with students, cooperation with local bookies for betting on high school football games and students engaging in frequent sexual activity with teachers, both on and off school grounds. Teachers helping students cheat on exams and the proverbial last straw, something involving the football team and a mature sheep.

This last one may sound worse than it actually was as the school's mascot was, after all, a ram.

Go Rams!

Paddy Kelly

At the week-long federal hearings in D.C., to their credit, the teachers vehemently denied ever helping students cheat on exams.

Even teachers have lines they won't cross.

Looking back on it, it's hard to imagine a more stifling atmosphere then a place where, for kids under 18, school was little more than a surrogate day care center with crime education classes on the side. The neighborhood grocery stores were surrounded by iron bars, there were daily shootings and the cops were never to be seen. Hell, it was the cops, when they were there, who were doing most of the shooting. The rest of the time it was the cops who were getting shot at.

Chance often stated later that he took two of the most important lessons in his life away from that inner-city war zone. His loss of the fear of death and an appreciation for the Black perspective.

The Blacks, Whites only comprised about ten percent of the neighborhood at the time, never saw Italians, Irish, Poles or French. Only Black and White. A distorted lens perspective which most of them would carry with them the rest of their lives.

They may have had good reason.

Having been stripped of their culture over the last 300 years and never really being afforded the opportunity to develop their own indigenous language or customs, they quite naturally had little appreciation for anything from somewhere as distant as planet Europe. They were probably the first as a people in the U.S. to come to grips with the reality that America truly was the land of the free where even the Presidential Suite at the Hotel Hilton was open to anyone. As long as you could afford it. A quiant system inherited from our English cousins

Point is, it was the Blacks who taught young Chance how to run, dance, play American football, baseball,

Politically Erect

music, how to fight and how to . . . well you know. Women.

The nickname 'Whitey' was never taken offensively by Chance but worn as a badge of honor, of belonging, to the point where life-long bonds were formed. It was with this maybe-not-so-unique point of view that Billy Chance set out to pursue what he was taught to believe is that noblest of all professions, medicine.

All he'd have to do is finish high school, (something no one else in his family had ever done before), find a shit load of money, (something else no one else in his family had ever done), and get accepted to college, something no one . . . well . . . you get the idea.

After that of course he'd have to find a shit load more money, get accepted to and graduate from med school.

Being poverty stricken in the extreme, the fastest, most reliable route available leading to an education in the medical arts was the U.S. military. That, and people tended not to trust you with narcotics and sharp instruments if you'd done hard time so, due to their limited earning potential and long term prospects, death and prison had been immediately ruled out as a career paths.

But, fortunatly there was a solution.

Billy had once read on a protest sign that war was good business. The protest sign was being brandished by somebody at Harvard and Harvard was an Ivy League school. It was the law of averages that anybody at Harvard must be smart and as luck would have it there just happened to be a war on and what'a ya know? America was recruiting! Billy Chance had a brain storm, (or a brain cramp, depending on how you look at it). He would go to war.

Back at City University New York, when Chance

started his journey into adulthood, career and a new life according to the dictates of the American Dream by accidentally stumbling into an athletic scholarship, Professor Carroll told him that over 80% of Classic Western literature opened with the protagonist coming back from or embarking on a journey.

Little did Billy realize, as he sat at his desk in the middle of the Burmese jungle, that when he started this journey yesterday, nearlynforty years ago, that he would wind up in this place, here, where he was now.

Maybe that's because Professor Carroll never mentioned that, in those old Greek stories, no matter where the hero started from, he never wound up where he intended. Or, just as those wily ancient Greeks intended, the journey was never real, only metaphorical.

Additionally, war would turn out to be nothtng like in the John Wayne, WWII movies Billy was raised on.

That Chance would learn the hard way.

Politically Erect

UNCHECKED CAPITALISM WILL ALWAYS OVERCOME DEMOCRACY

Paddy Kelly

```
William W. Chance Jr.
Apt 1106, Bldg 1
Federal Housing Project
Duncan Ave. Jersey City, N.J.

SA William W. Chance III
U.S. Naval Air Station,
Keflavik, Iceland
```

January 24, 1973

Dear Mom;

Happy New Year! Coming up on my one year anniversary in the Nav and still no orders to Corps School. Guess they had no sense of humor about me quitting weather school. That plus with the war winding down they're probably not too keen on sending too many of us to expensive schools. I'm told it's well over half a million to train one corpsman.

Things same here, nothing much happening. We had a condition Charlie twice last week, that means no one's allowed outside. Winds hit 145 mph at ground level and temps dropped to 65 below. It's not usually that cold. It rarely dips below minus 50.

I was in a bowling alley when the storm hit, so we were locked in all night until the next day and then again all day into part of the next

Politically Erect

night. But these folks have it all figured out. Where ever you're trapped the owners have to give you food and shelter. They keep track, no matter how much the people eat and drink, and the government compensates them later.

Next time a storm hits I'll have to head for a bar. Jeff, a Marine buddy up here, says he's gonna head for a brothel.

Minor tremors again late last night but earthquake season is nearly over. There's nothing like buildings shaking and streets splitting open in front of you to remind you of the insignificance of . . . well . . . pretty much everything.

Whale meat again for lunch. Not bad once you get used to it.

Dad found any work yet? Hope you guys are hanging in there.

Love you guys.

Me

Paddy Kelly

REMEMBER HUNGARY!
REMEMBER CZECHOSLOVAKIA!
REMEMBER VIET NAM!
VOTE COMMUNIST!

TANKS FOR THE MEMORIES.

Politically Erect

CHAPTER TWO

It was dark. Then again it was always dark. Except for around noon when it was a hazy grey for about forty to forty-five minutes. Then it got dark again. No wonder these guys kept sailing around sailing for new lands!

The grey, metal tubular bunk beds of the 1st Division barracks which lined both sides of the over-sized Quonset hut were exactly one yard apart and numbered exactly three dozen, 18 per side.

1st Division was where they stuck the non-quals, the Enlisted men who had no rank, rate or political connections. In other words, Navy losers. At the time there were only about a half dozen men assigned to 1st Division

The fifty year old deck had been waxed to a nice even warp on both sides and there was a single row of bare light bulbs strung down the center of the overhead.

Billy laid awake one night and pondered those light bulbs and realized an interesting social phenomenon.

Being all about the same age, the men of the 1st D were all raised on WWII movies, you know, the ones where all the patriotic guys go off to war and the women faithfully await their return.

The dirty little secret of how many of those WWII wives and sweethearts actually bailed on the ones they had 'given their hearts to' while those guys were away getting their asses shot off had leaked out over the years but most of the guys signing up or getting drafted to fight in The Nam quickly learned about the dirty little secret of the near 90% divorce rate in the U.S. Navy during that war.

Paddy Kelly

However, some didn't, until it was too late.

The light bulbs, strategically dangled just high enough to prevent a drunk sailor from punching them out when he came back from a rip-snorting bender, all pissed off becuse he just found out through the United States Postal Service that his fiancée, (French for 'who I'm fucking now'), back home in Bald Knob, Arkansas was fucking his best friend's brains out which was why the 1st Division Enlisted barracks at NAS Keflavik spent more money on light bulbs per annum than the Officers Quarters, mess hall and the headquarters buildings combined.

The fact that the letter usually ended with, *'It's not you. It's me.'* was a dead giveaway and probably was what sent him over the top and sank him into an alcohol induced stupor for a week or more.

However, therapy for this fucked-up-like-a-soup-sandwich-in-the-rain situation was thoughtfully provided for by the shipmates of the division. A particularly nasty porno picture from one of the plethora of a multitude of available magazines was torn out, the offending female's head was cut from the wallet photo he always carried and was pasted over it. The new montage, along with the *Dear John* letter was posted on the *Board of Shame* in the barracks.

The light bulb protection stratagy, stringing them higher than normal, worked pretty well until some drunk discovered the long handled broom quietly cowering in the corner. Which is why there was usually a case of 50 replacement bulbs permanently stashed in the closet.

It was late January just after 01:00 in the a.m. and over in the North bay of the Enlisted barracks everyone was tucked in nice and cozy for the night, soundly snoring and farting away when, somewhere in the distance, there was a muffled explosion. It was far enough away that maybe it didn't even happen. Maybe it was part of a dream, that half-awake, half-asleep dream state that may or may not end in a sudden return to reality when some asshole on Night Watch throws on the lights, and starts banging on the bed posts with his night stick and yelling; "GET THE FUCK UP!"

Slowly but steadily a ground tremor grew in force and intensity as the pipe metal beds starting slowly walking across the deck.

"GET THE FUCK UP!" Someone yelled from somewhere as a large window cracked and fell to the deck letting the old flow in.

"What the hell was that?" A voice from the other side of the room called out as the suspended light bulbs started gently swaying.

"GET THE FUCK UP!" Billy sat up in his bunk. Someone had switched on a light but the power generators were failing.

The bulb nearest his bunk quickly came up to full intensity then, along with the rrest of them, as if sensing the need to contribute to the surrealism of the moment, faded down to an eerie, yellow-ish dim, thirty watt glow where they slowly but rhythmically pulsated struggling to power themselves back up.

Still in his skivvies, the skinny Hispanic kid, Joey Hernandez got up and steered himself towards the head.

"Pro'ly yust another . . ." His words trailed off as he stared out the broken, over-sized picture window on the port side of the barracks. Several others joined him. Billy hopped down off his bunk and caught sight of the group huddled around the window, mesmerized like a pack of dogs staring at a freshly cut side of beef hanging in a butcher's window.

Billy made way over to the window. The red-orange

fire ball fanning out across the distant horizon slowly gave birth to a smoke plume which mushroomed in slow motion and rose tens of thousands of feet into the air. Its appearance was so sudden, its speed so lethargic that their minds raced to catch up much less comprehend what their eyes were feeding their brains.

The phosphorescence light of the mushroom cloud revealed the details of the barren, midnight landscape over 100 kilometers away, south on the Vestmannaeyjar Islands.

Billy immediately realized the irony of the full color poster on the back of the barrack's door;

What to do in case of nuclear attack;

1. Drop your trousers.
2. Bend over and spread your legs.
3. Kiss your ass good-bye.

He didn't laugh.

He had signed up less than six months ago to get the hell out of the Jersey City slum his family had fallen into and now, that it was the beginning of the end, Duncan Avenue was the first thing that sprang to mind.

"They blew it! The fucking bastards blew it!" Someone said.

"No fucking way!"

"They told us it would start here!" Someone contributed.

"At least the fuckers were straight up about that!" Came another despondent response.

No one turned, no one looked away from the big window. They just stared and waited for the radiation blast they were told about in training. The real war to end all wars had actually begun.

Politically Erect

"Should be here in less than a minute!"

"Thanks for the fuckin' update!" J.D. snapped.

"We ain't got no NBC suites!" Hernandez panicked.

"Tell me you're not that fucking stupid!" J.D. weakly uttered as he fell back and sat on the edge of his rack. "NBC suits or no NBC suites we're already toast."

Strangely, no one really panicked instead an all pervasive group mood ensued. They accepted their fate, curiously relaxed and let their minds wonder. Would it hurt? How long would it take? What would the folks back home read in the dailies?

More importantly, what would Walter Cronkite say?!

"Good evening ladies and gentlemen, this is Walter Cronkite with the CBS Evening News. This just in – some inconsiderate, unthinking, self-centered bastards in Washington, Moscow or Beijing have decided to fry the world by pushing the button! That's right, THE button! Consequently, we're all fucking toast!" (Right hand drifts to his ear mike)

"I have just been informed that tomorrow night's CBS Evening News will be indefinitely postponed.

And that's the way it is this Tuesday night, January the 23rd."

They all felt pretty stupid fifteen minutes later when one by one it gradually dawned on them that no one's skin was peeling off and no one was puking their guts up which was just about the time a senior petty officer broke into the quarters and gave them the good news.

He explained it was only a Class 4, subduction-zone, strato-volcanic eruption with an accompanying earthquake registering 6.7 to 7.0 on the Richter scale, which, if it kept rising could engulf the entire south western peninsula of the country including their rinky-dink little naval air station, the capital city and 210,000 Icelanders.

He disapeared back out the door as quickly as he had come and the men all breathed a sigh of relief.

At least it wasn't The Bomb.

******

In January of 1973 if you were stationed in Keflavik, Iceland you were so fuckin' far from Uncle Ho and his minions of death that no matter which direction you went in you'd be going towards Viet Nam. And while Viet Nam was unquestionably a helluv'a lot more dangerous, that didn't mean being stationed in Keflavik Naval Air Station you were out of harm's way. Not by a long shot.

While in Viet Nam you had to contend with enemy fire, racial tensions, a population of indig which either didn't want you there or wanted you to do all the fightin' and dyin' for them, all you had in Iceland were earthquakes, volcanoes, 100 MPH winds, ice storms and 50-80 degrees below zero temperatures. But, like in Nam, you still slept with one eye open. And the other one only half shut. Racial tensions weren't an issue in Iceland. Females, military and civilians, were banned from the air station. Except for taking a vacation, blacks simply weren't allowed in country.

As Chance never met a black guy who wanted be stationed in Iceland, (or a white guy who wanted to be stationed there), this never seemed to be an issue.

But even if there were no restrictions on who could be there, everyone still ate, slept and shit with the next earthquake, 100 mile an hour ice storm or possible

Politically Erect

volcano or earthqauke in the front of their minds. At least in a couple of categories, regardless of where you were things stood more or less even in Nam or Kef.

Because you were always getting fucked one way or the other, incompetent leadership and VD remained mutually common problems.

It was incompetent leadership that caused Billy to realize he could never be a 'career sailor', the respectful term for someone intending to spend twenty years or more of their life in the armed forces and it was in the Kef Air Station Enlisted Men's Lounge, the morning after the eruption, that Billy C. first encountered Chief Boatswain's Mate Eugene Amos Stump.

With a cup of steaming hot coffee in one hand, a smoldering, filterless cigarette in the other and both feet up on the U.S. Navy issue end table in front of him, Stump was watching the Armed Forces News on the single channel, 1967, B&W, T.V. set. The story currently airing dealt with the racial violence perpetrating America and centered across the southern states.

Apparently, according to the report, a young black sailor, home on leave from Viet Nam, had been found heavily shackled and drowned in a small backwoods lake in Mississippi. Stump let out a low grunt at the announcement, sucked on his cigarette and slurped some more of his viscous, mud-thick coffee.

"Just like a nigga'. Steal more chains'n he kin swim wit." Stump mumbled at the T.V. no doubt secure in the knowledge the news commentator could hear him.

Stump was a bitter, little anorexic man who apparently associated status with keys because he had a ring of them on his belt that weighed more than he did and which announced his approach three blocks prior to his arrival. This caused him to lean slightly to one side but he cleverly balanced the incongruity by constantly carrying a large mug of coffee in his other hand to bring him back to upright.

When he saluted you could see he had a permanent crook in his right index finger from years of holding thousands of mugs of coffee and a hardened nicotine addict could live off the scrapings of his teeth and finger nails for the better part of a month.

To call him a redneck racist from Arkansas wouldn't be quite fair for two reasons. One, because no one was sure he was actually from Arkansas and two, it wouldn't be fair to redneck racists from Arkansas. He hated everyone nearly the same, he just reserved a special hatred for blacks.

Hispanics, Europeans, Canadians and especially 'Dem God-damned Yankees!'

One of the first stories any FNG, (Fucking New Guy), would hear about Stump was about the time he actually put the entire 1st Division on report, not as a unit, that would be mutiny, but one man at a time. The heinous, war-time charges?

Following one morning's inspection the decks and heads weren't clean enough to suit him.

The guys in Personnel, one of which used to be in 1st Division under Stump, took the extra trouble to calculate that it would cost the Nav upwards of $75,000 to prosecute and punish 17 enlisted men, lock them up and shut down the entire division for 30 days. Conscientious sailor that he was, he felt it his duty to bring this to the C.O.'s attention. You know, to save money, what with a war on and all.

As senior enlisted ranks go, save for the Master Chief of the Navy of which there's only one, there's Chief, Senior Chief and Master Chief being the highest enlisted rank. The used-to-be-Senior Chief now Chief Stump no longer had any sense of humor.

'LIFER' is the disrespectful term for a career sailor, Lazy Inconsiderate Fucker Expecting Retirement. Stump was a LIFER.

Unfortunately he was also the head of 1st Division.

****

In the Vestmannaeyjar archipelago, just south east of the capital, lies an eight square mile island called Heimaey and, the morning after the eruption of the Eldfell volcano is where Billy Chance came to the conclusion that Icelanders truly were god's frozen people.

With a population of 5,000 inhabitants, 10,000 sheep, an unknown number of dogs and a very large quantity of freshly caught fish, (after all, when you live in a country where 90% of the national economy depends on fishing, everything has to be taken into account), and virtually no flat bottomed boats, the planned evacuation from the volcano stricken island was going to take a bit of planning.

In contrast to this, with the brand new baby mountain being born of Mother Earth's bosom at the rate of 10 to 20 meters an hour, Heimaey island was no place for bureaucracy.

Within hours of the eruption at about 03:30 that morning the Prime Minister of Iceland, his cabinet and the whole Althung, or Parliament, were in full swing mobilizing literally the entire population of the country to organize the rescue efforts.

Of course the Chosen Frozen of the 1st Division on their year-long camp out over at Naval Air Station,

Paddy Kelly

Keflavik Iceland, or NAVAIRSTAKEFICE in Nav Speak, were not ones to stand idly by while a volcano erupted only miles away threatening 5,000 helpless civilians, a bunch of sheep and a shit load of fish.

Besides, there were women on that island and where the troops were inside the air base the female to male ratio was an unacceptable zero to three thousand. Unless you counted the three fifty-something year old, 200 pound cooks in the chow hall. Noboady did.

Just as imortantly you couldn't see the volcano good enough.

So with the base so far away from the action how could they get to go home lookin' like heroes if they didn't get over there and start saving all those drop dead gorgeous Vikingettes on the island, rumored to outnumber the men 10 to 1?

No math required.

To show how brave he was, the base Commander of NAVAIRSTAKEFICE immediately radioed NAVFORATCMND, (Naval Forces Atlantic Command), and volunteered everyone on the base to fly over to the tiny island and pitch in with the rescue effort.

NAVFORATCMND sent a twixt message to USNAVCMNDPENT, (United States Naval Forces Command Pentagon), regarding the situation and after an emergency huddle with their mouthpieces, (Navy lawyers), USNAVCMNDPENT sat-comm'ed NAVFORATCMND who radioed the Commander of NAVAIRSTAKEFICE back that, because it was such a dangerous situation, what with the volcano still rising up out of the sea like an inflamed hemorrhoid on Poseidon's ass, the Navy couldn't **make** the men volunteer. Too dangerous. They could only do that if there was proof of an impending Communist threat.

As no proof that the Communists had actually

Politically Erect

initiated the volcano was forthcoming, the Commander would have to **order** the men to volunteer on their own.

Billy Chance and the rest of 1st Division knew this chain of events to be fact because the Crew Chief of the first C-130 Hercules to attempt to land on the island passed the word to the 'volunteers' while they were in flight. In flight being pelted by large chunks of volcanic rock just before they fishtailed 180 degrees onto the improvised, grass runway then skidded to a backwards halt on the formerly grassy field serving as the experimental runway on Heimaey Island. Approximately a yard from the edge of a 200 foot sheer cliff.

It was hailed as a textbook landing.

So, after they revived the co-pilot and got the pilot a clean change of underwear, they taxied the plane back into the wind and the green faced Crew Chief stowed his last, full-to-the-brim barf bag and lowered the three yard long ramp. The men of 1st Division, NAVAIRSTAKEFICE, prepared to storm the tiny, undefended island and do battle with the firebreathing dragon attempting to consume said island.

Fortunately Billy, the first sailor almost off the airplane, was one of the two men in 1st Division to have a high school diploma, and so was able to summon all the knowledge he had been given by his geometry, algebra and calculus teachers to astutely calculate that the 18 inches from the leading edge of the plane's ramp to that 200 foot sheer cliff wasn't quite enough to allow 50 fully loaded sailors and marines to hurry up and get off the aircraft before it was pounded into an expensive piece of junk by the constant hail of fist sized chunks of volcanic rock currently pelting them.

Some time later word finally reached the cockpit, (the men reckoned sent by carrier pigeon), to taxi the airplane forward a few yards, which they did allowing the men to scramble off the by now considerably dinged up C-130 Hercules which immediately took off again dragging the half open ramp down the runway with it.

The newly arrived saviors of the minuscule enclave of Viking descendants were immediately thrown into that most military of phenomena, organised pandemonium, when one by one in rapid succession, amidst the hail of volcanic rock, they came to realize that before leaving the base nobody had thought to issue them helmets.

Fuck me, Alice!

**

It was no happy coincidence that the colors of the U.S. Navy were blue and gold. Sentenced to eight years at All Saints Primary School in Jersey City, New Jersey is where a young Billy Chance and his classmates were sadistically compelled to prominently wear on their uniforms, in bright gold, capital letters on a field of Navy blue, the abbreviation of the school they attended.

The Jersey City was a tough enough place for a ten year old to survive in the jungle of the inner city without having to walk around all day with "ASS" plastered on his tie and across the breast of his dark blue blazer.

It was in the archdiocese of ASS that Chance's interest in medicine first blossomed, stemming from an incident he witnessed by pure chance.

One afternoon when coming home from school he saw a common neighborhood visitor parked outside an apartment house on his block. A white, Cadillac ambulance, red roof light flashing away. Attendants were evacuating two casualties, both black men, while two

Politically Erect

police officers were handcuffing two women, also black.

One of the blood soaked men, large tags of flesh flapping from his face in rhythm as he limped down the long set of granite steps outside the front entrance, was being held up by one ambulance attendant, who was also saturated in blood from the man's multiple stab and slash wounds. The second casualty was being carried down the steps of the tall front porch on a stretcher, covered in a blood-soaked, linen sheet. A fourth attendant dutifully trailed behind, carrying a severed arm eloquently dressed in the sleeve of a formerly white, linen shirt with a gold cuff-link. One of the cops had a blood stained butcher knife and a large meat clever, placing both in the squad car.

A neighbor was relating to the other cop that the two men were playing cards, an argument erupted which deteriorated into a punch up, during which the two faithful women dutifully armed their men.

A schoolmate Chance had been heading home with, Gilbert, the only black kid afforded the privileged of being an ASS student, casually commented as they watched the fourth medic place the blood dripping, severed arm on the stretcher with the dying man.

A short while later, after the ambulance, cops and rubber neckers had gone about their business, the two boys silently stared down at the crusted over puddle of blood on the side-walk.

They stared for a long time, and not yet jaded by the utter indifference of the city slums, had nothing to say. Eventually they left the elderly Jewish landlady to her scrubbing of the front steps and journeyed on.

It was a little ways down the street that Gilbert made everything come screaming into focus.

"Musta' bin playin' fo' money." He dryly commented.

Paddy Kelly

Gilbert's logic and perspective were immediately crystal clear to Chance.

No less than in any African nation or Asian Third World country, violence in the U.S., in addition to being the basis for all American society, was a way of life.

Particularly where money was involved.

*

After the last of the aircraft were called back to the mainland to reload with food, clean water and medical supplies and as these were the first American rescue personnel to reach the island, it was left to the individual troops to locate their assembly points which had been picked at random from a WWII map back in Keflavik and so were scattered throughout the island of Heimaey. The village was small enough that only a half dozen units had made it over to the island before the CH-47's had been recalled due to weather, so availability of assembly points wasn't much of a problem.

Once on the ground, the wind shifted seaward and they were no longer pelted with dried lava and ash.

The troops had been assembled by unit and the 1st Division was assembled next to the four storied hospital where they were informed they had been assigned a two kilometre search quadrant just south of the village which would angle them straight into the erupting volcano.

The two Marine units, one M.P. and one Infantry platoon, assembled and the grunts were prepped and moved out within 20 minutes. The M.P.'s, assigned to find and arrest looters and hand them over to the locals, gathered inside the only grocery store in the village. As they liaised with the civilian translators the concept of looting caused some confusion to the handful of

Politically Erect

Icelanders present.

"Excuse me Lieutenant. What means looting?" The senior translator, a policeman named Sloany inquired.

Sloany had been flown in from Reykjavik due to the fact that Heimaey never needed a policeman before and so didn't have one.

Sloany was six foot seven inches, easily tipped the scales at 270 and always stood ram rod straight. He once took out three British armed robbers in the capital and freed a hostage. Despite the fact that The Icelandic police force doesn't carry guns.

"I'm sorry, I was told you were a policeman." The senior Marine M.P. replied.

"I **am** a policeman, what has that got to do with my English vocabulary?" The Lieutenant found this enigmatic. "So what is looting?" Sloany repeated.

"You know! Looting! Stealing things from other people's houses that don't belong to you! Looting!"

"That's ridiculous, who would do such a thing?! Besides, what would they steal? Someone's fish?" The locals got a chuckle out of that. The Marine officer failed to see the humor.

"Lieutenant, if I may interrupt." Under the misimpression the guy was going to explain things to Sloany, the L.T. gestured, more out of frustration than curiosity, to the younger translator, a fisherman from the village. The fisherman addressed the marine.

"Sir, in Iceland, we have 1 prison, it's in the capital. In this prison there are 5 cells –"

"Are you trying to tell me there are only **five people** in prison in this entire country?!"

"Well . . . there are usually some people in the coastal jails, but only for a short time, until they are sober enough to drive home."

Paddy Kelly

"What happens if six people have to go to prison?"

"They just go home and when a cell is free the police call them and they come and report for prison."

Theoretically, human facial muscles are not supposed to be able to contort in the particular combinations which were being demonstrated by the U.S.M.C. L.T.

"What happens if somebody murders somebody, he just gets to go home?!"

The young translator smiled, but the policeman and the others, most of whom spoke English, laughed themselves silly. The L.T., your basic gung ho M.P. officer type who no doubt harbored dreams of a luminous career in the criminal sciences solving impossible homicide cases after he got out of the military, again didn't get the joke.

"Mr. Lieutenant, sir, the last murder in Iceland was in 1956, and that was a drunk driver who ran down his girl friend for sleeping with another man."

"Well did he go to prison?"

"Yes. For twenty years I think."

"Well where did you keep him?"

"We didn't. You did."

"What?!"

"He was a U.S. Soldier." Sloany interjected.

The next day the M.P. Company was re-assigned to the infantry guys working on keeping the island's tiny runway clear for resupply.

Occasionally some of them were siphoned off for trash runs.

With frequent wind shifts the volcanic spew of molten ash and Volkswagen-sized boulders, which were now to the seaward of the island, rendered it temporarily safe to head outside the buildings being used as refuge, which begged the question, out to where?

Back at the hospital all five members of 1st Division

Politically Erect

there were receiving their life saving and safety briefing as a grizzly old Chief Petty Officer named Anderson from Headquarters Company was handing out shovels and picks.

"Chief, what exactly are we supposed to do here? Nearly everything is buried ass deep in ash!" J.D. queried.

"Well, Seaman Apprentice, everything is buried. I'm standin' here handin' out picks and shovels. See if you can paint yerself a picture!" Puzzled looks were exchanged as the chief continued. "Don't look so glum boys, time for your safety briefin'! Pay attention to the winds. When they shift ya'll gonna have auto-mo-bile sized boulders headin' your way. But don't be too scared. Division says they gonna try and send over some helmets. Additionally, I'm well informed that the winds only shift about every fit'teen minutes. Also, ya'll get within' one klick o' that big red bitch, walk softly. Ya'll could be on a sub-ster-aenian step, ledge, or shelf or sumthin'."

"Chief, give us a break! What the fuck is that?"

"Pic'cha yerself walking on a sheet o' glass, underneath o' which, is about a yard or two of space, underneath o' which that is a mile deep, raging pool of fast movin', red hot lather! Underneath o' which is a place you boys is gonna see soon enough when you dies."

"Chief! Ju gotta be shittin' us!" Hernandez pointessly protested.

"I wouldn't shit you Hernandez! You're my favourite turd!" The group stared at each other, out at the pyroclastic flow less than half a mile away then back at the Chief.

"Lastly but not leastly, should you need to enter any

homes, residences, domiciles, places of bidness or buildin's, don't any of you dumbshits go lightin' matches or lighters so's you kin see better. We lost us a coupla' marines earlier this mornin'. Apparently there was a gas main busted open in a house where they was lookin' for survivors. Poor bastards got blowed ta shit." Reality suddenly set in. "Questions? No? Good. Carry on men! You too, Hernandez."

An hour later the intrepid but not so motivated expedition was wandering through their assigned sector, in no particular direction.

"I don't know why they gave us these fuckin' maps. There's no more streets, signs, roads or landmarks! Just one big field of the fuckin' black ash!" J.D. the designated complainer bitched as they meandered out across the ash strewn landscape.

Roof tops and fragments of roof tops hinted at where streets or roads might have once stood but, devoid of not only signs of any kind but with half the island blown away and a good part of the southern coast consumed by the eruption, there were also no recognizable land features.

The constant odor of sulphur and ash permeated the air and the light layer of snow blanketing the rolling landscape created an even more surrealistic panorama.

"Where's the fuckin' dinosaurs?" Someone commented as they pushed on towards where they were told the southern tip of the small village used to be. Their compasses were of no use as they were too far north on the globe and the out of date maps had no correction for the unusually high magnetic deviation coupled with the magnetic field strength could be referenced.

A mere two hours after disembarking the C-130 Chance, Hernandez, J.D. and Chilli Pepper with the FNG tagging along bumped into Jeffrey L. Davis, a

Politically Erect

Marine Corporal from the Twin Cities in Minnesota.

Now swollen to a search and rescue party of six junior enlisted men, none of whom had any kind of technical training in anything much less search and rescue operations on a sparsely inhabited, North Atlantic island featuring a still erupting volcano, they pushed on through the haze in search of whatever it was they were supposed to be searching for, confident in the belief that when they found it, they would know what it was.

"Twin Cities huh?" Billy reaffirmed.

"Yeah. Father's got a small waste disposal operation back there." Davis responded. Chunks of black ash crunched beneath them with every footstep.

"So it was either hauling shit or looking for the shit, huh?" J.D. proded.

"One way to look at it I guess." The FNG added.

"Who you with?" Chance asked the Marine.

"Just got here, yesterday." Corporal New Guy replied, his pick and shovel slung over his shoulder.

"Welcome to The Rock." J.D. quipped.

"Welcome to First Division." Chilli tagged.

"How do you know I'll be in First Division? I ain't got no orders yet!" Davis was incensed at the suggestion that he would be assigned to 1st Division.

"You got a rate?" J.D. asked.

"Not yet."

"You got rank comin'?"

"No."

"You got connections in the Department of The Navy?" Billy inquired.

"Shit! My dad's a garbage man in East Saint Paul."

"You remember that big, fat Personnelman First Class who checked you in yesterday when you showed up here?"

"Yeah?"

"You offer him a blow job?"

"Fuck no! I ain't queer!"

"Welcome to First Division!" Chilli congratulated.

Without warning, as they crested a small hill, Chance stopped dead in his tracks and stared straight ahead.

"JESUS it's fucking magnificent!"

"What?!" J.D. queried as he climbed the rise to stand next to Chance.

"The dawn of earth!" He gestured out over the island.

The barren landscape extended out for two or three kilometres, nearly flat then, as if Satan had opened a gateway to hell with the rising mountain acting as an open deck hatch, abruptly gave way to the pure white of the gargantuan steam clouds of the violently erupting mountain which intermingled with the reds and oranges of the pyroclastic flow. The titanic steam vapors drifted up and out to meld with the low hanging cumulus clouds. All of which was set against an endless azure sky and an emerald green sea.

"Did you fucking drop before we boarded the aircraft?" J.D. asked.

"NO! But this would've been the acid trip to end all acid trips! This must be what it was like at the dawn of the earth!" Chance confidently conjectured. Chilli pulled up besides them.

"MAN! Fuck Lucy In The Sky with Diamonds! This is mashed potatoes in the sky with ketchup and mustard!"

"You're a regular Hemingway Chilli." Chance isued the backhand compliment.

"I say we head out straight towards that big nasty bitch until we can't go no further!" Hernandez suggested.

"Then what?! Take our dicks out and piss on it?" J.D. argued.

Politically Erect

"Then spread out and see can we find somethin' of that town we supposed to be helpin'!"

"Fuck the dawn of the earth! I feel like I'm on fuckin' Mars!" J.D. threw in.

"Mars is red." Chance mumbled.

"What?!"

"Mars is the Red Planet."

"How da fuck you know? You ever been there?"

By now, nearly 20 hours into the eruption, the oversized hill the eruption had been had grown to a small mountain and had exploded out the west side of itself to form a giant dish of black ice cream with a big dolop of strawberry sauce oozing from a wedge scooped out of the center.

The fearless, intepid explorers pushed on.

"How the fuck do I knowit's red? I'll tell you how I know. My parents are married, they loved me and so I have something you can't even spell."

"What's that wise guy?"

"An edge-a-macation." Suddenly Chance stopped and started hopping up and down in place.

"Hey Billy, you crackin' up or what?"

"Shut up! Come here. Listen!" He pointed to the ground under his feet as they all moved to him. A distinct metallic sound could be heard.

"Sounds like somebody pushin' in the side of a van with his hand." J.D. observed.

"Start diggin'!" Billy yelled and they went at it as if it were a race. In no time they had uncovered part of the red cab of a large tractor trailer.

"Shit! There's somebody inside!" They frantically dug themselves into a pretty good sweat until they could open the driver's side door and when they did it was a rigor mortise riddled body that fell over on its side in front of them.

They stared in silence down at the contorted face, mouth locked open in a final death scream, hands broken off at the wrists as they still gripped the steering wheel.

"We're in fuckin' Pompeii!" Chilli quietly offered as a eulogy surreptitiously taking a step or two backwards.

"He was young!"

"Wasn't that young."

"Wasn't getting' any older!"

"Where's his eyes?"

"Evaporated." Billy observed.

"That sucks."

"He never knew what happened."

"Never saw it coming, ya mean!" J.D. added.

"You sick man!" Chilli chastised.

"Should we bury him?"

"He was buried asshole! We just dug him up!" J.D. barked.

"See if he has any I.D. on him, we'll get a rough bearing, and report him to the M.P.'s when we get back." Chance suggested.

As he spoke, Billy was struck by a strange tinge of guilt which washed over him at not being more shocked at the young man's gruesome death.

Must'a been drivin' for money. He thought.

*

Politically Erect

"WE HAVE DONE SO MUCH FOR SO LONG WITH SO LITTLE THAT WE ARE NOW QUALIFIED TO DO ANYTHING WITH NOTHING"

- Sign over Seabees' H. Q. Quonset.

Paddy Kelly

CHAPTER THREE

Billy's formative years as a young American left a strong impression on his inner psyche in that he had become politicized before he knew what the word meant.

Initially he appeared to be headed for a scholarly, academic life. Then in 1957, coincidently the same year Eisenhower asked Congress to send troops to South East Asia, Billy began his first year of primary education.

While the U.S.S.R was conducting its first successful atmospheric nuclear tests and America was marketing their revolutionary device, the Frisbee, disaster struck for Billy.

The Russians also launched *Sputnik* and the God-fearing peoples of the U.S. of A. collectively pissed themselves and went into meltdown. The Washington Brain Trust, panic stricken by the impending Red tidal wave which was obviously lapping at the shores of The Land of the Free, quickly assembled in one of their secret rooms that nearly everyone knew about because it was so heavily surrounded by lawyers, lobbyists and press, huddled up and put their heads together.

Seeing as how The Red Armageddon was obviously right around the corner, they'd figured they'd better get their collective asses in gear and do something pronto.

Following days and days and weeks and weeks of back biting, finger pointing and playing the blame game, they did what Washington politicians usually do when they haven't got the faintest idea of what the hell to do: they turned to the corporate lobbyists who in turn quickly held secret meetings in their dozens of private homes, retreats and ranches across the country, huddled up and put their heads together.

Politically Erect

This was not called passing the buck. It was called, 'consultation'.

Then, following days and days and weeks and weeks of figuring out how they could bilk the taxpayer for as much as possible and still make it appear as though they had hit on a solution, they advised the D.C. authorities that the only way to stave off the impending Communist hoard takeover of the Free World was to turn generation after generation of naive young kids into ridiculously brilliant mathematicians, physicists engineers and rocket scientists thereby ensuring sustained, unimpeded growth in the fields of Physics, Quantum Mechanics, propellant technology and all other aspects, facets and angles of Rocket Science. And in a short twenty to thirty short years, the logic argued, they would catch up to the Russians. Twenty years conservative estimate.

Of course the folks up in Detroit, alias "Motor Capital of the World", envisioning endless production lines churning off into the distant future, were pretty chuffed about this plan, and threw their complete political weight behind said operations. The Congressmen were happy, the Industrialists were pleased and a terror stricken American public were temporarily appeased.

Then when Russia launched a dog into orbit, the Boys on the Hill doubled down and counter punched by flooding the nation with legislation meant to saturate the country with millions of budding little Werner von Braun's and eliminate all those superfluous and pointless occupations based in The Humanities. Any high school graj-a-matit who dared to sign on in college to study Art, History or god forbid that most useless of all useless disciplines, Literature, was immediately and forever branded unpatriotic, a Pinko and probably, given a semester or two, was destined to bloom into a full-blown Commie!

Furthermore, said turn coats were duly warned that any such heinous act of treason would be entered into his or her Permanent Record.

That's right, THE Permanent Record!

Billy didn't take too well to the new and improved primary school program and so it took him 4 years to reach third grade. As more and more moronic regulations regarding math requirements metastasized across the U.S. school system, it became a race as to whether or not he would graduate high school before his 26th birthday.

And so it was that Billy Chance and his peers basked in the not-so-liberal, post war atmosphere of the American education system.

Until disaster again struck.

A few years later an essentially useless Texas politician named Lyndon B. Johnson was appointed president by a crazed little nobody who redefined the one-man one-vote paradigm. His name was Lee Harvey Oswald.

Johnson, a backwards ass oil baron, cowboy-wanna-be, who threw a temper tantrum when John Glen's wife refused to receive him in her home because she was embarrassed about her speech impediment, inherited the reins of power.

As further testament to LBJ's manhood he collapsed on his desk in the Oval Office crying like a baby when word of the Tet Offensive reached him. The commies broke the truce they had brokered. Again. Not the last time the Indians outsmarted the Cowboy.

It was around that time Johnson's brain trust decided that every man, woman and child, (born or unborn), had to reorient their lives and throw themselves heart and

Politically Erect

soul into the space race.

No doubt a good part of the reason the U.S. was so far behind the Russkies was due to all the curricular time wasted on Twain, Hawthorne, Steinbeck, Hemingway and their Pinko sympathies acting as detriments to the progress of Western civilization.

Oh Romeo, oh Romeo, where for art thou Comrade?
Hark! Through yon window! Is that a red, light I see?!

It was rumoured that if you read Marx, Lenin or Trotsky backwards you could hear Stalin talking to you.

Thank Christ LBJ and Lady Bird had such a hard time with polysyllabic lexicon, otherwise they might've accidentally read a Vonnegut novel.

Major school funding suffered. Arts and lit programs were struck from the curriculae and all available extra funds were diverted to the maths and sciences. Thousands of students were by-passed or left behind if they didn't achieve seemingly arbitrary grade levels in maths and physics in primary and junior high school.

This is when, while in these primary years, Billy along with a fair amount of America's pre-teen adolescents, lost all interest in school. So much for socialism and LBJ's "Great Society".

A few years later in high school, as happened about a dozen times a month and with his dad again out of work, Billy skipped school to make money shining shoes, doing deliveries and any other menial job which drifted down the river and welled up through the sewer into the lower parts of Jersey City.

Billy was finally called into the school principal's office, the six foot four inch tall, 325 pound school principle known as Sister Alice Martina, alias SAM, where he was given due warning that if he missed one more day, he would be expelled. This after he had already been put on double secret probation.

Then one day he awoke like many Americans, dismayed and frustrated by the constant threat of nuclear war, the depressed state of the economy and the lack of a future for anyone who couldn't explain the mathematics of the adiabatic process of thermodynamics. But mostly he had decided to, once and for all, kick the school habit.

Knowing it was his last chance before he was expelled he dressed, grabbed his shoe shine box and with grit and determination, went out to make some money with the words *fuck school!* like a neon sign outside at an all-night saloon flashing in his brain.

Once again, fate intervened and he never got caught for ditching school that day as it was the great President John F. Kennedy who came to his rescue.

That day was the morning of November 22nd, 1963.

The rescue was accomplished as JFK had the unforeseen consideration to be assassinated that morning and spare Billy the humiliation and annoyance of being sent back to SAM's forboding inner sanctum.

That day, as he stared up at the ffiteen inch, wall mounted, black and white T.V. with the eighty to a hundred patrons crammed into a dark smelly *O'Brien's Bar* on Duncan Avenue in Jersey City watching the police, FBI, Secret Service and CIA surround Dealey Plaza in Houston as Walter Cronkite on the CBS news described the police, FBI, Secret Service and CIA surrounding Dealey Plaza in Houston, two thoughts sprang to mind.

WOW! Something really important just happened, and SHIT! This is really gonna be bad for business.

Politically Erect

On that day, to his shock and elation, Billy Chance became a dyed-in-the-wool American capitalist as the emotional upheaval in *O'Brien's* caused by Kennedy's murder, motivated the half bagged patrons to give him money, mostly bills not just coins, without having to shine a single shoe.

God bless America! Became his new mantra as he ran home to proudly hand over the loot to his too old-before-her-years mother.

He was further puzzled when no sooner had word of the assassination spread to the schools, offices and houses in the neighborhood and people poured into the streets and the entire country seemed to grind to a halt. He was eleven and couldn't understand why grown men were crying, black women were screaming, balling their eyes out and passing out in the streets. But he did remember something that was probably his first glint of 'political' awareness.

There was a grey-haired, red-face Irishman at the bar that afternoon who shook his head, threw back his whiskey and muttered to himself, 'The Bastards finely got him!'

It would be for years that Billy would have intermittent flashbacks of the last time so many people stayed glued to their T.V. sets for so long, not counting the night the Beatles were on the *Ed Sullivan Show* of course.

It was only a month earlier during what history now calls the *Cuban Missile Crisis*, that networks actually cancelled Ed Sullivan to continue covering the news of the superpower standoff.

But at that point in late November American politics wasn't going to change for such a trivial thing as morality or justice, much less for a 'Mick, Catholic

Paddy Kelly

president who pandered to Niggers!'
Kennedy won the battles, but lost the war.

***

Following the eruption of the Heimaey volcano on the 23rd everyone on the mainland naturally volunteered to assist in the evacuation. In 48 hours the island was inundated to the point the population ballooned to three times its original size.

As there were no opeational shops anywhere to be had in the tiny village, supplies were shipped over from the mainland on a daily basis.

There was however, one small restaurant, with about four or five tables, in the middle of that tiny speck of land and the couple who owned it along with their three redunkulessly beautiful blond-haired, blue eyed daughters elected to stay and man the restaurant as a feed station to the troops who were there to evacuate the civilian women and children and attempt to save as much property as possible. Everyone had to eat in thirty minute shifts on a 24 hour rotational basis and needless to say the perpetual lines were long.

After so many months in country Chance had a pretty good handle on the language and as one of the put-Angelina-Jolie-to-shame daughters made her way past the lines of unbathed, stinking Marines and sailors, hauling a 50 pound sack of spuds over her shoulder, the Jarhead behind him tapped him on the shoulder with a question.

"Hey Chance, do these Mojenny's understand English?" Infected with his unwarranted sense of over confidence and superiority Billy unhesitatingly replied.

"In the capital yes. But in these outlying

Politically Erect

providences, not likely."

"GREAT!" Came the Jarhead's ecstatic reply.

"Why?" Asked Billy as they both watched her reach the top of the stairs, fling the sack of spuds to the floor and dust her hands off.

"Because I'd ride her like Seattle Slew! I'm talkin' suckin' her brains out through her crotch!"

With no discernible accent, sense of humor or change in facial expression the girl looked down on the two ignorant members of the foreign, invading navy.

"We are very grateful for your efforts to save our island, our homes and our property. My family and I have chosen to remain here, at great physical risk, to feed you, for free. The least you could do is not act so . . . American."

ENEMY FIRE FIVE O'CLOCK! MAYDAY, MAYDAY, MAYDAY! WE'RE GOING IN! MAYDAY!

Mouth open, the dumbfounded Marine turned to Chance who just shrugged.

"Maybe she went to school on the main land." Billy humbly suggested.

Just as the girl turned from the top of the narrow staircase a small rumble crept through the building immediately followed by a tremendous explosion in the distance. Bodies lined up along the wall leading down the stairs tumbled over, a wall cracked, women and Air Force personnel screamed and men cursed.

"Fuck it's another earthquake!" Someone uttered.

"They're called tremors!"

"It's neither!" Yelled an immense Marine as he dug his way out of the pile of stunned bodies. "It's that Big Red Bitch laughing at our pathetic efforts to stop her consuming this island! Well you know what?!" He stood straight up and made for the exit door. "FUCK YOU BITCH!!" Despite his size he was the first one out the door.

Chance and the unknown, horny Marine were right behind him and when they cleared the building with the ground still shaking, just as they broke into the dark of the Icelandic noon Billy spotted J.D. and Chilli Pepper running as best they could on the wavy ground in the opposite direction of a small crowd of rescue personnel.

"1st Division's ordered to report to the hospital, let's go!" J.D. yelled over.

"What's going on?" Chance asked as they headed out as fast as they dared in the dark, wreckage strewn street.

"Apparently there's still some patients in the hospital!"

"Ain't that where patients should be?" Chilli threw in his two cents.

"Not when the roof's cracked and there's hot ash and cold wet snow a coupl'a yards deep piled up on that roof!"

Given the size of the village they hadn't far to run and a few minutes later, as the tremors finally died down they reached the north face of the five storied, concrete block structure.

"Now what?!" Chance spotted an unusually large pile of picks and shovels about fifty yards away in the open, as if they had been brought in by truck and dumped off in a hurry.

"Chilli, Hernandez, grab us some shovels and picks. J.D., I'm goin' inside to find somebody in charge. Run around back and see if you can see the Chief. Meet back here in two minutes. If you can't see anyone come straight back, no point running around like headless chickens! Meet you guys back here in two!"

Politically Erect

Inside Chance found organized chaos. By bed, wheelchair and gurney hospital staff were evacuating about two dozen non-ambulatory patients through the front door as members of the local, one truck, fire brigade rushed in with large jacks, timbers and assorted other shoring up equipment. Adjacent to the lobby a nurse and an orderly were systematically dashing through the rooms and disconnecting the oxygen supply lines. Chance made his way to what used to be an information desk where a middle-aged, heavy set nurse was alternately collecting records, throwing them into a heavy cardboard box and directing staff members.

"Are you in charge?!" He asked.

"Sorry, I don't speak English!" She replied. Billy switched to Icelandic.

"I have some men here from the American Navy. How can we help?" The emergency generators began to fail and the high intensity spots lining the corridors started to fade.

"We have enough help to get the patients out! Better if you take your men on the roof. Do you have shovels?"

"Yes!"

"Then go! Please hurry!" By the time Billy was back outside the men of 1st Division were assembled, all five of them and each had a large snow shovel and a pick in hand as well as a Navy issue steel helmet slung over his canteen.

"Chance, what's the story? I couldn't find nobody." J. D. inquired.

"The staff have the patient situ handled. We need to get our asses on the roof and start shovelling the rocks and snow off as fast as we can."

"Well than, what the hell we standin' here for?!"

Paddy Kelly

Chilli Pepper was the first in the door with the others close behind.

As they fought their way up to the first floor, past staff carrying patients on litters or in wheel chairs a fire fighter stopped them as they started their way upstairs.

"Where you are going please?"

"We have to get up on the roof and start shovelling off the ash and snow while you guys shore up the cross members."

"Good idea but when the roof shifted it has jammed both access hatches. They will now not open."

"We can't access the roof through the normal hatches. They're jammed." Chance translated to the group behind him in the stairwell.

"What the fuck we supposed to do, fly?!" J.D. commented.

"How did your men get on the roof?" Chance asked the fire fighter.

"My men are not on the roof."

"Shit! Okay, then. Com'on!" He indicated to the guys. "I got an idea."

"I was afraid of that!" J.D. chimed in.

Chance and company made it to the fifth floor where he steered them to a small, abandoned treatment room and used the "D" handle of his shovel to break out a window which led out onto a two foot ledge which ran around the entire perimeter of the building on each floor.

"Hey Wildman, what's you doing?" FNG asked.

"From the ledge we can boost each other up onto the roof!" Chance worked the excess glass out of the frame and carefully climbed through out onto the ledge. "Hand me my shovel." He called back through the window.

"Jew can use mine if jew like." Chance was startled and nearly lost his footing. Standing next to him outside

Politically Erect

on the ledge was Chilli Pepper.

"How the fuck . . . ?" Chilli pointed to an adjoining open window.

"Jew yust have to turn dee handle, Mang. Dee window, eess no locked."

With everyone outside it was a simple matter to climb up the corner of the building to the roof, toss the shovels up and layout a plan. Just then two things happened in rapid succession.

The wind shifted and they were pelted with a hail of ash rocks and, in the far corner of the roof, they spotted a Construction Battalion driver at the controls of a small bulldozer which wasn't moving. Some particularly large chunks of ash were falling from the sky.

"SHIT! GETTIN' REAL OVER HERE! GETTIN' REAL!" J.D. shouted as they quickly donned helmets. Chance made for the stationary bulldozer and jumped up on the tread to talk to the Seabee Chief Petty Officer hunkered down under the steel plate welded to the topside of the frame acting as a roof.

"Morning Chief! Nice day if it don't rain, huh? Run outta gas?"

"Negative! They're sending a CH-47 over to lift me outta' here. Roof can't take the weight. We had no access to the engineering plans so the brass decided to risk it with this mini dozer. The risk didn't work. Roof cracked in about ten different places."

"Good to know!"

Just then they heard rotor blades growing louder as they slapped through the airborne ash.

"Get your guys doin' what you can to clear as much of this snow and ash off'a here and as soon as I get this thing back on the ground I'll get some more Seabees up here!"

Paddy Kelly

"Roger that Chief. Will do!" A set of four cables were lowered from the chopper as it approached.

"I gotta dee dee mau the A.O. my ride's here!" The Chief donned his hard hat and stood by to man the cables dangling from the belly of the chopper as it drifted into position overhead. The massive backwash made it impossible for anybody to do anything so the guys from 1st Division huddled together, off to the side to watch the show.

With hand signals the Crew Chief in the CH-47 indicated to the Seabee that, due to power lines on the chopper's port side, he needed to back his bulldozer up a bit to facilitate the hook up. A thumbs up signalled he understood and the chopper climbed straight up to eliminate as much of the rotorwash as possible so the Seabee could see what he was doing.

Apparently he did something wrong because as soon as the rotorwash eased up and the dust cleared the only thing Billy and the guys could see was the underbelly of the dozer as it slid in slow motion off the edge of the roof and disappeared into the grey abyss the air had become.

"MAN! That's fucked up like a soup sandwich in the rain!" Chilli commented.

They dropped their shovels and ran to the edge of the roof, fell to their bellies and crawled to the ledge, cautiously looking over. There, laying spread-eagled on the fourth floor ledge was the chief, vigorously shaking his head to clear the cobwebs while the machine lay ass end up crumpled on its plow blade, five stories below.

"YOU OKAY CHIEF?" Billy called down as the Chief looked up.

"DAMN! That shit'll sure-as-hell wake your ass up!" The Chief shot back." J.D. leaned over to Chance.

"Ya know, that's what I like about working with

senior enlisted men. Always showing you new and innovative ways to do things."

Suddenly from somewhere on the perimeter of the town, a few hundred meters to the east, there was a gas explosion in a house and the roof, half consumed by a raging blaze, was partially blown off. Chilli Pepper and the others looked up from where they were laying next to J.D.

"SHIT! Guess we're gonna need another coupl'a Marines!"

Chilli was destined to be a T.V. news commentator.

Paddy Kelly

BEST THING ABOUT BEING HIGH.
THE VIEW.

Politically Erect

William W. Chance Jr.
Apt 1106,Bldg 1
Federal Housing Project
Duncan Ave. Jersey City, N. J.

SN William W. Chance III
U.S. Naval Air Station,
Kevlavik, Iceland

Dear Mom;   April 27, 1973

Well, orders to Corps school finally came through! Chief gave me a heads up this morning at chow. They must be scraping the bottom of the barrel if they want me, but no complaints! It's been two years since I accidentally on purpose got booted out of Weather School just so's I could be a Corpsman and get over there.
I know you weren't over the moon about me signing up but with the scholarships gone there wasn't much choice if I wanted to finish college.
Mail seems to be running about two weeks from here to there so by the time you get this I should have arrived in San Diego and started training. It's about a two and a half month course then we either get orders to a Naval Regional Medical Center or somewhere else. 'Somewhere else' ould be a thousand other places, so don't go losing any sleep please.

                              Love, me.

p.s.- Got the news cousin Shirley's getting married. Great news. When's she due?

CHAPTER FOUR

More so than in any other walk of life, the Navy is about waiting. Waiting to ship out to basic training, waiting to start training, waiting to finish training, waiting for your first set of orders to your first duty station to come through and finally waiting to ship out.

Following a two year wait on a four year enlistment Chance's wait for orders was over.

A few months after they didn't get nuked, Chance's crew, were still rotating two weeks on and two weeks off of Heimaey Island and fighting the still spewing volcano.

One morning, while digging their way down to the door of a small fish warehouse to look for non-survivors, crusty old Chief Anderson made his way out to the site in a beat up, grey Willy's to find the exhausted search and rescue-turned digging crew sitting in the dark against the mostly excavated warehouse wall.

"Shit! We got company!" J.D. alerted the gang.

"He say anything we say we yust sit down five minutes ago." Chilli Pepper offered.

"What'a we say when he asks where we been diggin' all this time after he notices there's no hole?"

"Right over there, by that cargo door." Chance pointed to a bend in the warehouse about 30 yards ahead of where they were all plopped down.

"It's only half exposed! We been here over two hours!"

"Fuckin' wind keeps shiftin'! What can we do?" Billy shrugged.

"Yeah, fuckin' wind keeps shiftin'! I like that! Nice one Chance."

Politically Erect

"Thank you Corporal."

The jeep drove a little ways past the guys, did a 180 and pulled up onto a clear spot where a small office building used to be.

"Chance, get the fuck over here, on the double!" Chance dropped his shovel and, through the grey, ash strewn atmosphere, scurried over to the open top jeep. Due to the possibility of bad juju rubbing off on them everybody else hung back.

"Morning Chief! You're looking very strack this morning. Great day to be in the Nav, isn't it Chief?"

"Cut the bullshit asshole!"

"Cutting the bullshit Chief."

"I got a problem Seaman Chance."

"Chief Anderson, I for one firmly believe, that due to the incredibly professional job, you as leader of this rescue detail are doing here in the absence of a Senior Chief, I mean Chief Stump, you well deserve a promotion to Senior Chief if not Master . . ." Anderson was in no way surreptitious regarding the look he cast in Chance's direction. It was enough. "Cutting the bullshit Chief."

Just then J.D., wanting to snoop in and get the skinny walked over to Anderson, who remained seated in the jeep as Chance leaned on the rear fender.

"We didn't do it Chief!"

"Didn't do what?!"

"Whatever it is we're accused of Chief."

"B.D. this is an A-B conversation boy, so why don't you see your way outta here!" J.D. quickly backed away, both hands in the air.

"Roger that Chief, will do ASAP! Ahh. . . just one thing Chief Anderson."

Anderson replied with a 'What the fuck is it?'

expression.

"It's J.D. Chief, not B.D." J.D. meekly corrected.

"Since when do you spell 'broke' with a 'J'?" J.D became masked in confusion. Anderson proceeded to clarify.

"If 'D' is for 'Dick', then 'B' must be for 'Broke'!" The Chief barked. J.D. melded into the background.

"Effective communication! Hallmark of good leadership. Sorry we ain't done here Chief, but the damn wind –"

"That ain't my problem shit head. My problem is what am I gonna do when you're gone and I ain't got nobody left here who can read and write above a third grade level and whose parents are married?" Anderson's lexicon might have been seen as intentionally insulting but he was the kind of individual who believed in giving a man his due.

The Chief handed a manila envelope with the official U.S.N. seal to the soon-to-be Navy Hospital Corpsman Chance. The chief didn't bother to dismount the jeep, he just pulled up a little closer to the group and tossed the rest of the mail at them, then backed up again along side Billy who had by now torn open the envelope to find orders to San Diego Hospital Corps School to attend the next class which was to convene in two weeks.

"There's a medi-vac chopper coming out to the island day after tomorrow at zero seven hundred in the a. m. Make sure your dumb ass is on it!" He put the vehicle into gear and prepared to leave.

"Aye aye Chief! Hey Chief!"

"What?"

"Been a privaldge working with you."

"Fuck off dirtbag."

"SeriouslyChief, love you."

Anderson purposely spun the tires as he pulled out

Politically Erect

which caused him to fishtail and spray the resting troops with snow and the gravel-like volcanic ash.

"It's his way of saying h loves us!" Billy shouted over to them as they dusted off the debris.

Just then the wind suddenly shifted and the guys were bombarded with a rain of hot ash embers. They dropped their tools and made a bee line through the hazy light for the relative safety of the warehouse they had been excavating. Scrambling in through a smashed window they tumbled to the freezing, concrete floor and helped each other up.

Forty five minutes later the volcanic storm hadn't abated but they had found a large mound of some kind of packing material and fashioned some crude sleeping pads. Two hours into it they voted to spend the night and bedded down.

"Hey Billy?" Chilli called from his reclined position through the darkness of the storehouse.

"Yeah Chilli?"

"When you make Chief do they issue jew a gut like Anderson's or do jew have to supply it?"

"I believe it takes years of conscientious and fastidious dedication Chili." Billy answered while perusing his orders. No one had to read them to know what they said.

"Hey Doc! Congratulations!" Davis complimented Chance across the black, barren room of dried ash-filled stalls which had traded in their stacks of fresh cod for piles of three month old volcanic spew.

"Guess we gonna have some stories when we get back to the world of round doorknobs."

"He ain't no Doc yet!" Snapped J.D.

"Appreciate the vote of confidence Jerk Dick."

"In four months he will be. If he keeps his ass and

nose clean." Chilli defended.
"Good luck with that!"
"Hey Chance."
"Yeah J.D.?"
"Congrats asshole! Finally got your orders."
"Yeah, yeah I did."
"And I just got one thing to say to you."
"Yeah? What's that?"
"Good night Mary Sue." Billy answered and that was the signal for everyone to bed down as best they could.
"Good night everybody."
"Good night John Boy." Chilli threw in.
"Night Ben."
"Night Daddy!"
"Night Jim Bob!" J.D. Said.
"Night Mama." Billy answered.
"Fuck you Chance!"

*

1st Division had been on Heimaey island for the full week to ten days allowed by the station C.O. and now had a week off back on the mainland before they could be ordered to re-volunteer, so that night they had all decided to hang out in Room 401.

On the top floor, (deck in Navy speak), of the men's dormitory, (enlisted men's barracks), of the Kevlavik Naval Air Station, Iceland, (NAVSTAKEFICE), was the room that didn't exist. Room 401.

The door of Room 401 simply read:

'Swab Locker'
(Broom Closet in Civilian speak)

Politically Erect

Although not really any kind of mop closet, (swab locker in Navy speak), to anyone above the rank of Petty Officer 3rd Class, Room 401 was always locked and the key was always strictly controlled. There was a reason for that.

The secret of Room 401 had been passed down from successive generations of junior sailors, airmen and Marines since just after 1957 when the new U.S. squadrons first rotated into the country as the Brits signedover the base and left. The squadrons had continued to do so every six months ever since. According to international contract the Icelanders owned anything left in country for one day over six months. To get around this clause the U.S. rotated the three air squadrons and their airplanes every 180 days.

The squadrons were one fighter squadron, one bomber squadron and the most threateningly ominous of all, one sub hunter-killer squadron.

The hunter-killer squadron didn't have much to do all day, they just hunted and killed submarines. Specifically Soviet submarines. However in the entire 40 or so years of The Cold War, (no relation to Iceland), no one had ever heard of them hunting and killing any Soviet submarines, just hunting them. This is because there was an unwritten agreement between the hunter-killer squadrons of the Americans and the H-K submarines of the Soviets that read something like; 'If you are not killing us we are not killing you.'

The whole thing was really just a giant video game with the American techies against the Russian techies where everybody lived with a daily fear of the outbreak of nuclear war accidently being triggered by some new comer to the game who inadvertantly entered the wrong codes somewhere on one of those big, spooky machines they called computers.

So, due to some sharp Icelandic lawyers, (from the firm of Needlebaumsson, Steinsson, & Bernsteinsson), who negotiated the 180 day clause in the contract, combined with some desperate, anti-commie, paranoid American politicians and an unwritten but strictly enforced non-fraternization policy between the lower enlisted, middle enlisted and officers, aggravated by the constant isolation and darkness, the mysteries of Room 401 had remained undiscovered.

This combination of events allowed the lower enlisted to have a place where they too could kick back, relax and fry the shit out of their young brains.

After all, the officers had unlimited access to Sangiovese di Romagna and Meremma Toscana, Johnny Walker, (Red, Black and Blue labels), Cuban cigars and Jameson's 1750. The senior enlisted had their hangouts with Budweiser, Moosehead and Jack Daniels, so the lower enlisted had access to marijuana.

Hashish, mescaline, peyote, THC, valium, Librium, Benzedrine, red jackets, black Bennies, white jackets, the occasional snort of coke and that king of all recreational pharmaceuticals, lysergic acid diethylamide, alias LSD. (Navy speak equivalent not found).

Room 401 was a regular pharmacy minus certified pharmacists and with a very select clientelé.

Furnished with over stuffed, ripped chairs, broken stools and cracked lamps fished out of the large Dempsey dumpsters used for garbage, there was a wall-to-wall rug who's original color was indiscernible, (obtained on a midnight raid), a large frame hanging on one wall with no picture in it and an assortment of home made bongs. The whole room had been painted in paints stolen from the officer's stores, mixing all the leftover colors borrowed from said stores which resulted in a

Politically Erect

tasteful dark purple. As the sailors who never sailed reckoned that they would spend the majority of their time in Room 401 staring up at the ceiling, it too was painted in the same dark purple.

Several black lights, some *Cream*, *Doors* and *Hendrix* albums added just the right ambiance.

That night blotter, a tiny 1/8th of an inch square piece of paper saturated with LSD, was on the menu and, after neatly and reverently placing their tabs under their tongues, some of the guys toked up with some Panama Red to jump start their blast off and patiently await the magic fairies to come and visit.

Billy sat in one of the over stuffed chairs off to the side and prepared to watch the show.

Chance had seen what smack and crack had done to the blacks of his neighborhood and so had shied away from Lady Chemical's advances in the past. Despite living in it's heyday, he knew absolutely nothing about the drug world and, as he wasn't married, had not yet taken up drinking.

Sitting there watching, about an hour into the festivities, which by now consisted solely of everyone who had dropped acid, meaning everyone but Chance, sitting around mesmerized by things only they could see, he was fascinated. Fascinated by the lengths they were going through to convince him they were 'tripping'.

Bizarre facial gesticulations were universal and Chilli had taken to talking to the lamp on the end table next to him. Billy watched him for the better part of ten minutes but despite the fact that Chilli spoke without pause, the table lamp never answered.

Acid was the 1st Division's drug of choice for a simple reason. The corpsmen were able to mix it up in the dispensary from federally controlled substances at a cost of about $5 a pint. They reckoned that as they, being members of the United States Navy, were federal employees they had the right to control the substances. The fact that a strong tab of blotter only required one drop and sold for $1 combined with the fact that you could get 10,000+ drops out of a pint never entered into it. Or so the corpsmen told everyone.

"Hey Billy! How's things?" J.D. squatted with his hand on Billy's knee in front of Chance who sat upright in the big brown, overstuffed chair.

"Good. Good. Just checkin' out the show."

"Yeah, kinda' cool ain't it? How ya feelin?"

"Good, fine." Chance glanced over at Chilli who was nodding in agreement at the lamp.

"I can't believe you guys actually think you're going through all these hallucinations from that tiny little piece of paper under your tongue."

"You mean . . . this tiny little piece of paper?" J. D. held up a hit of blotter with a tiny picture stamped on it. Billy leaned over and examined it.

"For real? Mickey Mouse?!"

"Manufacturer's Good Housekeeping Seal of Approval Dude! Gotta know where this shit came from. Every manufacturer has his own mark. A logo, kind'a like Pepsi or Coke."

"I'm guessin' you're not a Pepsi kind of a guy."

J.D. didn't answer he just waved the blotter in front of Billy.

"No thanks Dude. I'm good." J.D. smiled like the Cheshire Cat. "I like you man! You're good people."

"I like you too Dude." Billy paid attention to J.D.'s hand on his knee. It hadn't moved but he was ready to bolt if it did.

"No man! I mean you're cool. You take people for what they are and don't judge. That's a pretty big fuckin'

Politically Erect

deal now days." Billy shrugged in modesty. "Tell ya what Billy, I'm gonna do something good for you. I'm gonna change your life for the better."

Very thoughtful! Mused Billy.

"I'm gonna play a record for you Dude." J.D. continued. "You like the *Airplane*?" J.D. asked. Billy smiled and nodded.

"Snuck over the Village one time and hung out on the roof of the Fillmore with a friend and listened to them play." Billy related.

"Nice! Catch ya later. Hope ya dig the tunes." He walked away. "Billy!" J.D. called back.

"Yo?"

"Fasten your seat belt dude." J.D smiled over at Chilli who gave a thumbs up and then smiled back. Billy saw this and smiled back at Chilli. J.D. moved to the record player and set up *Surrealistic Pillow* and gently turned the volume to '10'.

A few minutes later someone gave a blood curdling war whoop as the guitar march intro of *White Rabbit* crept into the room. Chance closed his eyes, sat back and absorbed the music. All eyes casually turned to Billy.

Billy gradually began to feel physically tired but strangely, ove the next twenty minutes his mind began to slowly but steadily pick up the pace.

After he had mentally reviewed all the courses he had taken in his first year at City University of New York before joining up in the Navy he smiled at some of the good times he remembered there, especially about some of the pretty girls. He breathed deeply.

He remembered the gymnastics team. Suddenly he was competing for City University against one of the Ivy league schools. Princeton, then Yale and he 'felt' rather than 'saw' the Payne Whitney Gymnasium where they beat Yale.

He walked out of the ivy covered gym building after the meet and a single engine Piper Cub, engine running, was out on the lawn. Inside the cockpit was the easy chair he was sitting in. Immediately after climbing into it the chair, the aeroplane began to physically breathe.

He let an eye lid slide open. *White Rabbit* seemed to be playing again and he wondered why they had kept playing it over and over for so long. The walls seemed to slowly undulate.

"Change the fuckin' record!" He yelled over to J.D. who was now sitting off to his right.

"Billy, I just put it on! Let it finish first." The Cheshire Cat's body turned into J.D.'s but his huge set of iridescent teeth still dominated his face. Chance realized something was different.

Glancing around the room he wondered why someone had turned on the lights and why they seemed just a little dimmer than usual. Everyone else was staring at the ceiling so he looked up. The overhead light was not lit. He perused the room. Everything was crystal clear. He could discern everyone's features, their facial expressions and postures. He could see in the dark!

He looked to his left where Chilli smiled and nodded at the lamp as he shook hands with it.

"What'a you lookin' at?!" The lamp angrily snapped at Billy.

Suddenly, as he willed his body to stand, he had a sinking feeling and tried to sit up straight but the arms of the overstuffed easy chair slowly began to envelop his hands. The chair's respirations increased noticeably. Just as he marveled at that the seat of the chair seemed to be swallowing him, slowly, softly but steadily. There was no fear, just breathless exhilaration.

Just as his head sank below the seat cushion to be

Politically Erect

completely engulfed as if he were a late night furniture snack, he glanced at the record player where Gracie Slick was yelling something about a girl named Alice.

He heard the last of music, with his eyes.

It would be a full twenty-four hours after gently touching down back on terra firma before Billy regained any semblance of coherence. Forty-eight hours before he could think straight.

After he came around, it was difficult to discern what was real and what wasn't. But one thing was certain. The world now made sense like it never had before thanks to J.D. and that spiked bottle of Coke Cola he slipped Billy earlier that evening.

**

A few days later, once back on Heimaey Island, the guys were given what would be their last assignment. Prepare and standby to unload choppers.

"Hey Chief. If we gonna fight this thing like the Mojacks with sea water and fire hoses we're gonna need a shit load'a P-250's!" Corporal Davis reasoned.

P-250's are ingenious man portable, high powered, gas operated pumps. They were developed for the U. S. Navy to be used in damage control when a vessel was taking on water and are capable of sucking up 250 gallons of water a minute and putting it some place else.

'Mojack' is the quaint military term for male Icelanders used by those who lived their lives in the narrow confines of American racism. The no less racist but also inherited from the Brits is 'Mojenny' for women.

Like something out of a John Wayne movie the words were no sooner out of his mouth when a reinforced wing of Chinooks with Con Ex cargo boxes in belly slings broke over the horizon and came drifting towards them.

"Hey Chief, what's in the Con Ex's?" J.D. asked.

"A shit load of P-250's! Now get your sorry ass over to the C.P. and tell that worthless, tits-on-a-bull lieutenant that the birds are coming in!"

"Aye aye ,Chief!" J.D. double timed down the hill and headed for the Command Post.

"Rest of you lazy bastards, get over there and help unsling them Con Ex's and let's get them there pumps out to them crazy Mojacks!"

By midnight, fifty fire fighters and over 100 sailors were manning about three dozen U.S. Navy issue P-250 pumps, nearly five miles of fire hose, stretching from the harbor all the way back to the leading edge of the pyroclastic flow and dousing the Big Red Bitch with ice cold, Icelandic sea water.

Chance, soaked in sweat from hauling gear and helping man a nozzle less than three meters from the lava flow, sauntered up to Chief Anderson who stood on top of one of the pumps surveying the battle.

"What'a ya think Chief?" Billy called up to the Chief. Anderson folded his arms across his bloated belly, chewed his cigar to the other side of his mouth and spit.

"Son-of-a-bitch if it don't look like them god-damned, crazy Mojacks ain't got that there lather flow stopped dead in her tracks!" Billy likewise folded his arms across his chest, put a foot up on the chief's pump and surveyed the midnight scene from *Dante' Inferno*.

"Sum-bitch!" Billy parroted as he turned his head and spit.

Politically Erect

It was 21:15, on the 8th of May, Chance's last night on The Rock, and he lay in the top rack of his bunk bed, hands folded behind his head staring up at Miss January duct taped to the overhead. He was torn between getting shit faced that night and taking it easy.

"You going over the U.S.O. tonight?" He asked Davis, now a permanent member of 1st Division and who was comfortably reclined in the bottom rack.

Jarheads and squids never shared rooms, but on The Rock, due to the fact that no troop buildings had been torn down since the great escalation during WWII, barracks space was decidedly a buyer's market. As long as you kept your assigned space squared away, your rack made and a minimum compliment of uniforms in your locker, no one gave a shit where you slept.

"Naah! Waste of time." Davis shot back. "Same old shit. Shit Led Zeppelin recordings, shit watered down beer and the same shit old ugly bastards I gotta see all day. Nothing but a sausage fest."

"You sure?"

"The only difference between the U.S.O. and the Titanic is Titanic had a band."

"Well this U.S.O. show apparently brought their own juke box and they flew in some strippers this morning. You know, just to show us what we ain't got or probably ain't never gonna get as long as we're stuck on this rock. There's a strip show at 22:00."

Jeff was already off his rack, on the deck and in front of his locker pulling on his trousers before Billy finished the word 'show'.

"Let's go!" Davis said.

Like most buildings on the airbase the Enlisted Men's Club was a rectangular, cinder block affair with a steel trussed roof and corrugated steel roofing. Essentially a no frills, big empty space littered with chairs and small, round two-top tables, enough to hold hundreds of horny, drunk sailors, Marines and airmen as well as the odd, unfortunate civilian who somehow got lost on his way to some civilized destination.

Apparently the girls who would dance that night had top shelf, professional representation because the P.R. department had spared no expense in their promotion of tonight's show.

There were not **one** but **two** hand lettered posters at the entrance to the club.

> BLAH, BLAH BLAH BLAH, BLAH!
> Starring...
> *Dale Swallow!*
> co-Star of the #1 Smash Hit Feature...
> "Debbie Does Dallas III!"

Inside the six-fifty to seven hundred seat massive, warehouse-like space there was a wall-to-wall stage, off to the left side was a back wall to front wall bar and of course dozens upon dozens of cheap, pressed wood, two top tables with cheap metal chairs.

With the money left over from the poster campaign, the U.S.O. P.R. people had invested heavily in pink and purple balloons which festooned the place. Every corner and nearly the entire ceiling.

Reminiscent of a 1930's union hall, the place was already packed with restless sailors and Marines and so Billy and Davis ambled up to the bar, ordered 4 tequila sunrises each and decided to hang out and stake their claim there.

After a few minutes the lights dimmed and, without ado, the show suddenly started when a slightly overweight 30-something, dressed in a green vest blouse, matching sparkly hot pants, and platform shoes walked on stage with a portable Vicktrola and a long extension cord. She sat both on the stage and ran the cord back into the wing, stage right.

Apparently the Stage-hands' union was on strike.

There was a long pause liberally punctuated with cat calls and she re-emerged with a record album, opened the Vicktrola and put it on.

She perused the guys in the front seats and picked out a burley Marine.

"Could you hand me up a table please?"

"Why? You need something tall and hard to set that on, Sweetheart?"

"Yeah, I do! But it has to be longer than two inches!" Amongst a shower of hoots and cat calls the Marine quietly handed up the table. She sat the record player on it, set the needle in the groove and for the next ten minutes danced, gyrated and stripped down to her undies to Sly and the Family Stone.

A few minutes later it mercifully ended and there was a ripple of applause as she gathered her garments and left.

"Great show." Davis quipped.

"She's why God gave man the secret of alcohol." Billy lifted his drink.

It was around thirty minutes later that the 'feature' act appeared who turned out to be a much younger, early twenties something, brown haired girl, and much better looking, than the former 'B' team members they had been enduring. Miss Swallow took the stage and her choice of repartee was Led Zeppelin's *Been a Long Time*. And she could dance.

She appeared to be getting a good reception from the testosterone saturated crowd as a few over enthusiastic troops in the far corner had a slight disagreement concerning the seating arrangements. Two black eyes were negotiated for two broken bottles, a bruised fist and a busted chair and the matter was considered settled.

As the hooting and hollering steadily built to a crescendo
and just as the future hooker seductively removed her top, somebody burst in through the back doors screaming like a banshee.

"THE LIGHTS ARE OUT! THE LIGHTS ARE OUT!"

The Lights in that part of the world meant the Aurora Borealis alias the Northern Lights. As most of the Naval base's compliment had shipped in before the Aurora season, they hadn't yet had the privilege.

There were no virgins in the hall so everyone had seen breasts and at least two vaginas, one of which they didn't remember, but no one had seen the Aurora before which meant, discounting the time it took for the 400 plus troops to squeeze through the only double door, the place emptied in about 17 seconds flat.

Billy had seen the Aurora before and so, glancing out to a Kawasaki 350 parked outside the adjoining barracks, he suddenly conceived of a way to make his last night in Iceland a memorable one.

Bursting through the front door Chance drove the Kawi up to the foot of the stage and spoke up to the pissed off young stripper who was redonning her top.

"Well?" He looke up at her. "You coming or you wanna just stand there all night in your underwear?!" Dumbfounded she stared out across the ramshackled, abandoned hall. The scene looked like Schofield Barracks on the morning of the 7th of December back in '41.

Several, partially deflated balloons floated aimlessly

across the wrecked tables and spilled drinks in broken glasses coated the floor everywhere.

The Led Zeppelin record had reached the end of the groove and the P.A. system emitted a rhythmic scratching sound reminiscent of a giant insect trying to get into the wrecked room from somewhere on the roof. Off to the side of the room a single passed-out drunk was draped, unconscious over a table.

"Ahh, what-the-fuck?" She shrugged. "Might as well. Can't dance." Chance turned the bike, back wheel to the stage as she gathered her things, threw her coat over her shoulders and hopped on the back of the borrowed Kawasaki. Weaving through the tables they drove through the club, out the door and off into, what would have been had they been any place else, the sunset. But they were in Keflavik, Iceland in late April, so they drove off into the Aurora Borealis instead.

**

The next morning just after 06:00 hundred Billy was met outside the barracks by the single jeep assigned to First Division to be driven over to the airfield to catch the next bird back to the land of round doorknobs.

As Chance was driven away J.D. and Chilli sat, arms propped on the windowsill of the second deck bedroom window watching Billy finally ride off into the sunset.

"You ain't about to cry or nuthin' like that, are ya?" Chilli nodded over to J.D. and asked.

"Fuck you! Why would I cry?!" J.D. shot back.

"The eternal bond between brothers-in-arms, comradeship and brotherly love."

"Horseshit. Ten minutes after he's wheels up on the

Paddy Kelly

runway nobody'll remember his god damned name."

"'Cept Chief Stump!" Chilli said.

"'Cept Chief Stump. Here's to fuckin' the Stump." They both saluted with the middle finger.

Due to heavy cross winds the flight had been delayed for two hours, but now Billy stared silently out the port side window of the Iceland Air 707 as they gained speed and gently lifted off the icy runway. The plane's intercom crackled to life and in a mild Icelandic accent, the pilot came on.

"Ladies and gentlemen as we take a slight deviation from our scheduled course please allow me to show you something you'll remember for the rest of your life." The hundred or so passengers sat up and listened. "New York City has the Empire State Building, Paris has the Eiffel Tower and Egypt has the Great Pyramid at Giza." The captain continued. As the plane gently banked then leveled off the surrealistic sight of the gargantuan mushroom cloud created by a still erupting Eldfell volcano on Heimaey filled the port side of the aircraft.

No one spoke, no one moved. Suddenly the low hum of the aircraft seemed to slowly fade to silence and seconds turned to minutes as they floated above the last throes of the young parcel of earth still being born to the newest continent on the planet.

No one said it, but all thought it, and felt it. The majesty of the sight was a stark reminder of man's insignificance to the universe.

"For the rest of your life! No shit!" Billy involuntarily mouthed to himself as he stared out the small window. "Hell, maybe longer." Chance's mind flashed back to when he was fourteen. He and a friend saved up $5 each, swore each other to secrecy and ditched school to sneak off over the Hudson River to New York City to take a 20 minute joy ride in a tour

Politically Erect

plane around Manhattan Island.

Coasting over the tallest buildings in the world on that clear sunny day in the Beaver DeHavilland the adrenaline rush, which had actually kicked in on the subway ride on the way over into Manhattan and lingered for days after, was fuelled by a mixture of the new facet of danger and doing something no one in his family had ever done before: flew in plane. Also knowing that if his parents found out, his father would go postal on him added a bit of excitement.

I'm gonna jump out of one these things someday! Billy promised himself as he stared mesmerised out of the plane's small window.

"Sir. Sir!" Billy's time tripping was disrupted by the beautiful, blond Icelandic Stew tapping him on the shoulder. "Sir you must fasten your safety belt, please. There could be danger."

He glanced down at his unfastened seat belt.

"Yes, of course I'm sorry." He buckled up and returned to staring out the small window. Another massive explosion blew out of the top of the now half mile high mountain and he could discern small dark specs of rescue workers scattering in all directions. "Wouldn't want to do anything dangerous, would we?" He said to himself. The plane banked away and the flight continued until they climbed above the point where the gargantuan mushroom cloud slowly evaporated from sight into the azure sky.

Evaporated as he hoped his memories of The Rock never would.

*

Paddy Kelly

**FAMILY,
THE GIFT THAT KEEPS ON TAKING.**

CHAPTER FIVE

On the flight back to The States Chance fully realized his mother would be hurt that he didn't talk about stopping home enroute from Iceland in his latest letter, so when he knocked on the steel front door of their apartment on the eleventh floor of the projects, she clearly realized he meant to surprise her. At least that was his cover story. It seemed to work.

"You little bastard!" She lovingly exclaimed as he stepped through the door into the sparsely furnished front room. "How long can you stay?"

"I've got five or six days before reporting aboard."

"Where you going for school?" The man behind the newspaper across the room inquired as a thin plum of cigarette smoke slowly drifting up to the ceiling.

His father sat behind a full sheet spread of his news bible, *The New York Daily News*. Burning away, a cigarette dangled from his mouth.

"Dad! At least open a window will ya! This isn't the Forties anymore!" Billy crossed the room and cranked open the steel framed twelve inch by twenty inch "jump proof" window. It didn't help much. "San Diego." He answered.

"Then where?"

"Guys drop out along the way so no orders till we finish the course."

"Papers're reporting they arrested another couple hundred hippies trying to cross the border into Canada! Yellow bastards!"

"Joe, don't start already!" His mom snapped across the cramped room. Billy noticed the 1963 Motorola TV still held pride of place centered against the right hand wall. The faux mahogany cabinet doors were closed over so's not to reveal the mising cathode ray tube or any tubes for that matter. It ws just an empty cabinet.

Billy dropped his sea bag on the deck, pulled off his pea coat and meandered into the three foot wide kitchen.

"There's not much in there." Mom called out to him. "Sean didn't get to the store yet."

"No prob mom! Just looking for a little juice."

"Well if you had called . . ."

You never call! Or write enough! How the hell am I suppossed to know that you're alright, goddamn it!?

"There was no time between flights ma!"

I'm a big boy now ma! Don't need you to wipe my nose anymore!

Still entrenched behind the newspaper his father smiled at the banter then quickly scowled again at the newspaper.

"God damn Republicans!" He quietly mumbled. "God damned CBS!" His opinion on anything was never left to doubt. Elicited or not.

Mom listend carefully and pretended to ignore the political commentary as she sat gently rocking and knitting in the opposite corner.

"Crazy bastards!"

"Language Joe!"

Guy never shuts up about his God dmned politics! Knit one, pearl two.

"Some guy from California saved up his pension, and is flying to Sweden to get himself changed into a girl!" Joe scowled.

"Good! Now he'll know how it feels to be one of us!" She quippted. *Knit one, pearl three.* "How the hell are they even gonna do that?" She genuinly quieried.

Knit two, pearl four. Knit one, pearl two.

Politically Erect

With a glass of juice in hand Billy paused in the doorway, took in the scene and imagined the chaos their understanding of the world had become, as the reality of their hopelessly out dated political beleif system gradually revealed itself. As the ominous predictions of the Sixties came to fruition and their wholesale rejection of how corrupt the system they were raised to believe in really was and had become combined to set off the five Stages of Death and Dying on a national level, socially speaking. Denial, anger, bargaining, depression and acceptence. Billy reminded himself that they would never reach the fifth stage.

For better or for worse, they truly were representitive of their generation of Americans.

"Where's everyone else?" Billy enquired.

"Pat's moved out and living with her boyfriend. Debbie's working, Chris is moved in with his girlfriend and the little kids are in school."

Despite the fact that the 'little kids', the five youngest, were all teenagers now they were still referred to as 'little kids'.

"Pat's getting married next month." Mom announced.

"Nice! When's she due?" Billy teased.

"Don't be a smart ass!" Mom chastized.

"June!" His dad volunteered from behind the tabloid.

"Oh, nice." Billy declared.

"This country's going to hell!" Dad turned the page. "Ever since those two Left Wing bastards got in, the country's been going to hell!" Anyone who didn't agree with Joe Chance's politics was, by default, a Left Winger.

"So Dad, how do you really feel?"

"Go ahead and laugh! You'll see someday! They'll catch that slimy bastard Nixon in the act, believe you me!" He lit another Marlboro with the still burning butt of the last cigarette. "What we need in this country is someone the people can trust! Someone like Reagan!"

"Ronald Reagan, the movie actor?" Billy challenged.

"He was so good in *Bedtime for Bonzo*!" Mom volunteered.

"Well he's a governor now, and damned qualified!" Joe argued.

"Enough politics!" Mom demanded. "I almost forgot, Chris said to meet him over in the City tonight at seven."

"Nice one! Where?"

"*Trader Vic's* on 59th Street."

*

Military training instills a unique sense of punctuality in most people so at seven sharp Billy turned the corner in front of the Plaza Hotel onto 59th and entered *Trader Vic's*.

The faux, over-the-top Polynesian decor was topped off with the huge, hand carved Hawaiian, dugout canoe used in *Mutiny on the Bounty* with Marlon Brando.

His brother was at the bar.

"Why are we here?" Billy asked once in ear shot.

Just then an attractive, bare foot twenty something in a bikini top and grass skirt sashayed by with a tray of drinks and smiled at them. Her long black hair swished acrossed her curvaceous buttocks as she passed. "Never mind." Billy added.

"Two Jameson's." Chris ordered. "So, Mr. Navy Man! You look good!"

"Fuck you too!" They shook hands. "I reiterate, why are really we here?"

"Heide's got a surprise for you!"

"You two finally get married?"

Politically Erect

"No. But don't tell mom. We told her we were. Only way she wouldn't give me too much shit about co-habitating."

"Co-habitating! Somebody got a thesaurus for Chrictmas."

"Fuck you. Come on." Chris grabbed the drinks and slid off the stool.

"Oh my god! You're living in sin! Good for you. Where to?" Billy quippted.

"We'll grab a table. The girls should be here by half past."

"'The girls'?!" Billy stopped dead in hs tracks. "Not another blind date!" Chris took the drinks and ushered Billy to a table directly under the gargantuan canoe and took the seat opposite.

"You'll like her, she's in the Coast Guard."

"Oh good, I like the tall ones!"

"How do you know she's tall?"

"She must be if she's a Coastie! You have to be six foot tall to join the Coast Guard."

"Really?! I never knew that."

"In case the ship sinks, you can walk ashore!"

"Yeah, good one. Use that on her, I'm sure you'll wind up in bed. ALONE!"

As this was Heidei's third attempt at matchmaking Billy, there was an awkward pause.

"Sorry about springing this on you, bro. It was Heide's idea."

"I appreciate it man. I really do. But we both know she's not gonna show."

"Bullshit! I met her, she's cool."

"Twenty bucks!" Billy challenged and held out his hand. Chris took it and they shook.

"Easiest twenty I'll make all day!" Chris boasted.

Paddy Kelly

"Oh! You stop giving blow jobs?"

"Fuck you Popeye! Anyway, you know what they say . . ."

"You say, 'there's plenty of fish in the sea' and I'll punch you out and take your whiskey!" Billy threatned.

They toasted, downed their shots and Chris signaled for two refills.

"So, how goes the war?"

"Joey Cusak bought it."

"The guy from the gym team?"

"Yeah. Land mine. Richie Horn was sent back after two tours with his mind completly scrambled and both knees torn up. Jumped out of a chopper into a rice paddy up to his waist. The bird started taking fire and when they pulled him out and into the bird they tore both knees out of their sockets. Permanent disability. He'll never work again."

"That's fucked! He was a good guy."

"'Was' being the operative word. Guy's a vegtable now. Bullets don't ask for your resume before they tag you."

"What'a your chances of going over?"

"This country will never be the same after all this is over. Regardles of who wins." Billy let out, cautiously avoiding the question and the fact that he had already volunteered, several times.

"How do you mean, 'who wins'?"

"If you saw the state of our military you'd shit a brick!"

"How do you mean?"

"I could never do it but I gotta be honest, I don't blame those guys running to Canada. It's nothing like the Press paint it. The rampant racisim on both sides, the idiot poiticians telling the idiot field grade officers what to do and how to do it. Hell, the majority of enlisted are

Politically Erect

uneducated minorities or redneck whites who had a choice of doing jail time or going to war. Half the Army grunts can't even spell their names. Most of the rest joined the service because the garbage cans froze over in the Winter and there was nothing else to eat. Most senior enlisted are all hillbillies from the Ozarks and all the Second War vets that are still in are counting the days until they're out."

"You think we're not gonna win? We'll give up to the Communists?!" Genuine shock laced the challenge.

"People in this country are slow to catch on. Slow to catch on to the fact that this ain't W. W. Two. The Big One. The good fight to crush the NAZI's, save Europe and reinstitute the American way of life."

"When'd you get so political?" Chris challenged.

"Political hell! I'm the American politician's worst nightmare."

"What, a commie?"

"Worse. A reader!" Chris didn't quite get the gist but Billy continued. "Half the problem with America, half the reason the D.C. clowns get away with what they get away with is these fucking people don't read. The book is quickly becoming a thing of the past. Replaced by the idiot box! Ther's a lot of other news sources out there besides NBC, CBS, ABC and the *New York Post*. Problem is, America doesn't know that."

"I read!"

"*Playboy* and *Penthouse* are not ranked as literature!"

"Hey that *Forum Section* uses some pretty diverse vocabulary!" Chris defended.

"Yeah, who knew there were twenty-seven words for tits?!"

"Who do you reccomend I read Mr. Worldly?"

"There's this guy writes for *Rollling Stone*, Hunter

Paddy Kelly

Thompson, called Nixon the biggest scumbag in politics. I think he's got his finger on the pulse. Completely different writing style. Nixon certainly may be the biggest scumbag ever to soil the Oval Office, but he sure as hell isn't going to be the last and that's not the worst of it. There's going to be bigger, more twisted assholes signing up and finding bigger and better ways of buying themselves the election as time goes on."

"So what's all that mean?"

"I'm not sure but I'm not sure I want to be around here when that starts going down."

They talked for four more drinks until Billy had finished venting and steered the conversation around to Chris and his girl Heidi.

Finally, Billy glanced up at the bar clock. It was five minutes to nine. Two more large whiskeies later it was obvious the blind date was going to be a no show.

Billy smirked.

"Well, there's always one good thing whether the glass is half full or half empty." Chris proposed as he handed over a crisp new twenty.

"Yeah, what's that?" Billy asked.

"Either way there's room for more alcohol!" He said as he peeled off a twenty and passed it to Billy.

****

A few short days later Chance stood dumbfounded at the display just inside the main entrance, which dominated the quarter deck, (big ass lobby), of the Naval Hospital Corps School, San Diego.

"These guys **must have** been out'a their fucking minds!" The words involuntarily slipped from between his lips.

He was just outside the auditorium of the main

Politically Erect

administration building of the base. He continued to stare, mesmerized, at the massive wall festooned with eight and a half by eleven, black and white photos in thin, wooden trim frames appropriatly painted black.

Each was of a smiling young sailor in his dress blues and white dixie cup cover. Healthy, young men who had served in the U.S. Navy Medical Corps. All graduates of the course. All with numerous awards to their name.

All dead.

Below each photo was a short blurt explaining the horrible mutilation most underwent and then the way in which each had died and the scraps of metal and ribbon they were awarded for what they did.

Congressional Medal of Honor winners, Silver Star citations, Bronze Star commendations were all complimented by hundreds of other awards listed without photos, as there wasn't enough room, off to the side on a series of large bronze plaques, 50 names to a plaque. He picked one and read the citation.

. . . and after sustaining several life threatening wounds himself, HM3 Kenworth continued to expose himself to enemy fire in order to save the four wounded Marines. Silver Star, Purple Heart awarded posthumously.

After the enemy grenade, which failed to detonate as he dove upon it, HM2 O'Brien threw it back at the NVA position and proceeded to man the M30 machine gun, subduing the remainder of the enemy fire and then, single-handedly, carried the three Marines to safety.

Making multiple trips, under heavy fire, HM3 Wachowski tended through the night, the five wounded

Paddy Kelly

Marines all of which went on to full recovery. Bronze Star and Purple Heart awarded. Posthumously.

"**Were** outta their fucking minds!" Billy added.

As the enemy over ran their position HM3 Turner continued to tend his wounded Marines as he assisted in fighting off the enemy flooding into the field dispensary being credited with seven enemy kills. Refusing to board the Medevac chopper until all the Marines were safely aboard, he was consequently wounded and unable to board where, upon his insistence, he manned an M203 and neutralized an enemy armored 113, and imposed a further unknown number of multiple enemy casualties before succumbing to enemy fire.
Congressional Medal of Honor, Medal of Valor, Purple Heart awarded.
Posthumously.

After twenty-five uninterrupted minutes all the citations began to run together.

Balboa Naval Regional Medical Center, San Diego nestled in the extreme south west corner of the country, was one of the two Naval Hospital Corps schools the Nav had and Chance would be there for the next four and a half to five months.

The Hospital Corpsman is an interesting rate for several reasons. Unhindered by those pesky lawsuits which hamstring civilian practitioners, corpsmen are able to give injections, suture wounds, diagnose, administer therapy and write prescriptions. All the stuff nurses are not allowed to do. Now, nurses being officer types and HM's being enlisted types, this occasionally causes some friction.

On the other hand, most HM's being male types and

Politically Erect

most nurses being female types . . . they usually managed to come to amenable and sometimes simultaneous, agreements.

Billy eventually realized it was time to shove off and head out for the standard 'Welcome Aboard' meet and greet ceremony which, based on past experience, would be the last time they would be treated as human beings.

As it was late April and 95 degrees outside with no hint of the pounding heat letting up, it was only logical Chance assume he was to report to the school's auditorium which lay conveniently just behind the massive awards wall he had been previously perusing.

However, Petty Officer Chance had no way of knowing that it happened this was the day the O.W.G.C., alias Officer's Wives Garden Club, decided they should have their semi-annual garden awards ceremony of course to be held in said auditorium.

This month featured cacti of the Southwest.

Fifteen minutes later, outside on the blazing parade ground, in front of a small, portable podium, the dog and pony show began.

Standing in formation on the parade ground, all in dress blues, 'Cracker Jacks' in the vernacular, the 45 students were welcomed by a full Admiral with more fruit salad on his chest and scrambled eggs on the bill of his cap then in all the kitchens of all the Denny's on Interstate Route 80.

After establishing his magnitude by leisurely taking the podium and clearing his throat the Admiral launched into the opening act.

"You are about to become a member of the only Enlisted Corps of the U.S. Navy." The assembled cadre, oozing sweat, but at least partially impressed, paid attention.

Paddy Kelly

"Due to the need for Hospital Corpsmen in a vast array of foreign, domestic, and shipboard duty stations, as well as with United States Marine Corps units, the Hospital Corps is also the largest rating in the United States Navy." With a slight breee the temperature cooled slightly and the impression level rose.

"Your level of training here will be such that when you get out and apply for college credit, in no less than fourteen states you will automatically qualify as a basic EMT and thus be able to work as a paramedic." Impression level 7.5 and rising. "Thereby sparing your poor parents the further burden of paying for your education!"

8.7 and stable.

"In no less than seven other states you will be entitled to challenge the AARN exams, there-by allowing you employment as a Associate Registered Nurse." Thoughts of being killed or mutilated were pushed from the fore as murmurs of approval permeated the humid air. "Welcome to the Great Lakes Regional Medical Center!"

Next up on stage was a short stubby, salt and pepper haired Master Chief named Tennyson. Walking the tightrope between hard ass and professional, Tennyson had to consider the brass present, the few females in the audience and the few guests sitting in the relative safety of their air conditioned cars parked behind the troops.

"This ain't the fuckin' Boy Scouts and we ain't sendin' ya'll on no God damned campin' trip!" Tennyson came from the old school of political correctness. "They's a reason United States Navy Corpsmen gots 22 Congressioanal Medals of Honors, 174 Navy Crosses, 946 Silver Stars and 1,583 Bronze Stars." He allowed a dramatic pause." All in spite of 1,500 KIA times four wounded!"

Next came an orientation speech from a Chief with

Politically Erect

ribbons from just above his left tit to just below his left ball. Billy mused the Chief probably had to take off his jacket to look left.

It was introduced that this guy would be their Class Mentor, (babysitter).

Babysitter was an important job slot as Uncle Sam was about to spend nearly the equivalent of the price of an M-72 tank on each of these baby do-gooders and so wasn't particularly keen on anything marginal washing them out of the program. Especially since over in the Nam Charles was particularly enthusiastic about taking out Corpsmen and medics on his campaign to Communize the civilized planet one third world country at a time.

Chance didn't immediately recognise him as a chief in the United States Navy due to two factors. One he spoke without using 'ya'll' for all personal pronouns or 'they's' for the third singular and he wasn't sporting a spare tire. No balcony above the playground, that is he wasn't suffering from Dunlap's disease, as his belly hadn't dun-lapped over his belt. He looked like he took care of himself, a habit he picked up while spending seventeen years with the Marines. He was Chief Wajenski. From, as Billy would later learn, Jersey City, New Jersey.

"Being the sharp troops you are, you have no doubt noticed there are an appreciable number of female sailors in the area and I know what you're thinking. Don't!"

Standing at ease, all heads craned the area and that's when Chance saw her two ranks back. One of only four females in the class. Dark hair, blue eyes and a body to stop a nine day clock. Disaster immediately struck when she smiled back.

It's all over but the cryin'! Billy pleasantly thought to

himself as the Chief droned on.

"Same goes for alcohol, drugs and any other forms of sex you may be considering. You people are here to learn how to save lives. So pay attention!"

Last upon the showcase was an officer who would be their class leader, a Lieutenant Junior Grade, appropriately named Willy, who was immediately christened Lieutenant Limpwrist by the entire class. He was an over the top gay who made Liberache look straight. Oddly enough he was from San Francisco. He had failed his nursing exam twice and sought refuge in the military. The Navy being more tolerant of gays then the Army, who demanded that it's officers at least act like men, he was able to slip in, so to speak. No pun intended.

"The mess hall is that way and in one hour you will fall in out side the admin building annex to march to class. ATTENTION! FALL OUT!" Any attempted vocal masculinity evaded him.

This being the first opportunity for the students to meet each other there was light convcrsation and greetings on the way to the mess hall for breakfast. A tall, lanky guy with blond hair approached Billy as they walked.

"Terry Burns out'a Athens. My friends call me Ridgerunner!" He proudly drawled brandishing his hand. Billy shook it.

"Billy Chance, Jersey City."

"I's a paramedic back in Athens. That's in Georgia. This jeer course is'a gonna be a piece of pie fer fellas like me. Is you a paramedic or sumthin'?"

"No." Billy politely returned with his eyes glued on the dark haired corpswave just ahead of them. "Nice to meet you." Billy imagined he was talking to the perfectly symetrical ass gently swaying three or four

Politically Erect

yards ahead.

"Well I thinks that –"

"Sorry Terry, my ride's waiting. I gotta run." He smoothly pulled up alongside of her and matched step.

"Mind if I ask you a question?" He asked while she feigned nonchalance. "Do your eyes hurt?" She slowed her pace and shot him a quizzical glance. "Because they're killing me!"

She remained stone faced but there appeared to be a hint of a smile fighting to escape as she picked up her pace again and headed down the slight incline of the stone path which lead to the entrance of the Enlisted Mess.

Minutes later they were in the massive, cafeteria styled chow line.

"Twelve." She said to him while perusing the vegetables.

"What?" They slid their trays down the rails as the line moved forward.

"Three for boldness. Nine for originality."

Score one for the home team! Billy congratulated himself. They found a table and sat.

"So where you from?" He asked.

"And the crowd sighs as his score drops to a ten." She said. "Really? That's your follow-up swing?"

"Oh, you wanna play hardball?!"

"That depends on how hard you swing, Slugger."

"How hard do you like it?" She fought back a smirk. He rationed himself to three second stares straining to avoid overt breast scans. "I love your hair. Perfect combination, light eyes and dark hair."

"I like your hair as well." She reciprocated in earnest. "Dusky blond, not that phoney beach boy, bleached blond look. Back home that was all the rage. Looked ridiculous for mid-westerners. So tell me . . ." She leaned into him across the table. "Does the carpet match the drapes?"

He stopped eating and leaned in as well. "Not sure, I don't do carpet. My floors are made of wood."

Just then Ridgerunner's homing beacon zeroed in on the two and he plopped his tray down and took a seat.

"Hey ya'll! What's cookin'?" He dropped his tray on the table.

"Nothing, anymore." She said as she gathered the contents of her tray and reached for her purse.

"You got a name?" Chance asked.

"Connie, Connie Shepherd." She said as she stood to leave.

"I hear there's a theater somewhere on base. You free this Friday, Connie, Connie Shepherd?"

"I'll check my calendar and get back to you." She lifted her tray and headed out.

Both of them watched her as she floated across the floor and into the crowd.

"Psst!" Ridgerunner reached over and tapped Billy on the shoulder.

"What?!" Chance snapped as he maintained a cross hairs on her perfectly heart-shaped gluteus maximus. Terry leaned in closer and whispered.

"I bet she ain't really got no calendar!" Ridgerunner confided.

Billy turned and stared at him.

**

At the rate hospital corpsmen were getting wacked over in Nam, with the exception of failure to maintain academic standards, few candidates washed out of the

Politically Erect

program. There were however, exceptions.

The first two months of the four month course featured the required array of subject matter, Anatomy & Physiology, Advanced First Aid, Materia Medica & Toxicology, Minor Surgery etc . . . Tests and practical performance exams were given every Friday and, except for one incident things went off uneventfully.

Pressure for the 'must pass' areas in the school was increased as word came down from the Pentagon declaring that tech school failures were to be immediatly reassigned out to 'any available slot' in the fleet. Taken to mean any shit job available usually in a sea-going slot or someplace like Keflavik, Iceland.

It was in the eighth week that they were given their final anatomy exam, a must pass area, which came in the form of a two hour practical.

By now the original 45 candidates had been whittled down to 32 and this exam was considered a mile stone. Out of 150 questions students could only fail eight in total.

Ridgerunner, who had been passing by the skin of his teeth so far, seemed particularly giddy that morning as they filed into the basement morgue of the hospital. Billy wondered had Terry, who was also shit at memorization, figured out some way to beat the test? As he had several times before.

Inside the large, white tiled room were eight previously autopsied cadavers which had been laid out on standard, stainless steel tables in four rows of two and draped with white sheets. An M.D. or R.N. evaluator was stationed at the head of each table and, by previously selected teams of four, the students were directed to their appropriately numbered tables.

As the teams moved towards their assigned tables

Paddy Kelly

Ridgerunner, in a seperate group from Chance, winked at Billy and secretly pulled a slice of roast beef wrapped in a piece of aluminium foil from his pocket mouthing the words; 'From the chowhall!' over to Billy and smiling before quickly putting it back in his pocket. Apparently Ridgerunner had a plan. However, there was something Ridgerunner could not have anticipated.

Lieutenant J.G. Limpwrist, the most squeamish nurse in the U.S.N. Hospital Corps, would be his team's evaluator. Given what Ridgerunner had in mind, this made him nearly squeal with delight.

The senior officer on deck, a Commander from the surgical ward, stepped forward and spoke up.

"Once each team member has his clip board, pen and test sheet at the ready your evaluator will expose your cadaver and you will have sitxty minutes to correctly identify the one hundred and fifty anatomical features labelled by the various numbered pins." He scanned the room then continued. "You will turn your sheets over and your evaluator will continue with the one-on-one verbal testing portion of your practicle. Are there any questions?" There were none and with everthing set, the evaluators all gave the okay and the signal was given.

"You may begin. Good luck." The sheets were slid from the corpses and the students, two on each side of the table, got down to business.

The atmosphere was serious as the evaluators watched, the students wrote and the Commander meandered.

About forty minutes into the proceedings Ridgerunner, two cadavers down from Chance's, began to peer intently into the cadaver's abdominal cavity. Lieutenant Limpwrist immediately took notice.

"Problem Petty Officer Burns?"

"No sir!" Burns shot back. A few minutes later the

Politically Erect

same scenario played out, only now Burns was in the vicinity of the cadaver's opened right thigh. Lt. Limpwrist watched him intently.

"Petty Officer Burns, did you prepare at all for this practical?"

"Why yes sir, I studied real hard like." Lt. Limpwrist, harboring no love for the Southerner, wasn't convinced and decided to focus on Terry.

Meanwhile Billy and the other three in his team had been filling in the blanks at an appreciable rate and were nearly finished.

Five minutes later Ridgerunner, using his pen, was retracting organ after organ as if he had lost a piece of jewellery inside the cadaver. Lt. Limpwrist lost all patience.

"Petty Officer Burns, exactly what the hell are you doing?!"

Ridgerunner popped up straight holding a medium Kelly forceps from which dangled the thick slice of rare roast beef.

"I was just a wonderin', ya'lll ain't never taught us nuthin' about what this here muscle is." He held up the slice of beef.

"Let me see that!" Lt. Limpwrist demanded and started around the table towards Burns.

"Maybe if I kin taste it I kin tell!" He took a big bite and chewed, consuming half the slice before Limpwrist reached him.

In the entire history of the Spanish Inquisition, the Nazi torture chambers or the long list of cinematic failures such as *Plan Nine From Outter Space*, *Santa Clause Conquers the Martians* or *Myra Breckenridge*, no victim or group there of, could have matched the consecutive, female-like screams which flooded the cavernous chamber as Lt. Limpwrist grabbed his own face, turned ghost white and began shaking at the knees.

Despite steadying himself on the dissection table frame, Lt. Limpwrist fell to his knees, still screaming and if not for the quick action of two of the other students, would have cracked his scull on the floor when he passed out cold.

During the ensuing pandemonium all the instructors scurried to the scene. The commander sent for ammonia capsules and supervised Limpwrist's revival and the now unsupervised students, quickly and quietly traded answers. Terry stood off to the side watching the event and calmly finished his snack.

Rumor has it that there's a plaque in one of the barrack heads, (toilets), at the San Diego school to Petty Officer Third Class Terry Burns of Athens, Georgia which reads;

"For selfless bravery in the face of the enemy!"

No longer a candidate for membership in the U.S. Navy Medical Corps, Ridgerunner would have to find employment elsewhere in the U.S. Navy. But he would be remembered at NAVHOSCORSCHOOLSANDIEGO for a very, very long time.

*

Time seemed to fly by and evolution followed evolution as one by one each module was tested, completed and checked off the list.

Billy and Connie kept regular company and had started to get a little more serious. They spent most of their off time together, studied together and had even managed to make it off base to a motel once or twice and

Politically Erect

back in time for curfew.

Now two weeks from graduation and accepting the fact that there was little or no chance that they would be stationed together, they promised each other two things. They would take leave and meet up once they had reached their respective duty stations whenever they could and they would spend their last two day weekend following graduation together in town.

Now in the sixteenth week, finals in all the remaining subjects loomed and the practicals came hot and heavy until only the last evolution remained, the combat field test.

As women were banned from front line combat, and the obstacle courses would be run carrying patients, this would be for males only. Severe injuries to students were not uncommon and, as it was a live fire training excercise, there had even been a handful of deaths over the years.

Any Women's Libbers that might have been around quietly kept to themselves.

Within the scope of 'training' few events in a troop's military career are as exciting as a final exam in the form of a practical exercise. Throw into the mix that it's a live fire exercise and, without being a white man strolling through the South Bronx at three o'clock in the morning with a flashy gold watch and fifty dollar bills hanging out of your pockets, it's about as close to death as you can get.

In this particular exercise Chance's squad were given the task of supporting a Marine infantry company which had the training task of safeguarding some armor which had the training task of navigating seven miles through a wooded area until they reached the open staging area where the Marines and the tanks along with the armored personnel carriers, known as one-one-three's, would stand down and later convert to the real life mission of getting on trains and ships and sailing off to Viet Nam.

Due to his growing up in the unrestrained racial and political violence of Jersey City Chance had seen an inordinate amount of death for his age.

Once while raiding parked box cars full of food he and some other primary school classmates were moving quietly across the open tracks of the switching yard to avoid the yard cops. One of the bulls sighted them and gave chase. Mikey Spinozzi was two tracks behind him when Chance turned to yell at him to move his ass. Mikey was suddenly replaced by a swiftly moving, 100 ton locomotive. The shredded, pulverized remnants of the crate of tinned soup Mikey was carrying was all that was left of where Mikey used to be.

But Chance had yet to come across the truly 'freakish' side of death. On the second day of the exercise as he doubled timed down the embankment in response to the cry of 'Corpsman up!', that fact was about change.

In what was supposed to be a training exercise, he was met with something every corpsmen or troop dreads and no one ever wants to experience, friendly fire.

The M113 armored personnel carrier was developed to safely transport troops. However, somehow during the exercise, a young Marine, during a bivouac, had rolled down a short embankment onto a road while still asleep in his sleeping bag and had been run over by the 12 ton one-one-three.

By the time Chance responded a senior medic stationed with the Marines had made it to the scene. Billy immediately noted the three expended morphine syrettes on the ground next to the kneeling corpsman.

The Marine was completely squashed from the waist down at a forty-five degree angle and what used to be his

Politically Erect

intestines and other abdominal organs dripped from the treads of the track. The young private was still completely conscious but didn't seem to be fully aware of what was happening.

"Am I gonna be okay, Doc?" He asked Billy.

"GIVE ME YOUR MORPHINE!" The HM1 demanded.

"But he's already had –"

School protocol dictated each corpsmen was issued three ampules of ¼ grain of morphine each and no patient was to receive more than one ampule every four to six hours, regardless of injury.

"GIVE ME YOUR FUCKING MORPHINE NOW, GOD DAMN IT!!" The senior petty officer ordered while carefully blocking the marine's vision of the injury with his own body.

The usaul crowd hadn't gathered yet which partially explained why the senior corpsman worked in such a hurry. Billy made eye contact with the HM1 and by his blazing red eyes he semed posessed.

It was in that few seconds Billy Chance learned more about emergency medicine then he had in the last fifteen weeks.

He dug into his M-1 med bag and handed over all three of his morphine syrettes. He stood by, helplessly, as the HM1 quickly injected all three of Billy's ampules in rapid succession into the Marine's left arm, the last directly into his vein.

Within seconds the young victim's eyes glazed over, his respirations quickened and he began to convulse. Chance watched half understanding, half disbelieving and fell to his knees.

After a short minute the convulsions gradually subsided, slowed then turned to sporadic twitching. The young Marine's blue eyes stared out into the distance, glistened then slowly glazed over.

Billy fell back on his heels as the senior corpsman reached over and closed the young man's eyes.

✭

It was a day later with minutes to spare that Billy, accompanied by J.J. Johnson, a guy he sometimes paled around with, dismounted the the Navy shuttle bus on Fourth Avenue in the Gaslamp Quarter section of San Diego, an area Connie suggested. They jumped off the bus across from the prearranged rendezvous and wandered across the street to the Holiday Inn and stood outside to wait for her to show up.

"So you gettin' serious with this chick or what?"

"Why, you writing a book?" Billy cracked.

"Yeah, maybe I am." J.J. defended.

"Well, leave that chapter out!"

It would be the first time they were to meet in three weeks and spend time together prior to shipping out and reporting aboard their respective duty stations. Connie got a set of one year orders to Lakehurst Naval Air Station in New Jersey while Billy drew orders to Balboa Regional Medical Center in San Diego. Literally across the street from the school.

Ten minutes later, just across the road, a Yellow cab pulled up to the curb. The cab pulled away and Connie stood there waiting for an opening in the evening traffic to cross. She didn't have to wait long.

Wrapped in a thigh length, low cut white linen dress and wearing five inch black heels, it was like the parting of the Red Sea that cars stopped for her, horns blared and men stared.

Who said the world isn't black and white?! Billy

Politically Erect

declared to himself as he caught site of her.

As she crossed the street in slow motion, her raven black hair flowing in the evening breeze and her azure blue eyes with a body that would make a man harder then Chinese arithmatic, their two jaws simoultaneously hit the ground.

Immpecably made up, she looked like the kind'a girl they cast in B comedies for sex appeal to keep the audience paying attention when the gags were weak or when the dialogue was wearing thin.

"Congrats on your nomination!" J.J. whispered.

"What nomination?" Chance whispered back.

"The Noble Prize nomination! If you didn't get the telegram yet you will."

"What the hell you talkin' about? Prize for what?!"

"For finding the cure for homosexuality!"

"Stow it asshole!"

"Man it's a good thing my hands are not made of sandpaper! Because when I pop wood tonight they'd be sawdust all over the sheets!" J.J. quietly declared.

"You've got a real romantic streak in you, you know that?"

"Well, actually my mother always said –"

"Fuck off will ya! In case you haven't noticed this is a date!"

"Aren't you even gonna introduce me?" J.J. pleaded.

"NO now fuck off!" Neither took his eyes off the stunning figure approaching them.

"Give me one good reason!"

"I'll give you five good reasons." Billy held up a clenched fist. "But mostly I don't want her to bail on me two minutes after she gets here when she sees the company I keep! Now shove off!"

"But couldn't I-?"

Paddy Kelly

"NO!"

"What about if I just-?" Johnson persisted.

"If you're still here by the time she reaches the curb I'm gonna tell her your a pole smoker!"

"Hope you can't get it up!" J.J. snapped as he turned and headed into the hotel bar to start on the night's elbow bender.

"Hey, Hospialman Chance!" Connie greeted.

"Hey yourself, Corpswave Shepherd!"

"What happened to your dumpy little friend?"

"Oh, he sends his apologies but he suddenly remembered a previous engagement which he formally forgot about."

"Oh, okay. So, what's on the agenda, sailor boy?" She took his arm and they started to walk.

"I thought dinner somewhere, maybe a show afterwards."

"Dinner huh?"

"Yeah. Maybe some Chinese? One of the guys in my section told me about this cozy little place over on Pacific."

"If you don't mind, I took the liberty of making reservations somewhere else." She counted.

"Okay. Where?"

A great little place about a block over." She took him by the hand and led on.

"What's it called?"

"Don't worry, you'll like it!"

"Okay, I trust you. But I'm curious, what's it called?"

"Motel 6!"

Several hours, a half dozen beers and several soaking wet sheets later, it was nearly midnight, they were showered and decided to to go out and forage for food along the main drag.

Five or six blocks from the motel Billy stopped and

Politically Erect

pointed up.

A two foot by three foot neon sign over the doorway crackled while it struggled to fully illuminate as it flashed.

Willie Choy's Chop Suey Haven.

As they passed under the intermittant buzzing and entered the late night joint they were swallowed up by a dark, high ceilinged room festooned with large red, ornate, plastic lanterns. The hand painted murals on the side walls seemed to reach back to the vanishing point as the room streched the entire length of the city block with the rear area cordoned off by a pair of swinging aluminum kitchen doors one of which was propped open.

The long narrow room, crammed wall-to-wall with two top tables and bentwood chairs displayed no visible aisle. Billy mused that a diner with a bladder problem would be hard pressed to reach the toilets in time for the obstacle course the worn furniture presented.

Actually, the tiny gray head peaking just above the counter top was all of a woman, Billy guessed was old enough to have workrd on the original Great Wall, sat behind the tall counter just off to the left. It was only when she stepped up on the something stashed behind the counter that they could see was actually standing and was less than four foot tall.

"Herro! You eat?" She greeted with a near toothless grin.

"Yes please." Connie answered.

"You stay? You go?"

"For take away please." Billy added.

"What you rike?" She asked in perfect broken

Paddy Kelly

English.

They ordered and as the old one scribbled out the order on a carbon pad, Billy nudged Connie and nodded towards the back.

From between the single open aluminum door they caught sight of a significantly older man squatted low on the kitchen floor, arms dangling over his knees. His white Fu Mnachu brushed the floor between his wide open legs and from the sound of The Late Show blaring up through the restaurant and the eerie whitish glow on his face two facts were obvious; the old guy probably didn't understand most of what he was watching and he was half deaf.

The old woman, order check in hand, eased herself down off whatever she was perched on, waddled around in front of the counter and proceeded to shout back to the old man in Mandarin. There was no response.

How fat was she Johnny? Ed McMahon asked. The audience laughed.

The visibly annoyed homunculus of a woman took exactly half a step forward and yelled again, a fraction louder.

Billy and Connie deduced she must have cosmically transferred her anger because this time the 200 year old man's Fu Man Chu danced rythmically below his chin as he screamed back.

Defiantly slow he stood upright and shuffled to the huge stove. Implements clanged, a wok banged and flames roared.

Ten minutes later, two over sized, brown grocery bags cradled in his arms, bumping nearly every chair in his path the old man serpentinely shuffled to the front, plopped the bags down on a table and grumbled his way back to his cave.

"Ten fitty!" The old woman declared. Shocked at the

Politically Erect

price for so large amount Billy gave her fifteen dollars and five minutes later the two young sailors were sitting on a bench manipulating chop sticks from large containers of steamed rice and moo goo gai pan to their mouths.

Later, their hunger satiated but half the food remainig, they wandered the winding, chilly streets crunching fortune cookies until they could eat no more when they came on a small cluster of hobos huddled arund a pair of large oil drums filled with burning scraps of wood.

"Get yo asses up in here boy! Ya'll wanna freeze half to def?" The hobo captain insisted.

"Well thank you for the invitation to share your hearth, kind sir!" Connie blandished with a bow.

"Hey, any you guys want an egg roll?" Billy offered. Two of them accepted and the large white food containers made the rounds.

Walking back in no real dirction they found themselves about a block away from the motel.

They stopped and held each other close.

"Guess we've had enough food to last the weekend." Connie declared.

"Till we get back to the base!"

"You really want to go back to the base?"

"Where else we gonna go? It's quarter after three in the morning. The last shuttle goes at three thirty."

"Weve got the room until eleven tomarrow!" Connie suggested.

"Sweetheart, it is tomarrow!"

"Well in that case . . ." She took off her heels and began running in the direction of the motel. " . . . last one in bed naked's a fat, old Master Cheif!"

Paddy Kelly

★

It was now over a week since the M113 incident and Billy had heard nothing concerning the subject of the ballsy HM1 who risked his career and a prison sentence when he euthanized the fatally wounded Marine and now Chance's mind was on graduation which lie only six hours away.

A military barracks housing up to 300 hundred troops, sleeping side-by-side in two long rows of an open plan, sealed up wooden building with only a single 32 inch door at either end is a place no one relishes to be. Especially when it's one of the antiquated WWII styled barracks.

The accumulated methane content due to flatulence alone was so lethal that if weaponized, would defeat any enemy foreign or domestic.

Fortunately by the time Billy came to serve, with the exception of the barraks and team houses of the Special Forces units, there were few WWII structures left.

Now the Navy boasted modern housing with university styled dormitories housing one, two and four man rooms and heads with single shower stalls as opposed to the old prison styled, gang showers.

Even though modernized, the buildings still required an all night fire watch and it was Billy Chance who had pulled the duty the last night before graduation. Nothing ever really happened so all he actually had to do was walk up down the passageways with a baton and intercept and challenge strangers.

It was about four o'clock in the morning when a lone sailor, dressed only in his skivvies and, an unseen object concealed in his left hand, left his four man room, headed down the passageway to the head and went inside.

Politically Erect

He was young, looked almost too young to be in the military, was baby-faced with blue eyes, close cropped, dirty blond hair and a slight build. The kind of kid no conscientious warden would put in with the general population. Except maybe in Texas where they'd do it for sport, then take bets on how long he'd last.

The young corpsman pulled the lanyard on the fluorescent light over the sink and stared into the mirror for an inordinate period of time. He appeared not to recognise the guy who, bathed in eerie, incandecent light, stared back at him.

There was no telling what he was thinking but whatever it was he came to some kind of an inevitable conclusion, because the next thing he did was to produce a large straight razor then slowly and systematically deeply slash both wrists slicing skin, severing tendon and completely opening both radial arteries and all ancillary vessels. As he stood there profusely bleeding into the sink, he remembered what one of his instructors had said in class about how most suicides use the bath tub to do this. They fill it with hot water to accelerate exsanguination: death due to massive blood loss. 'Bleed out' is how the cops would describe it.

Being a good troop he was careful not to drip blood on the deck as he dutifully put the rubber stopper in the drain and turned on the hot water then immersed his leaking wrists.

It was seconds later that HM3 Chance wandered in to take a piss and he saw the kid wobbling in front of the sink and walked over to him and laid a hand on his shoulder.

"Hey mate, you okay?" Chance recognised the kid from another squad but didn't know his name. The kid looked over and gave Chance a smirk. "Look what I did." He calmly said, and then looked down at the reality he had imposed on himself.

Billy glanced down into the large pool of bloody water in the sink then back at the kid's pale white face.

"SHIT!" The kid's legs suddenly gave way and Billy caught him. "It's alright, just do as I tell ya. Ya gonna be okay!" Chance laid the kid on the floor, and using his own skivvy shirt made a single wrap around the wrists, placed the wounds face to and tightly tied the kid's wrists together. This stopped the bleeding, but there was well over a pint of blood in the sink, and close to that amount again now as the water over flowed onto the deck, there was an indiscernible amount of blood lost all together.

"Can't do it." The kid uttered. "Just can't." He began to shiver.

"What the fuck's wrong with you, man! We're done! This place is history, we graduate today! Why would you do this?!" He asked cradling the kid's head.

"I don't . . . want to . . . go . . . to Nam."

"Maybe you'll get non-combat orders!"

"If they ship me over there I might die!" His speech was now at a whisper. "That's all. Don't wanna . . . die in . . . the Nam."

His head fell off to the side, unconscious and Billy reflexively felt for a carotid pulse. There was none. The pupils of his glassed over eyes were fixed, dilated and non reactive.

With the gently over flowing sink splashing to the floor behind him Chance used his fingers to close the boy's eye lids over, and with a blood soaked hand gently set his head on the tiled floor, stood to turn off the water and looked down at the kid's pale, chalky face. Suddenly He saw the scene from outside himself as if he were standing in the doorway looking in.

"Probably never even been laid." Billy muttered.

Politically Erect

Jesus Christ! He thought to himself. *Is this gonna be the cycle from now on? Every time I finish a school or change a duty stations someone has to die?*

The following brief investigation revealed that the kid was from just outside Dallas where he got drunk on his 21st birthday and hit a police squad car. The judge gave him a choice, two years in the State Pen or sign up in the military.

With the highest overall combat casualty rate in the U.S. miliatry the corps school class's first casualty had not even made it to graduation.

Paddy Kelly

GENITALS PREFER BLONDS.

Politically Erect

William W. Chance Jr.
Apt 1106,Bldg 1
Federal Housing Project
Duncan Ave. Jersey City, N. J.

HM3 William W. Chance III
U.S. Naval Hospital Command
San Diego, California

Dear Mom;   August 24, 1974

Graduation was last week and school was a real education. You'll be happy to know my next duty station is The Regional Medical Center in San Diego. The orders are for a year and it's pretty certain the war will be over by then.

Sorry to hear about Dad losing his job, it's tough enough for someone without high school as it is, but after that GM, Ford and Chevy fiasco and all the closures, even the unskilled labor market is drying up now.

Don't go doing a jig or making wedding plans but I met a girl. Details to follow.

Will try and send some money next month when I get paid.

Sorry to hear about Uncle Pete dying.

Love you guys.

p. s. - Don't tell dad I called him 'unskilled' labor! He'll kick my ass.

Paddy Kelly

CHAPTER SIX

Balboa Naval Regional Medical Center
San Diego, California

The United States Navy had over 200 ratings and of those nearly every one was subject to get orders to Nam, with most staying state-side and only a small percentage of the ones which would go to Nam having any chance of seeing any action. However, the Hospital ratings, being members of the only Enlisted Corps in the Navy, were slightly different.

Discounting the plethora of technicians and administrative personnel which comprised the medical corps' sub-ratings, most of which who would also never see the inside of the war zone, this left with the line corpsmen. The non-line corpsmen, if you were one of the medical sub-ratings, you were either going on to a comfy seven to three clinic job or going to war.

As the war wasn't going so well for the Yanks in '74, 90% of everybody from Class 137-74 was pretty well assured they were not going to a comfy, state-side clinic job.

Billy reported to the personnel office that morning after graduation as directed to receive his orders, took his place in line and a half hour later was handed a thin 8 1/2 by 11 manila envelope. Stepping away from the window he opened the envelope which contained six copies of orders. Orders to the Naval Regional Medical Center, Balboa, San Diego.

Again his requests for or land duty or ship board assignment in the South China Sea had been ignored.

"Hey what about travel pay?!" He yelled back into the window to the clerk.

Politically Erect

"There's a base-to-base bus. Comes every two to three hours! It's free." An hour and a half later he was stepping off the bus at his new home for the next year.

A personnelman checked him at the personnel desk then escorted him to the hospital where he would serve on administrative duty for the first week while he unerwent base orientation.

"Welcome ta NRMC, San Diego." The overweight, black, PN2 sarcastically greeted. Billy was amused at how his white Dixie cup cover precariously balanced on a large tuft of curly, non-regulation afro. Rather than walk he affected an exaggerated gait which meant to Billy he either wanted to reaffirm his 'blackness' or liked mocking passing cripples as they limped past the them enroute to the central hospital building.

"That be the hos-spit-tool." He was the kind of guy who talked 'at' people rather than 'to' them. Probably had little or no status back on the block, Billy figured and now after making rate, thought himself a cut above the rest. The rest of what wasn't exactly clear. "NRMC, San Diego, or as it is known to most of us with dicks 'n shit, 'Dyke Central'!"

Billy's head whipped back around as he ripped his eyes from the shapely nurse tightly shrink wrapped in her regulation dress whites.

"You're not serious!" Chance challenged.

"Navy's biggest secret. I dun know if they joins as dykes or if'n they do sumfin' to em in basic, but whatever it is, there it be. Place be full of rug munchers!"

Billy pondered the possibilities. *Dyke de Solé. Dyke and cover. Finger in the dyke! Huh, endless possibilities!*

Billy noted there was very little foot traffic and put it down to being late afternoon on the weekend. As they approached the bank of six double, glass doors which formed the main entrance to the fifteen story structure he noticed just inside the vestibule, dominating the entire right side of the lobby, an over sized reception desk manned by one junior corpsman floating in the middle of the massive space was lost in a magazine.

"You pulls desk duty fa da first week til they gets yall's clinic rotation squared away."

"What'a I do here?"

"Sit behind that big, McDonald's lookin' desk and give directions." He looked Billy up and down as if sizing him up for a fight. "Think you kin handle it, white boy?"

Chance resisted the temptation to comment on the correlation between his mentioning McDonald's and the size of his ass. Instead he just smiled, cocked his hat forward and assumed a cross armed defensive position.

"Shit Bro, if a uneducated nigga' from Alabama kin make PN2, I don't rekon I ain't gonna have me no problems, you dig. Bro!"

Save for a few minor scraps in basic training, which were quickly settled, Chance had managed to avoid the overt, rampant racism which plagued the U.S. Armed forces. A racism that was activly and heavily muzzled by order of the Pentagon and completely ignored by the popula press. Unfortunately that would not be the case throughout his time in the military.

Not prepared with a comeback, Lumpy just smirked and be-bopped on down the hall and out the front door as Chance shook his head and went around behind the reception desk.

Fuckin' clown! Billy mused to hmself.

"Hey." The slightly younger sailor acknowledged as he greeted Chance. They shook hands.

"Hey. Billy Chance, New Jersey."

"Jimmy Fagen, Arizona." He dismounted the chair

Politically Erect

and moved to Billy. "I'm going to head down to the restaurant, get a Pepsi. You want something?"

"No thanks, I'm good. Anything I need to know while you're gone?"

"Somebody comes in you direct them. Floor plan and directory are under the glass on the desk. Somebody calls, ask for the extension and connect them. They don't know the extension directory's right there under the desk." He headed out the side door of the closed-in desk area.

"Exciting!" Billy declared.

"That's about all the excitement you'll see around here, shipmate. It's Sunday. Nothing happens around a hospital on Sunday." Billy heard his footsteps echo through the hallway as he disappeared.

Restaurant? I thought it was called a mess hall? Billy again mused as he settled into the big high backed chair. He slowly perused the area as his eyes bounced from item to item.

"Desk, check. Phones, check. Brand new, Underwood-Olivetti, electric typewriter. Check. Keys operational?" He punched one of the keys. "Check!" He laughed to himself. "Join the Navy and see the world! Through a fucking porthole." Billy grunted.

In the next hour he studied the floor plan and gave directions to two visitors. He read the doctor's directory, flipped through a battered copy of a three year old *National Geographic* and restudied the floor plan. Then gave another vistor directions.

By around 16:00 the other guy still hadn't returned and Billy was getting a little hungry while wondering exactly how long it took an Arizonian to drink a Pepsi when a slightly dishevelled Senior Chief in khakis came through the front door, walked to the center of the deserted, massive lobby, glanced around the area then made for the desk.

Average height, medium build with salt and pepper hair with a slightly weathered face, Chance couldn't tell if the man was smiling or smirking. He wore no cover, his tie and collar were opened and he held his left arm across his chest.

"How can I help you Senior Chief?"

"Where's X-Ray from here?!" He demanded in no uncertain terms.

Opposite the entrance, othe right of the desk, just inside the lobby, was a wall festooned with a bank of double doors leading to the inner, upper and lower bowels of the gargantuan structure.

Billy pointed.

"Third set of doors on the right Chief."

The Chief turned and walked away form the desk. "Hey Senior Chief, you alright?" That's when Chance's pulse jumped from 60bpm to just over 200.

Aside from his injured arm the decorated war vet clutched a standard issue Colt .45 in his good hand.

Halfway across the lobby the Chief stopped, turned back and made eye contact with Chance.

No one can legitimately be criticized for how they react in a life or death situation but few people realize there are more than just the two, fight-or-flight reflexes. There's always the old duck'n'pray stratagy.

Billy sat still and quickly decided that if the right arm, the one holding the weapon, moved in any way he would make a dive for it and scramble for the side hall to his right.

Chance couldn't know that, returning home from his third tour in the war zone, while doing some repairs around the house that afternoon, the Chief discovered his wife's secret lover. A 19 year old Seaman Apprentice,

Politically Erect

(very low rank), who worked in personnel who also believed she was divorced. The boy toy had shown up at the house, the Senior Chief answered the door in his skivvys and the clueless kid stupidly asked for Doris. The ensuing fight resulted in some broken ribs, a fractured jaw, multiple contusions and abrasions and a fractured ankle.

The Cheif got a broken arm.

Long seconds passed. Billy and the Senior Chief were locked in a stare-off. The Chief's eyes seemed to say, "This is gonna be you in a few years." Billy's eyes signalled back, "Whatever it was Chief, it wasn't my doing!" Suddenly the Chief uncocked the .45, muttered a Clint Eastwood "Thanks." and walked off through the door marked 'X-Ray'.

Billy immediately grabbed the phone and contacted base security.

For whatever reason, probably because somebody had a brother-in-law with a security firm somewhere, the Nav had started to abandon the concept of Shore Patrol for internal policing matters and went to private security firms. Unfortunatly the guys they hired were kind'a like mall cops, only not as bright.

Fifteen minutes later a gaggle of them tactically came bursting through the front door like a mob at a Rolling Stones concert who were running late. There was a slight difference. This mob was armed with MP-5 machine guns, M-16's and Remington 12 gauges. All pointing at close range directly at Chance.

"ON THE DECK! HANDS BEHIND YOUR HEAD! TOSS YOUR WEAPON ACROSS THE FLOOR AND DON'T FUCKIN' MOVE!"

Great! Not just idiots, but armed idiots! Chance realized.

"You want me to put arms behind my head or don't move?"

"WHAT ARE YOU. SOME KIND'A SMART ASS?!"

"I'M THE QUARTERDECK OF WATCH! I'M THE ONE THAT CALLED YOU GUYS, ASSHOLE!"

"WHAT? WHERE'S YOUR WEAPON?!"

"I AIN'T GOT NO WEAPON! I'M THE GODAMNED DUTY CORPSMAN! **I CALLED YOU!**"

The rent-a-cop's radio squelched and he listened into his shoulder mic.

"Roger that." He turned to Billy. "Alright we got word there's some looney here with a gun and he's coming back out. Don't move, just act normal! Even though he's got a gun and is probably just another crazy vet, act normal,"

"Gun!? Big fuckin' deal! I'm from Jersey City. Everybody's got guns!"

The Keystone Cops dashed around the lobby and out the doors hiding behind bushes, planter pots and three foot high garbage cans.

Minutes later the Chief meandered back out into the lobby. Cleverly surrounding him in a full circle, the cocking of hammers and shotguns sounded like a dozen kids dragging sticks across a chain fence at a full run.

Figuring their aim probably wasn't any better than their judgement, Billy slowly hit the deck and waited.

The dismayed Senior Chief looked around, quietly lay his .45 on the deck and raised his good arm.

"I SAID BOTH HANDS!" The Chief struggled to comply but couldn't get his obviously broken arm above shoulder height.

"He's got a broken arm!" Chance yelled as he popped back up from behind the desk.

Politically Erect

"SHUT THE FUCK UP AND LET US DO OUR JOB!" The five foot four John Wayne ordered.

The security geeks nearly knocked each other over as they rushed him and Chance could see him pass out as they wrenched his broken arm behind his back to cuff him. The Chief went unconcious.

"Cops are the same everywhere." Billy murmured.

The Senior Chief's crime? Earller that day, when he came came in for treatment, he hadn't signed in at the desk before going to X-Ray. No one knew he was there.

Having been in the war zone so long, where an injured man is tended to immediatly and without a ton of paper work or buerocracy he mistakingly assumed here, like over there, he would be treated first and burocritized later.

Nothing happens around hospitals on Sunday? Fucking Pearl Harbor happened on a Sunday! Billy mused as the rent-a-cops dragged the unconcious chief out the door.

***

"I double timed it over to the port side to lend a hand beatin' them little yellow bastards off the rail as they tried to board!" The hoarse voice coming from underneath the tented sheet on the large hospital bed built in intensity as the old man's narrative progressed. "We'd already lost Jimmy Franks and both our Chinese Coolies! Wasn't NO WAY IN HELL I was gonna loose no more'a my men afore I got us back down the Yangtze and out to the fleet!"

Now in his third month of a six month rotation through the major wards of the NRMC, Chance listened to the war stories of the terminal ward's most well known, well liked and most interesting patient. The 89 year old 'Captain Jack' McCarthy, a pre-WWI era gunboat petty officer who started his warrior's career in 1900 at the age of fifteen when he first fought in the Philippine-American war in Manila Bay, then less than a year later received orders to go and join his first gunboat stationed on the Yangtze River during the Boxer Rebellion.

Around the age of thirty, he participated in the War for and occupation of Haiti, the occupation of Nicaragua in 1914 and later in 1915 the battle for control and subsequent occupation of the Dominican Republic during the Banana Wars before shipping out in 1916 to fight in the North Atlantic during World War I. He briefly served as an adviser for riverine tacticts during the Russian Civil War from 1921-22, had a bit of rest in his mid thirties until World War II kicked off then joined in that little get together.

He was refused service during the Korean War due to his age and was forcibly retired a Master Chief Engineer.

There were, up until the time, six enlisted individuals in the entire history of the U.S. military, to include the Army, Navy, Marines and Coast Guard, authorised to wear two extra rows of ribbons on their uniforms due to the fact that they had been awarded too many medals. Of the six he was the only one still breathing.

But, Jack was on the way out thanks to terminal syphilis. His chart contained a standing order that he be encouraged to interact with the staff as much as possible for an hour at least twice a day. So the nursing staff took it in turn to sit and listen to his stories, enter abbreviated renditions of them in the notes and report any, aside form the normal, strange behavoir.

Billy sat mesmerized and stopped writing as he stared at Captain Jack as he was reminicent of a kid sitting under a sheet on his bed disobediently reading a comic book after bedtime.

"Them anti-boarding party drills did their job that day I can tell ya!"

Another corpsman came into the room and approached Billy.

"You HM2 Chance?"

"Yeah, why?"

"Report to the C.O., on the double!"

"Fer what?"

"Dunno, but whatever it is it's on the double!"

He finished entering his nursing notes and wondering, *WTF?! What'd I do now?!* He said good afternoon to The Captain, left the T-Ward and made his way upstairs to the C.O.'s office where he knocked smartly three times on the steel grey door.

"ENTER!" He opened the door and stepped into the sparsely decorated office, assumed a spot front and center forward of the full bird's desk and saluted sharply. The Captain had her face buried in a personnel record with the yellow performance sheet flipped over the jacket.

She was the first female Chance had ever seen with WWII medals among the five rows on her chest. Plaques and photos, some of her standing on Omaha Beach immediately following the invasion, hung on the wall behind her.

"Petty Officer Chance? William Chance?" She asked without looking up.

"Reporting as ordered Ma'am!"

"Stand at ease."

"Thank you Ma'am."

"I have an interesting report here Petty Officer. From one of my junior nurses."

"Am I at liberty to ask which nurse, regarding what,

Captain? And may I just say, Ma'am, in my own defence . . ." She lowered the folder and stared across at him.

"You've nothing to defend Pettyofficer. I'm informing you I'm going to endorse Lieutenant Martin's recommendation to give you a special commendation!"

Chance literally felt weak kneed.

Who the fuck was Lieutenant Martin? He quickly thumbed through his memory files. *Linda, Janet, Janenne, Kathy, Natsha . . . ahh! Natasha! Carol? Nope, nothing.*

"For . . .?"

"For . . ." she read from the folder. "Quick thinking and presence of mind without which the patient, a one Petty Officer First Class Stinson would have surly aspirated his own fluids and drown. Chance's quick thinking and swiftness of action undoubtedlysaved the ptient's life. Petty Officer Second Class Chance has brought great credit to himself, the NRMC facility and the United States Medical Corps."

What the fuck?! Billy's mind raced through the entire last three months on the wards. Every incident, altercation and all the rounds he could remember and he couldn't recall a PO1 Stinson. *Who the hell was Lieutenant Martin and why the hell was he recommending me for a Special Commendation?*

"I asked if you had any comments Petty Officer Chance!"

"Er . . .no, no Ma'am. No questions at this time."

"Well then you'll report one half hour early for shift tomorrow, squared away as the Lieutenant informs me you always are, and we'll give you your commendation. You're dismissed."

"Yes Ma'am. Thank you Ma'am." He saluted, executed an about face and di di maued the area of operations as directed.

Politically Erect

★

Paddy Kelly

BEING IN THE MILITARY IS LIKE SMOKING DOPE

THE HARDER YOU SUCK, THE HIGHER YOU GET

CHAPTER SEVEN

NRMC Dispensary, San Diego
07:15 Sunday

The Korean War vintage, olive drab green, cracker box ambulance, with the big red cross in the white field on the sides, screamed through the base towards the docks at full throttle, flat out at 37 miles per hour.

"Why we drivin' with lights and siren? That fucker's as dead as he gonna get!" The passenger quandaried Chance as they took a turn a little too wide. Being early Sunday morning there was no other base traffic so disaster was averted.

"It's to let the Old Man know we're trying to beat the Press. They get a hold of the story and it'll be all over the front page tomorrow how another poor G.I. offed himself rather than go fight in the unjust, illegal war in support of the industrial-military complex supported by an unjust Congress." Chance explained.

"What the fuck you care what they print?"

They took the turn-off to the piers a little too tightly and came up on two wheels.

"I don't give a shit. I just like driving like Mario Andretti."

The passenger, HM3 Lee, a black kid out of the South Bronx, graduated from the Great Lakes course about a month after Chance finished up in San Diego. They now found themselves stationed together at the NRMC in San Diego.

"Dat's another thing, how come all you white boys always be callin' yall's commandin' officers 'the Old

Man' n' shit, like he's ya'll's grandpa n' shit?"

"Dunno Lee. Probably the same reason blacks can't conjugate."

"I don't know what that means, but I find out it's a insult I'm gonna –" They swerved as they took a turn and narrowly missed a double parked car. "Damn White Boy! Slow down!"

"We're only doing 35!" Billy argued.

"They still gonna run the story!" Lee insisted.

"Yeah but, if we beat them there, they'll have to run it without photos of the dead body."

"Well hell, step on it Hutch! I hates them racist, honkie, press mutha-fuckas!"

Billy liked Lee and had to smile at the fact that it was never really clear what Lee hated. Perhaps it was fashionable because he was young and black or perhaps he didn't know how else to express himself. But whatever it was, Lee hated it.

Billy was able to push it to 38 mph no problem, downhill, and a few minutes later they arrived on the extensive row of piers situated on the west coast docks wth no press in sight.

Two men, a short black security guard and the base commander who wore civvies, stood in the blazing sun on the edge of Pier 39 looking out into the bay as the ambulance pulled up. They were staring out at a dark blue lump gently bobbing in the water about 200 yards out in the harbor. Looking closer it appeared to be a dead sailor, what was affectionately known as a "floater." The two saluted the base C.O. and Billy approached him while Lee hung back.

"What'a we got sir?"

"The *Saratoga* reported a sailor A.W.O.L after missing ship's movement–"

"They put out nearly two months ago!"

Politically Erect

"Thanks for the update petty officer! Being the C.O. of the one of the largest deep water ports on the Western Seaboard housing the largest carrier fleet in the world I sometimes get confused and lose track of the really big boats under my command!"

"How you like your old man now?" Lee mumbled out of earshot.

"Yes sir. I mean, I know that Commander . . . that you know that the really big boats . . ." The full bird captain stared at him. "Shutting it sir."

"If I may be allowed to finish?"

"Yes sir. Please do. Finish. Sir."

"He's a family man, religious etc. . . and so doesn't fit the profile of a deserter. In addition his family and parents haven't heard from him either."

"I understand sir. We'll take the skiff and go out and get him."

"Good plan corpsman! You ever thought about being an officer?" Lee took a step further back away from the fallout zone. The C.O. wiped the sweat from his forehead.

"Well sir –"

"DON'T! NOW GET THE HELL OUT THERE! And make sure you get him on this side of those two yellow buoy markers before the Press get here! They get shots of him on the other side that's state property which means we have to notify the State Coroner and sit around out here with our thumbs up our asses until he gets his fat ass out'a bed from next to his fat-assed wife, has his coffee, cigarette and meanders out here. Got it?"

"Loud and clear sir! We're on it. Lee, let's go!" They climbed over the side and down into the aluminium Boston Whaler outboard which was permanently moored alongside the pier for just such purposes.

"When's the last time that guy got a blow job?" Lee cracked.

"You offering to give him one?"

"Man, fuck you white boy!" Lee shot back as he untied the bow line.

"I'm just sayin', that's one way to get rank."

"Very funny! Hope you keep your sense of humor when we get close up to that floater!"

"Actually, the C.O.'s not so bad."

"How you figure?"

"He reminds me of my grandfather." Chance quipped as he started the outboard.

"What, he don't get blow jobs either?" Lee parried.

"Gram the gaff pole and push off, Dr. Ruth!"

Ten minutes later, approaching the drifting corpse, Chance cut the skiff's single Johnston and they coasted up alongside the face down, gently bobbing body. Whoever he was he had definitely been a sailor as his tattered, gabardine shirt and bell bottomed trousers were U.S. Navy issue.

Chance manned the eight foot long gaffer's hook and gently pulled the body by the belt hauling it up to the port side of the skiff. Lee had removed his own shirt and was wrapping it around his face against the rising stench.

"He won't smell really bad until we get him out'a the water." Chance advised.

"OUTTA THE WATER? MAN YOU LOST YOUR FUCKIN' MIND OR WHAT? I ain't takin' no dead mutha-fucka out'a no fuckin' water!"

"Don't be a pussy! He ain't gonna bite ya!"

"I **know** he ain't gonna bite **my ass** cause I ain't takin' his ass out'a that water!"

"Then what the fuck do you propose?! One of us dive overboard and use him as a paddle board and push him into shore?"

Politically Erect

"Good idea, long as that one of us is **you**, cause I ain't wrestlin' no dead body out'a no water onto no muthafuckin boat!"

"ANYTIME, LADIES!" The Commander voice blated out from dickside

"Alright, god-damn it! Just take hold of his wrist while I reposition the gaffer hook and get a lanyard around his belt. I'll lash him off to the side and we'll coast him in where we can get more help."

Chance adjusted the gaff under the victim's belt and pulled him tight to the hull at the same time Lee moved in and daintily grabbed the victim's left wrist by his shirt cuff with two fingers being extra careful not to touch any dead flesh.

Focused on undoing the gaff pole and stowing it under the seats Billy heard a prolonged sucking sound followed by a thud topped off by a blood curdling, high pitched shriek.

When he turned to look aft, Lee was sitting on the back bench, holding the sailor's naked and blackened, left arm from the wrist to the exposed bone of the shoulder while the empty sleeve, still attached to the shirt, flaccidly floated next to the corpse. Billy smiled at Lee's terror.

"Great idea, I should've thought of that! Bring him on board piece at a time! Might take awhile, but good idea!" Lee threw the arm to the deck and kept cackling in disgust as he thrust his hands over the side and into the water to give them a vigorous scrubbing. The shirt around his face slipped off and the stench of rotten flesh filled his nostrils causing him to scramble for the shirt and re-tie his mask at which time he stared to wretch.

"Death's not contagious!" Billy chided.

"Man, fuck you! That shit . . . ain't funny!"

Paddy Kelly

Lee refused to touch the body so it took some effort on Billy's part to get them all back to pier side but once there, they tied off and had the dead sailor prepped, it was only a matter of teamwork to get him up and out of the water.

As the body was water logged it took all hands to man the one inch manila line Billy had rigged around the one armed sailor as they hauled him up and over the breaker wall and onto a waiting litter on the deck of the pier.

"Lee, grab the report pad out of the cracker box." Chance said as he squatted down next to the face up victim. "Look like our man Commander?"

"No. We've a recent photo from his wife." The C.O. handed Billy the photo. "James Loggerheit. White male, 23 years old, 155 pounds, blue eyes." *Eyes, not an issue*, Billy thought. The victim had no eyes. They'd been eaten away by fish. "That's not him." The Commander declared.

The victim tentatively appeared to be a 225-250 pound, six foot, Arabic or black male.

"Chance get a blanket out of your vehicle and cover the corpse."

"Aye sir."

"Search him for I.D." The commander said to the security guard just as a press van came around the corner.

"No sir!" The security guard snapped back.

"No sir?! I'm the god-damned base commander! I said search him!"

"No sir! I ain't in no Navy."

"You also ain't in no security service! As of Monday you're on unemployment, now get the hell outta here!" The useless rent-a-cop willingly hit the bricks.

Chance came back over with the blanket, lay it aside

Politically Erect

and knelt by the body. He systematically searched the four trouser pockets and the two shirt pockets. The left breast pocket yielded a laminated, U.S.N. issue, green I.D. card. He perused it and shook his head.

"Son-of-a-bitch!" He quietly said as he passed the card to the C.O. who read it aloud.

"James Loggerheit, white male. 23 years old, 155 pounds, blue eyes." The C.O. read aloud.

Eyes not an issue.

In the ambulance on the return trip with the body stowed in a black body bag in the back, Lee nd Chance spoke.

"Everyone drinks before a long deployment. Some guys over do it and when they put out to sea, especially if they're assigned to the casting off party, sometimes they go overboard, literally. Vessel of that size, 4,000, 5,000 plus compliment, they're not missed right away. Coupl'a months later, they turn up, lookin' like James Loggerheit."

Lee had been silently staring out the window.

"23 years old, used to be white, male. With used to have blue eyes." Lee mumbled making no attempt to hide the fact that he was dealing with some emotional shit. In an effort to ease the tension he sensed Billy continued.

"Flat tops loose one to three guys every time they put out. The Forrestal's lost six overboard so far this year!"

"You tryin' ta cheer me up, don't!" Lee snapped.

"First time that close to corpse?"

They slowed as the Marine guard waved them through the front gate.

"First time I ever seen a corpse!" Lee continued to stare out the window as they cruised out to the highway to head into the city morgue. "How come this shit don't bother you man? Is that some kind'a white boy shit that brothers don't know about?"

"Don't think so but, I can only speak for myself, I saw alot'a blood growing up. It's like people fucking you over all the time, you get used to it. Learn to turn it off." Chance looked over at Lee still staring out the window. "Why'd you go HM if you're so squeamish?"

"I ain't squeamish! I just don't like dead bodies, blood n' guts n' shit that's all. And I didn't pick it. My father used to own a TV repair store. I signed on for radioman."

"You had a guaranteed contract for radioman?! How the hell'd you wind up an HM?!"

"Guess some cracker figured HM was close enough to RM!"

"Watch that cracker shit, Boy!" Lee flipped him the finger and chuckled.

The mood turned more serious as they realized the stench of the corpse had started to permeate the space of the vehicle more intensely. They had the small side windows down but it was a pointless effort as the old vehicle was designed to be used on the frozen tundras of Korea during the war and so its main engineering considerations, heating and insulation, were counter productive in the relentless 100 degree San Diego heat.

"I'm gonna stop. Hop out and run around and open one of the back doors."

"Fuck that shit! Open BOTH doors!" Lee protested.

They pushed on but by the time they reached the bridge both had two surgical masks wrapped around their faces and Lee was permanently perched on the window ledge of the passenger's side hanging out the window.

Suddenly, as they slowly coasted along with the afternoon traffic, Chance started laughing uncontrollably through his two masks. Lee took a deep breath and

Politically Erect

ducked his head back into the cabin.

"What the hell you laughing at? Them fumes finally gettin' to your ass?!"

Billy pointed behind the ambulance. Lee ducked back outside in time to see a six vehicle space between them and the next car back.

A not so clever motorist in an open top Corvette Stingray quickly cut his way up the shoulder and into the wide open space.

It was only seconds before he found out why the space was there and quickly dropped back from the open doored ambulance.

The driver, his fashion model girlfriend trapped in the bucket seat next to him, frantically struggled to undo her head scarf and improvise a face mask.

He tried to swerve to the left and cut back into traffic but Pedro's Lawn and Garden pick-up, bristling with lawn mowers and garden tools, wouldn't fall back to open a space for him and the next dozen cars behind the pick-up, also in a hurry to get past Ground Zero, bunched closer to block the flashy guy driving the flashy car with the flashy girl.

By the time they had cleared the bridge and reached the Downtown area the model had lost her gastronomic struggle and had painted the passenger's side of the fire red Vette with a thick layer of partially digested bacon ad eggs. Continuing her impression of Jackson Pollock by dry heaving over the side.

"Looks like you're not the only one allergic to floaters!" Billy shouted out to Lee.

"Fuck both them movie stars! There's a war on! Everybody's gotta make sacrifices!" Lee yelled back.

Paddy Kelly

****

Four nights after Chance had received his commendation in a quiet ceremony in the C.O.'s office, the bi-monthly rotational night shift arrived meaning the ward staff had four days off before they would pull another two week shift, this time the 03:00 to 07:00 watch. And as had become the routine every rotation, there was a party some place.

"Hey Chance!"

"What?"

"The L.T. says to give you this." As he pushed the portable x-ray machine off the ward towards the elevator the x-ray tech handed Billy a homemade flyer run off on one of the hospital's only mimeograph machines. It announced a 1950's party at the beach-side penthouse apartment of three of the more well-to-do young nurses two of which whose fathers were admirals.

"Yeah, I know about this. Not going." He offered the invite back to the tech. "I got the Kawasaki packed and heading down to St. Augustine for -"

"Turn it over, jerkwad!" Chance did. On the back there was a hand written note.

Be there, Hero!

The writing was obviously female but to remove all doubt there was a red lipstick imprint just opposite. The tech peered over Billy's shoulder.

"Ride 'em cowboy!" He slapped his own butt as he moved down the hall and turned left.

"Huh. Augustine'll still be there in the morning." Billy muttered.

Politically Erect

****

When he wasn't under any sort of emotional strain and despite his young age, he spoke like a fortune cookie reminicent of an old, jaded mandarin. At other times he sounded like a perpetually upbeat, personal motivator. Still at others like a like a Bro from the Hood..

He hated Chinese food, said it was too slimy, and preferred pepperoni pizza, especially for breakfast. A Bruce Lee "phonetic", (fanatic) he had seen every B, C and D kung-fu movie ever made, but had not one day of martial arts training. At times he would sit for hours on end in the lotus position and mumble high pitched sounds to himself in a self fabricated mantra. Sometimes it would be what sounded like an obscure form of Mandarin, although he would freely admit that he spoke not one word of the language. No Chinese, no Japanese. No Taiwanese, no Vietnamese, Burmese or even Pekinese. None of the -eses. He attributed this to the fact that he came from a poor family with no education.

Now it is a fact that all over China Lee is a common name. However, in the South Bronx, New York there are very few blacks with Oriental monikers. Quite possibly Thomas Jefferson Lee from Flatbush Avenue was the only one.

This minor racial discrepancy, although not unnoticed by those outside the hospital staff, remained verbally untouched by mutual agreement. Several factors came together to create this situation.

First, Lee was a good corpsman and strongly adhered to the credo, 'patient first'.

Next he kept his nose clean and never got himself in trouble. But finally, his act was highly rehearsed and therefore very entertaining.

Lee was an interesting character. His on-again, off-again Chinese accent and contorted vocabulary is why Chance enjoyed working with him. He was, how you say? Enigmatic as well as entertaining.

If for nothing else Lee was easily worth tolerating just to observe each new black victim as they approached him with their 'right-on, power to the people, kill whitey' bullshit. Lee could give a shit about the universal struggle of his black brothers against 'The Man'.

Forced to participate in a conflict they didn't understand by a country they no longer or perhaps ever had loyalty to, the Blacks serving during Vietnam possibly had every right to harbor the resentment they did. It just so happened that in the millennia of human migratory patterns East Bumfuck, Texas, Arkansas or Louisiana was where their father's sperm and their mother's eggs had accidentally ended their great diaspora.

But the reality was that they were either going to to assimilate into the larger society or they weren't.

As it turned out some did, some didn't.

To most of the under twenties in Viet Nam, black, white or Hispanic, it was the unspellables bombing and shooting the unpronounceables. It was somebody else's war. The politicians, the industrialists. The old guys still imprinted with the glorious but faded and hopelessly out-of-date ideals of WWII.

In a land now transformed into a society where 'profit over people' was not only the daily mantra but the driving force, the youth were unable to reconcile what they saw as the double standard being held up to them. The elders couldn't comprehend why the youth didn't just put their heads down, get to work and 'build a life'

Politically Erect

for themselves same as they did. Back during World War II. Back in the days of 'The Big One'.

Back when things were more black and white.

In reality, as the Blacks saw it, their war was back on the streets of America. War against the abject poverty, unrestrained racism on both sides and utter hopelessness of their futures. A future which now hinged on whether or not they made the trip home on a commercial airliner wearing a uniform festooned with ribbons or were delivered back to their loved ones as a lump of scorched goo wrapped in a sandwich bag.

Few had any hope that either war would be won any time soon.

Hindsight is always fifty-fifty but in retrospect, it is interesting to note, Billy often pondered, that, of the U.S. leaders who advocated violence and those who advocated peace, which survived the Sixties and the fashionable wave of assassinations which American culture so enthusiastically seemed to advocate.

John F. Kennedy, dead. Medgar Evers, dead. Martin Luther King, dead. Alberta Williams King, dead. Robert Kennedy, dead. Yet those who lived by violence, Huey P. Newton, Bobby Seale, George Wallace and Richard Nixon, to name a few, not dead.

All Petty Officer Third Class Lee cared about was phoning home once a month to make sure his pay check reached his half blind, diabetic mother still living in the same South Bronx shit hole he had left behind.

Finally, there was a reason that would teach Chance a lesson he would remember for the rest of his life.

The fact that Lee wasn't always the Lee that he was now.

Paddy Kelly

***

Wherever possible blacks took great pains to segregate themselves from the whites in the U.S. military, particularly in the lower ranks. After hours social events were no exception. This was just fine by the whites as well. The Pentagon did all they could to downplay the overt racism on both sides, but their efforts did absolutely nothing to leson it.

This was extremely unfortunate for some, especially in the enlisted ranks. Lee and Chance were no exception. They had just begun to form a bond based on their team work and the fact that Lee had no desire to display false bravado in the face of the gruesome situations they were called on to deal with. This was balanced by the fact that Billy had control of his gut reflexes, especially when it was somebody else's guts spread all over the road. Both had learned from their parents that you judged a man by his ethics not his ethnicity.

So in an effort to snap Lee out of his recently encroaching depression Chance had convinced him to blow off the usual 'Brothers Only' weekend gig where all he'd get was another useless dose of militant whitey bashing with a side order of how the only way the American negro, (now called African-American), would rise to power was when all the Honkies were dead or the blacks got their own country. These armchair politics would be washed down with all the Thunderbird wine he could hold down until he puked.

The separate country thing was another goal both sides agreed upon and seemed to be actively working towards.

So, at the risk of being expelled from the black race, Lee accepted Billy's invite and tagged along to the party.

Politically Erect

★

Just south of San Diego lies Coronado Island, playground of the rich. Connected to the mainland by the two mile long Coronado Bridge from San Diego to the Island, it struck both young corpsmen, crossing the bridge by taxi, as the stuff of dreams.

It was early dusk and through the windshield of the white and green City Cab driving south from downtown, the sun was no longer visible. However, once the taxi climbed to the apex of the expansive bridge straddling the massive channel the burning red-orange horizon out over the Pacific stretched as far as could be seen in either direction.

It was the first time either of them had ever seen "The Coast" and compared to the industrial, steel grey, confines of New York or Jersey City, Chance and Lee both had the sensation they were on the other side of the known universe.

"JESUS! It's like something out of a movie set!" Billy commented.

"Or a God damned post card!" Lee tagged.

The Chicano driver shoke his head.

"Pinche gringos!" He murmured.

"What's that rhythmic pounding? Sounds like a giant's heart beat through a stethoscope!" The taxi driver didn't answer, he just pointed out to sea. Billy nearly fell out of the moving sedan.

Coming in sets of eight to twelve, about a mile out to sea, he could see the ten foot beach breakers which marked the inland border of a surf zone that started at least 100 to 200 meters on the seaward side of the beach.

It was ten mimutes later, therein on the south side of

Paddy Kelly

said beach, on the twenty-seventh floor of the Coronado Arms, at precisely twenty-one hundred hours and thirty-seven minutes Billy Chance and his trusty side kick, Doc Lee, left the soft, instrumental version of *Ina-gada-da-vida* seeping through the overhead speakers of the gold, mirrored elevator and stepped out into the black and green Carrera marbled hallway with the plush purple carpeting leading to suite number 2717.

They rang the bell and a moment later the door swung open to allow a blaring rendition of *Born To Be Wild* to assault their senses. They exchanged glances with the stoned woman holding the door and entered a future twenty-two hours neither of them could imagine or would soon forget.

*****

It was a strange sight at first, all their normally uniformed colleagues in not only civilian attire, but poorly done 50's costumes.

Despite the fliers designating the party was 1950's themed, no one could even remember the Fifties much less had lived through them, so their only reference to the fifth decade of 20th Century American culture was the poorly written T.V. sit-com *Happy Days*.

Of the thirty or so people present about half made an attempt at satisfying the theme's requirements and of those, half again were dressed as Fonzie. The rest, the few women included, had decided on Cha Chi.

Chance and Lee, niether in costume but both deciding to emulate the parents in *Happy Days*, scanned the room for the bar, spotted it and set off to one side of the ultra-mod room next to the full length picture window looking out across the picturesque Pacific.

A few minutes into their first drink a young, feeling

Politically Erect

on pain, tech approached them.

"Hey Doc, lemme ask you something."

"Sure." Billy responded.

"It is it possible to shoot booze?" He asked Chance. It was the x-ray tech who had passed him the flyer up on the ward the day before yesterday.

"What the hell you talking about?" Billy asked.

"I mean could I put some vodka in an I.V. bag, hook up a line and shoot it, straight into my vein? You know, to get a faster buzz?" In on hand he held up a liter bag of saline and an IV line with a 16 gauge needle plugged into the end and a quart bottle of Stoli's in t he other. "You know, I.V. like? I mean, it is alcohol so it's already sterile and all, right?!"

Billy stared at him then glanced over at Lee.

"I don't see why not." Chance offered. The tech smiled and headed off through the still sparse crowd.

"Are you crazy? He could die!" Lee challenged.

"He won't die. He won't get very drunk or get much of a buzz, but he won't die."

"Then why'd you tell him that?"

"Never met anybody that stupid." Billy shrugged and sipped his Tequila Sunrise. "On the other hand, if he does go into V-tach and arrests, there's no better place than being surrounded by twenty or thirty highly trained emergency med people."

Leaning on the fully stocked bar complete with professional bar tender Billy perused the room. He smiled at the thought of having moved up from room 401 of the enlisted barracks in Keflavik and the Hashish, mescaline, peyote, THC, valium, Librium, Benzedrine, red jackets, black Bennies, white jackets, the occasional snort of coke, and that king of all recreational pharmaceuticals, lysergic acid diethylamide, alias LSD, to the officers who had unlimited access to Sangiovese di Romagna and Meremma Toscana, Johnny Walker, (Red, Black and Blue labels), Cuban cigars and Jameson's 1750, thus skipping over the senior enlisted who had to make do with Budweiser, Moosehead and Jack Daniels.

At the other end of the bar he spotted a small gaggle of giggling nurses, like a bunch of kids about to go into *31 Flavors* with a fist full of dollar bills. They were carefully breaking up a fair sized rock of pharmaceutical coke and passing out cocktail straws which had been cut in half.

Suddenly the X-ray tech came shooting out of a back bedroom screaming like a Banshee flying out of the woods. He was holding his arm with the I.V. detached but the 16 gauge needle, still in the vein dripping blood.

"YOU ASSHOLE!" One of the three nurses who were renting the penthouse screamed across the room as the tech redecorated their white, shag carpet and ducked into the toilet.

"Told you he wouldn't die." Billy shrugged.

As he turned to place his drink on the bar Chance's attention was caught by a woman still in uniform. Chance had seen her around the wards but they never spoke.

Purposely designed to neutralize a woman's sexual appeal, the United States Navy uniform for females, (WAV's in NAV speak), could make any Bond girl look like somebody's spinstered old aunt. Apparently she had just gotten off shift and didn't have time to change. He watched as she, clothes bag drapped over her arm, ducked into a back room.

But when she re-emerged, minutes later, standing across the expansive, plushly carpeted living room, dressed in black, patent leather heels and a low cut, chiffon scarf dress, he was mesmerised. Then she stared and smiled. At him.

She coyly grinned across to him, picked the olive from her Martini and slowly mouthed it.

Then her alluring face came into focus jogging his memory. She was an LT on the General Medical ward.

Could this be the lieutenant who mysteriously fabricated and submitted the official report stating that he had saved a non-endangered patient's life by not actually performing a life-saving procedure she said he had but he hadn't?

Lee leaned in from behind and whispered into Billy's ear.

"This is the part where you walk up and, without babbling, drooling or exploding in your pants, strike up a conversation." He gently shoved the dumbfounded Chance from behind. "And check your ID card so your dumb ass don't forget your name when you open your mouth to speak."

Focused on not tripping, Billy awkwardly sashayed across the floor and around the chrome and glass furniture towards the radiating halo of back lighting which surrounded the woman's tall, lithe form.

Her chestnut brown hair gently waved in the breeze and her azure blue eyes sparkled like the twin stars of the constellation Gemini as the rest of the room was slowly washed out of focus by her nova-like radiance. The distance between them slowly closed and, as the orchestral music swelled and he stood within smelling distance, he suffered a near brush with sexual suicide when he opened his mouth to speak.

"I ahh . . . I. . ."

In his befuddled, mind altered state he had no way to notice that, although she could have easily posed for

Penthouse Magazine, she was at least ten years his senior.

The metamorphoses from how she appeared now and how he remembered her on the wards, camoflaged in her starched whites, into the Playboy Playmate of the Year goddess which now stood before him was unsettling. He instantly determined that if he were ever abducted by Tralfamadorians and encaged for observation on their home planet, she would be his Montana Wildhack.

"Sue, you can call me Sue." Suddenly the room snapped into focus and he was back on planet earth.

Her name was Sue Martin and she was from somewhere he'd never heard of in one of those southern states he didn't quite catch as the words seemed to ooze in slow motion from her pink glossed lips.

"Ahh . . ."

"You already said that."

"Yeah, ah sorry." Suddenly Billy started fidgeting with his wrist watch.

"Something wrong with your watch?"

"No, I don't think so. At least I hope not." He replied tapping the crystal of the time piece. "I just bought it. It's state-of-the-art ut very delicate and I was just testing it."

"State-of-the-art? What's so special about it?'

"It's cadmium powered, microscopically and atomically calibrated and uses alpha waves to telepathically signal to me." He explained as he held the watch to his ear.

"What's it saying to you now?" She sipped her drink and smirked.

"Well, it says you're not wearing any panties under that dress."

"Well it must be broken, because I **am** wearing panties!"

"Huh!" Billy exclaimed as he tapped the time piece

Politically Erect

again. "Damn thing must be about fifteen minutes fast!"

"So there is life in you!" She fired back.

"I've never had trouble rising to the occasion if that's what you mean." She smiled and drained her drink. Setting the glass on the lamp table to her left, she took his hand and led him down the hall to a back bedroom. As they passed through the doorway Chance pretended not to notice the tan line where her wedding ring had been.

Lee, who had crept up across the room unseen, peered down the hallway and upon hearing the bedroom door close over and the lock click home, sighed and turned back to gaze out upon the chrome and fur festooned room.

Moonlight had begun to shine through the ocean side picture window and, with the stereo temporarily on hiatus, the waves could just be heard breaking against the beach twenty-seven floors below.

"Huh!" Lee spoke to himself. "A black enlisted man from the inner city slums in a penthouse suite, on the beach full of white officers drinking Stella Artois! Whatever the hell Stella Artois means." After soaking in the awe-inspiring sea scape he polished off his beer and started back for the bar on the other side of the room.

As he ordered another Stella an attractive, well-built Hispanic in a mini skirt and black high heels tapped him on the shoulder. He recognized her as a lab tech from the Regional Medical Center.

She didn't speak but held up a small, clear plastic bag half full of some clear crystals, plucked a mixing straw from the bar and nodded towards a toilet. Lee smiled.

As they came into the oversized bathroom a young guy in a black, two sizes too large Fonzie wig, was down on his knees carefully placing single service ketchup packets under the rubber bumpers of the toilet seat and the rim of the toilet.

"Oye pendejo, vámonos!" She commanded. The prankster looked her up and down, shrugged and vámonosed. She slammed the door and locked it mufflling Pink Floyd.

Across the room through the other guests, the civilian bartender wiping down the bar observed the action as Lee and the girl emerged from the toilet a few minutes later. He began a runnuing commentery.

"It's late in the last quarter here at the Garden and several contenders have attempted to get the ball in the hole but her defensive line seems to be holding. Wait a minute, what do we have here?" He watched as they nodded to each other. "And . . . hold the phone! Looks like we have a last minute entry, just off the bench!" He watched as she took Lee by the hand and led him down the hall. "It appears to be a rookie corpsman . . . she's giving him an opening . . . and . . ." The two made their way into another bedroom and the door closed over.

"She shoots! He scores, and the crowd goes wild!"

*

Dormant winter foliage contrasted vividly with the encroaching dawn and 1969 Chevy Impalas lined William Howard Taft Street patiently waiting with a deceptive innocence. Their futuristic, chrome plated tail fins poised to impale some unsuspecting, young football hero going long for a forward pass.

Vague visions of Smitfield slowly coalesced in Billy's fogged mind as he clawed his way to consciousness the morning after the night before. The dream dissolved into daylight and he once again found himself in the realm of the living.

Politically Erect

Chance carefully opened one eye quickly realizing something was wrong.

"And he who doth remove the sword from my head shall be king!" He grabbed his temples with both hands. "FUCK!" He loudly whispered. Slowly at first, Chance adjusted his eyes to focus on the acanthus leaf and fruit mould surrounding the ceiling light fixture above the bed.

Where the fuck am I? Then his hand wandered up and over the silky smooth ass cocked towards him.

Oh yeah! His brain reminded himself.

Flipping back the top sheet Billy exposed Sue's long, lithe form. She lay on her left side, left arm extended with her top leg bent at the knee contently sleeping. With the rising sunlight filtering through the translucent shade, her tanned body took on the appearence of a full color Nagle print.

He struggled into his khaki trousers and left the room.

Lee, although stirring, remained slumped down and engulfed by the lime green, leather Rest-O-Matic in which he slept. Partially covered in nothing but a purple, paisley bed sheet draped about him like a cape, all five appendages of his 147 lb, five foot-nine frame rested in different orientations. This was a good thing because in order to count to twenty-one that morning Lee would have had to be naked.

Stepping over something or someone Billy surveyed the carnage inflicted on the penthouse living room as a result of the last thirteen and a half hours of debauchery.

Reflecting off the open Pacific the sun blasted into the room like a death ray from outer space but as the drunk and drugged, breathing corpses strewn about the room were only one step away from already being flatline, the sudden blast of intense sunlight never even phased them.

The room was deceptively large however, with three corpsmen, four techs, two corpswaves, five nurses, and a pharmacist, (without whom the party would have not been possible and who was held in high enough esteem, due to his immeasurable contribution to the evening's festivities, was afforded the couch to sleep on), strewn over every available centimeter of usable space, it was a challenge to calculate an azimuth to the kitchen.

Chance gazed out the kitchen window at the post card-like scene as he sipped some coffee.

"SATAN LIVES!" From out by the apartment's front door Lee's voice boomed through the air dripping with enough evil to make the Wicked Witch of the West proud.

The spine tingling screams which followed did not immediately penetrate Chance's deep fog or wake the others but the cries for help and the pleads for mercy apparently didn't go unheeded in the hallway as several neighbors popped their heads out to investigate. and were mixed with the sounds of men loudly declaring non-profane expletives such as, "OH MY GOD!" and "Unbelievable!"

The women's voices could be heard over the men's, retching and contributing to the chorus with phrases like, "OH MY GOD, I DIDN'T KNOW THEY COULD GET THAT BIG!"

A couple of them were oriented towards the begging for mercy type variety of panic.

The thud of what sounded like heavy books being dropped was tempered with the sound of a half dozen pairs of feet scurrying down the marbled hallway towards the elevators.

As the echoes of the Sunday morning callers faded own the hall and into the distance, Chance poked his

Politically Erect

head through the kitchen doorway and peered out the kitchen across the sea of humanity, sleeping undisturbed in the living room to see the wide opened front door, a pile of bibles strewn across the hall floor and Lee standing there with his arms raised high holding his blanket wide open, cape-like, head cocked back, laughing manically.

Returning to the half dozen eggs he was now preparing for breakfast Billy looked up as Lee wandered into the kitchen.

"Who was it?" Chance asked.

"Christians." Lee answered casually strolling in with one of the forsaken books open in his hand, as if he were reading.

"What'd they want?"

"Wanted me to help them find Jesus."

"Didn't know he was lost."

"You wanna read?" Lee now stood in the kitchen still half draped in his purple, paisley bed sheet cape as he offered a confiscated copy of *The Morman Bible*.

"No thanks. Saw the movie, wasn't impressd. God looked a little to much like Charlton Heston. What'd ya say to the little darlings?"

"Not much. Just gave them my theological perspective." Lee flashed open the sheet to reaveal, in all it's glory, his Afro-nakedness.

"I'm impressed."

"Bet you are white boy!" He wiggled his junk for emphasis.

"Two polysyllabic words in one sentence! Impressive."

"Fuck you."

"And he's back." Billy scooped the eggs from the pan onto a large plate. "You remember that kid, that kid from

Denver I told you about, the one in my class, off'd himself the night before graduation?"

"What about him?"

"In between sesions last night Lt. Martin -"

"That's one fine piece of -"

"Thanks for the update. In between sessions her and I got to talking. Turns out he had orders cut to come here."

"So the stupid little bastard wasn't goin' no where near Nam?"

"Probably not, but what was interesting was that his family is rich. Like oil and gas rich."

"How the fuck he get snagged into the Nav if he had money?!"

"Just lucky I guess. You want some eggs?"

"Hell yeah!"

"Pan's over there, butter's in the fridge." Billy instructed while he sat at the table and dug into his breakfast.

"Asshole!" Lee mumbled.

The toast popped up.

****

LIFE IS LIKE A SHIT SANDWICH.

THE MORE BREAD YOU HAVE,
THE LESS SHIT YOU HAVE TO EAT.

Paddy Kelly

CHAPTER EIGHT

The second thud was more pronounced and had moved around to the side of his head. The kitchen walls distorted and then began to evaporate.

Fucking Rod Serling shit! Billy thought.

Most people hated this Twilight Zone crap, the gradual distortion of reality experienced when in a life threatening situation for a prolonged period of time. But Chance began to anticipate it, and so was growing to like it. Worse yet the longer the danger seemed to last the more he seemed to like it. He remembered his father telling him, 'If you can't get out of something, get into it'.

John Yossarian would be proud.

Increasingly the steady diet of bizarre calls, strange incidents and odd occurrences began to cast life in the shadow of a no-man's-land somewhere between dream state and fantasy. The absolutes of the life he had been raised with, honesty, integrity, reliance on people in authority, in essence life making sense, were being eroded by the reality of the life he had experienced in the last two and half years.

Back home the regular occurance of riots, cops and National Guard troops indiscriminately slaughtering citizens, the blacks razing neighborhoods to the ground in some bizare form of racist anti-racist protest combined with the seemingly monthly political scandals all appeared to be locked in a freakish game of one-upmanship. The America he thought he knew was disintegrating as the world watched the whole thing on the Six O'clock News.

Anti Viet Nam fever, and by extension anti-military fever, infected every nook and cranny of American society. It was like a massive dose of nuclear fallout, from which there was no escape.

He had been told throughout the Fifties and Sixties that it was clearly only a matter of time before some asshole panicked and pushed the button to drop the big one. Now it was just a matter of who would take the decision to incinerate the world. A Russian, a Chinaman or a Yank?

Chance gradually became more aware of the muffled thud, thud in the back of his head again but ignored it. He looked over at Lee who wasn't there anymore. Instead he was looking across the kitchen of the high rise on Coronado Island.

As time progressed, it had become increasingly difficult to distinguish between the past present and future, what had happened, what was happening and what would happen. To add to the surrealism of life in the Navy, his dreams had gradually began to meld with reality until it was nearly impossible to differentiate the two.

Was it just an altered perspective brought on as a side effect of dropping acid or could I really be cracking up? No history in the family. So what was it? Time would tell.

As a third thud knocked his skull against the bulkhead of the ship the high pitched whine of the engines and the whuck-whuck-whuck of the rotor blades of the UH-1 slicing the air filled his ears. Suddenly he could see through his eyes again. Through the rain drenched side window he could see they were still on the ground.

"How long we been in this god damned chopper?" He yelled over at Lee. Suddenly the ship lifted slightly, tilted radically to port causing the rotor wing to narrowly miss a fence line. It seemed as though every time they gained a few feet in altitude the night wind and driving rain rose to the challenge and blew them back down onto the tarmac.

"'Bout half an hour." Lee shouted back. Although back on the ground, something didn't feel right. Looking out the side hatch again, Chance realized they were only a few feet off the deck and the pilot was fighting a losing battle to maintain his hover. The port side skid was twisted and bent upwards blocking the door from sliding opening and also making it impossible to land safely.

"Tower, tower, Eagle-One. Am unable to land, must cancel medevac. I say again, dust-off a no go. Advise alternate means of transport be arranged. Eagle-One, out." Like a Pink Floyd recitation the pilot's radio commands electronically echoed through the head set.

The pilot ordered everyone to evacuate through the starboard side door as he fought to maintain his hover. The two corpsmen, the crew chief and Marine co-pilot tumbled out of the increasingly gyrating chopper and half scurried, half crawled off through the wet sand to one side through the driving rain and managed to make it to the crest of a ridge about 100 meters beyond the fence line.

As he watched the pilot fight the wind and rain to maintain control of the ship Billy's mind flashed back to the vehemence of the war protests he had seen back in the States the night before he shipped out. They were accompnied by selective man-on-the-street interviews being broadcast on the CBS news.

"This war is bullshit man! We got no business buttin' our noses in other people's business!" The aggitated protestor yelled at the camera, hundreds of other sign wielding citizens in the background. Baton swinging police waded into the crowd.

Somehow all the men and values he had been raised

Politically Erect

to admire, the entire country had been raised to admire, had suddenly, overnight become the enemy of the people. The bad guys, the guys they were now wrong for looking up to.

From a safe distance on the beach in a small clearing, they watched as the UH-1 lazily zigzagged off at a dangerously low altitude, fighting the cross winds, out over the churning sea and faded into the night.

"Where's he going?" Lee asked the co-pilot.

"Can't land, gotta ditch in the water."

"In this shit? How's he gonna get back?" The tiny chopper was quickly swallowed up by the dark. The Marine Warrant officer just glanced at Lee as he removed his helmet and walked away.

"Air Sea Rescue's been notified." He sullenly called back over his shoulder as he trudged down the dune and through the sand. "They'll try and get him a boat." That's when it hit both corpsmen.

Like last month's tampons, they were all disposable.

★

"The decision's been made to attempt a tug rescue." Billy announced as he came back into the small lobby of the clinic. Lee was already behind the reception desk in the old easy chair drying himself off with a bath towel.

"A 'TUG' RESCUE?! As in 'tub boat' rescue, them little dinky assed boats you play with in the tub when youse five years old?! The ones that always swamp when you put the little piece of Alka-Selza tablet up they ass and let 'em go in the water?!"

"It's a 'tug' boat, a sea going tug."

"Oh hell no! This nigga ain't gettin' on nothing in this

storm smaller then a fuckin' flat top, you dig where I'm comin' from?!" Chance was busy packing a couple of extra I.V. bags for the anticipated longer trip. He hadn't expected the outburst but was amused how fast Lee dropped the Chinese act and reverted to his native Brooklynese Ebonics when he was rattled. "Pull that fuckin' U.S.S. John F. Kennedy up to the curb and I'll go out on that bad boy! Or the Lex, or the FDR! But a tub boat? You out'a your fuckin' mind!"

"Lee, that chopper pilot still hasn't been heard from, if he's still alive after ditching. Air evac didn't work. The only way through this weather out to that casualty is by sea."

"That guy out on that ship gonna die, he'd a been dead already! If he's still breathin' that I.D. corpsman can keep his ass alive till hurricane what-ever-the-fuck it is moves on!" For emphasis Lee gesticulated his point.

"Well command doesn't see it that way. Besides, just because the ship's doc is an Independent Duty corpsman doesn't mean he can work miracles. He's aboard a tender not a floating cardiac clinic! We're due at dock side in fifteen minutes." Billy headed for the door. "I got extra gear in a med bag packed, let's go! They're sending a jeep over."

Like a kid refusing to go to bed on a school night Lee reiterated his attitude by crossing his arms and slouching down in the easy chair.

"Huh! That's interesting." Billy commented as he moved to the door. Lee begrudgingly peaked up over the reception desk as Chance, who sensed Lee's reaction when he heard the chair cushions shift, stopped but didn't turn back around. "Guess my friends back in Jersey were right."

"Right about what exactly?!" Halfway through the door Chance stopped and turned.

Politically Erect

"At the party, the night before I shipped out, they said, 'never worry about goin' on a dangerous mission with a, you know..."

"Yeah I know, get to the point!"

"Never worry because they're afraid of the water, afraid of the dark and afraid of the cold. They won't go!"

"MAN! Fuck yo friends and the lame ass horse they rode in on!"

"I'm just sayin' Bro . . ."

"And don't give me that 'Bro' shit niether!"

*

Everything was wet. Everything all the time. Even their beds. Water washed through the main streets and roads of the city as if they were just tributaries of a mighty river. Hardly a day had gone by for the last week when they didn't see some kind of household good or another gently flowing down the main street. Hats, baskets, furniture, the occasional kid. Almost no matter where you were you had to shout to be heard.

Monsoon season in the Pacific.

Interesting that scenes like this were never on the recruiting posters, Billy mused.

The medium sized and smaller vessels would normally be safe inside San Diego's natural harbor but with hurricane force winds and monsoon rains predicted, the larger vessels, those which couldn't be safely docked and moored inside the cresent, had judiciaously been put out to sea, well north of the expected landfall of the storm. They would have to wait it out.

The accompanying cross winds were the main reason but increasing shore swells would rip hell out of the smaller vessels as well as the docks if they were left moored up in port and so they too were eventuall ordered to head out and wait for the weather to calm down. The only vessels left in the small man-made section of the harbor were the two tugs left over from the mass deployment recall back in '73.

Billy Chance, now riding shotgun through the wind, rain and dark, in a standard issue '52 Willy's jeep half filled with rain water, was headed for that harbor.

He turned and looked back at the rear seat where Lee was also covered in a dripping wet O.D. green poncho.

"This don't mean shit, so don't go readin' nuthin' into it!" Lee commanded still with crossed arms for emphasis. Billy held up both hands as a concession.

Their orders had been amended to proceed to the *U.S.S. Mary Elizabeth* via the first available sea-worthy craft to Medevac, (rescue), Machinist's Mate, (wrench jockey), First Class Jameson, a thirty-six year old, black male with a diagnosis of ACF, Acute Cardiac Failure, (bad shit).

"Heart failure?! You're pulling my middle one! We're risking our asses for a FUCKING CORPSE?!" Billy tactfully inquired of the driver. This was the first time they had heard of a provisional diagnosis.

"We don't know that yet!" Private Driver shouted back above the wind. "Commo's been out for over an hour!"

Translation: *Piss off Buddy! I wouldn't tell you even if I knew. I just want to dump your ass off and get the fuck out'a the rain and back into my warm, dry rack!*

"Who made the diagnosis?" *What ass hole is responsible for us being in this shit?* Billy yelled over to Private Driver, one hand cupped beside his mouth.

"The O.O.D. over at H.Q. got it from the C.O.! Must'a talked with an M.D. over in cardio." *Someone*

Politically Erect

with a helluva a lot more stripes than me!

"Fuck me Alice!" *Tell me this ship's HM trained at San Diego not Great Lakes.* Billy prayed to the gods of triage.

The rain, though less driving, continued as they pulled into the parking area of the docks. They headed for a far corner of the berthing area as the gradually easing swells joined with the sun threatening to peak over the horizon.

They rounded the corner of an enormous boat house and the slip below revealed their sea-worthy craft being prepared by a pair of young deck hands, both Boatswain's Mates. The younger one precariously balanced on the pitching fantail, waved to the jeep as he worked at coiling down an aft mooring line.

They watched the unknown private vanish with their topless limousineback into the pinkish-grey dark of the night. Or day, whatever the hell time it was. Biological clocks didn't work so well afte 24 hour shift in the E.R. with another 10 to 12 hours to go.

He and Lee walked across the expansive concrete dockside and down a personnel ramp to the wooden pier where Billy saw, for the first time close up, the vessel that would take them out.

As he watched the two young sailors work, his M-5 Med bag slung over his shoulder, Billy could sense their seamanship and realized that, finally, he had found 'the real Navy'. A place where there were no clerks, filing cabinets, cold steel decks or oily diesel smell. Just sailors. Sailors surrounded by sea soaked oak and wet hemp. Chance drew in a long, slow deep breath to fill his lungs and bask in the aroma. A broad smiled crossed his lips.

Chance noted that labled across the perfectly curved

Paddy Kelly

ass of the seasoned but pristine vessel was the name U.S.S. ERIN. But far from being misconstrued as ass antlers, a Panama City license plate or a tramp stamp, the meticulously hand lettered moniker proudly announced her identity leaving no doubt as to exactly who she was. Having read extensivly on the history of various navies through the centuries, Billy stood on the gently pitching dock and soaked in the romance of it all.

The sea going tug is the smallest ship in the U.S. fleet, yet one of the most important. Billy was mesmerized by what he felt was the most artistic creation afloat. The perfect symbiosis of hemp, timber, iron and brass. He let his eyes glide over how the beautiflyy woven, hemp fenders oozed over her rails as she roughly swayed in her berth, heaving in protest at her moorings like a Siren of the sea longing to break free and roam the waves.

His mind immediately flashed back to his early high school days in Jersey City when he and friends would cut class from their school which was perched high on the palisades overlooking the Hudson River and New York Harbor.

The ritual eventually progressed into ventures down to the mile and a half wide river where, from between the hundreds of burned out and abandoned wooden piers, they'd watch the ceaseless harbor traffic as if it were a TV show on the largest big screen in the world, the New York City skyline as a backdrop. Ships from Europe, Africa and Asia. Bristol, Durban and Singapore. Every port in the worLd.

Naturally, on warm days, this led to swimming. Naked of course. Couldn't very well wear wet underwear under your school trousers going back home.

This inevitably led to 'dares', the first of which was one of the last as well as the most daring for Jimmy

Politically Erect

Stinson. The dare was to swim along the Jersey side of the expansive river then across into one of the many tug lanes. Timing had to be perfect or you'd be spotted by the tug pilot which meant that the NYPD River Patrol would show up, fish you out and mom and dad would get An unpleasant phone call.

"Mrs. Kowalski? Sergeant O'Hara here, NYPD. We need you to came and collect your son down at the station house. We picked him up trying to hitch a ride on one'a the tugs in the river. Oh yeah, bring some clothes. He's naked.

Once you reached the tug lane, in order to complete the dare, you were expected to duck below the water level, resurface near the wake and latch onto the bow by a dangling line, a fender, a fixture or any means you could. The one who held on the longest was the winner.

After about half a dozen of what became known as 'Jersey City Sleigh Rides', little Jimmy Stinson became the undisputed champion when the alligator banded watch his uncle gave him for his birthday, the one he refused to take off no matter what, snagged a frayed cable hanging off the aft section of a barge being towed by a tug and Jimmy was towed, and nearly drowned, for forty minutes up stream halfway into North Bergen.

Until graduation day little Jimmy was known as "Ball-less Jimmy". Nothing to do with lack of courage, that he had proven in spades. The nick name was earned due to the fact that after he finally crawled up out of the freezing water nearly two miles upriver near Union City, his testicles had completely receded up into abdomen. He no longer had any balls.

"MAN! What the fuck stinks?!" Lee's voice snapped

Paddy Kelly

Billy out of his time tripping.

"That, my homeboy hobo, is the smell of wooden ships and iron men!" Billy slapped Lee on the back as he descended the ladder onto the tug's deck. Lee didn't respond, just hesitated on the pier. "Let's go bro! Time and tide wait for no man!" Billy prodded.

"I want a life jacket!" Lee looked down at Billy refusing to cross the short gang plank. His arms were crossed again.

"They got life jackets below, come on."

"I ain't getting' on that boat lessin' I got a life jacket!"

"Lee! You see those thick hemp hawsers tied off around those big iron bollards? We're still moored to the dock!" Lee was a statue. "If it sinks the worst can happen is that you'll fall on your ass as the boat hangs from the pier!" Billy pointed to a small pile of bright orange Mae Wests on the pier across from the base of the ladder. "Take one of those."

Historically she was the last of the ATA class tugs which were laid down near the end of WII when every rivet, bolt, gear and plank had been made by hand in a time when the word 'craft' wasn't spelled with a 'K' and didn't come in a box with macaroni and dehydrated, chemically laced cheese.

The young BM saw Billy smiling and called over to him. Billy drew closer and the kid, barley nineteen, who went into a well rehearsed spiel.

"Weighs in at 2,680 tons standard displacement, 32 hundred tones fully loaded. 182 foot by 47 foot by 13.5 foot at the beam. With 300 horse in her aft thruster." He pointed to the waterline below. "She can jimmy a 900 foot flat top like the Lex anywhere in port and flat out at sea she can push 16 knots!" He bragged as if he were the original engineer. Billy listened intently and was compelled to comment.

Politically Erect

"If the Vikings had these puppies nobody would have ever heard of the Spanish Armada and Queen Elizabeth would have died a name in a church ledger book!" Billy mumbled as he ran his hand over the port side rail oblivious to the fact that his words were lost like a fart in the wind.

"Man what the fuck you babblin' about?"

"Petty Officer Lee, your down-to-earth, home spun and insightful commentary is always a treat for the ears."

"Man I'm axin' a question! What's ya'll talkin' 'bout?"

"Marine engineering. Educational stuff. Doesn't concern you." Billy snipped.

Trying to discern whether or not he had just been insulted Lee, now wrapped snugly in a bright orange Mae West life vest over his poncho with his head like a Milk Dud atop an orange Halloween cupcake, walked the rest of the short way down the ramp and caught up as Bill was saluting the aft ensign from the gang plank and stepped aboard.

Lee ignored naval protocol and, as if walking on eggs, gingerly climbed down from the gangplank and over the rail, testing his footing on the gently rolling deck.

"Just for the record, I don't like this shit!" He informed Billy.

"You look like a burnt hot dog in an orange bun."

"Go fuck yourself!"

"Tell me something. You're squeamish, you have no intention of pursuing a medical career, you don't like getting up early and you can't swim. You put any thought into this before you signed up in te Navy?" Billy climbed the short bridge ladder up to the pilot house to get in out of the rain which seemed to have let up a bit.

Paddy Kelly

Lee followed as he answered.

"Plenty!" Lee barked. "It was either this or get drafted into the Army. Fuck you very much. The Army meant the infantry, not no, but fuck no! Which meant Nam. Fuck no! And I got a strict three 'fuck no!' limit when I make major decisions concernin' my future."

"And yet here you are in the Navy in a situation as potentially dangerous as being in Nam ?"

"Thank yu for remindin' me, fuck you very much!"

"I see your reasoning." Billy shrugged as he climbed up into the pilot house.

In the relative safety of the pilot house Billy removed his poncho and begun to admire the brass fixtures, the perfect lines of a well designed and hand, crafted sea going vessel. It was the first time HM2 Chance felt like he was in the United States Navy. The real Navy not just a loose confederation of military people executing government appointed jobs.

It was just as he was imagining what it might be like to pilot such a craft at sea that they were given a heartfelt, personal greeting from a big, burly, sleeves rolled-up, cigar-chewing, last-of-the-true-Sea Gods of the United States Navy. The kind that even most officers kowtow to.

A Master Chief Petty Officer Boatswain's Mate.

The big Master Chief, six foot three and pushing 245 pounds, stood in the hatchway under the glare of the over head pilot house lamp and casually crossed his arms. The Master Chief extended his warm salutations through his dangling cigar.

"I don't know which one'a you fuckin' pecker checkers got somebody ta get somebody ta get me up at zero-dark-fucking-thirty ta get underway in this shit! But as you may have observed from my overly cor-jial demeanor, I ain't no happy fuckin' camper at this fuckin'

Politically Erect

point in time! Now get the fuck below with that useless as tits-on-a-nun, dick on-a-priest Lieutenant and stay the fuck out'a my wheel house till we clear the breakwater! This ain't no Disneyland ride!"

Chance instantly liked him.

Two white streaks followed by a black, green and orange streak vanished out the aft hatch and down the bridge ladder.

"He's really a people person." BM3 Emerson, the guy who had been on the bow, assured the two corpsmen as he escorted them below.

As they entered the small crew space Chance, last in line, stopped and stared at the officer stretched out on one of the bunks, snoring like a P-250 pump with its suction hose only partially in the water.

Not quite able to bring himself to enter the room Billy stood in the hatchway. Lee took notice and, as he removed his poncho and re-donned his Mae West, he looked over at the sleeping lump of khaki.

"What's wrong witch you?" Lee asked. Billy continued to stare.

"You know that feeling ya get when a cop gives you a traffic ticket for doing seventy in a sixty zone, which you deserved because you were doin' seventy, but because police fines rise in an exponential manner on the secret police fine scale, and Leon Valley, Texas needs more revenue so they can 'fight crime', meaning buy more patrol cars to crash in high speed pursuits so they can be on the show *Cops,* so he writes it up at ninety knowing there's not a goddamned thing you can do about it, especially since you have out-of-state-plates?"

"I'm black! Whatta you think?."

"I kind'a feel like that. Only not as euphoric."

Why'd it have to be Roscoe? Roscoe the fuck-up.

Paddy Kelly

Roscoe the guy whose picture you would see in the encyclopedia when you looked up the phrase, 'fuck-up'. Roscoe the worst excuse on two feet for anything let alone a guy who was allowed sharp instruments and Class A narcotics! Billy fixated on how his fuckin' perpetually crooked glasses made him look like a pudgy, stupid Buddy Holly. (No offence Buddy.) Billy slumped to the deck and sat there.

Without a word Roscoe jumped up and stumbled to the head.

"Why so long face Billy-san?" Lee, easing back into form asked as they each picked a bunk and dumped their gear.

"Because we get to make this trip with the most hated man in the Vatican."

"Meaning?"

"The strongest argument for abortion yet conceived. Lieutenant Leroy 'Bubba' Roscoe.

"How you know him?"

"He was assigned to Balboa Regional but something happened and they dumped him off on the corps school. By day one everybody on the teaching staff realized he didn't have a clue what the fuck he was doing so they gave him a 'promotion' to administration where he couldn't do much damage."

"So how the hell'd wind up here?"

"Apparently he found a way to do more damage."

"He a M.D.?"

"Jury's still out. But . . . why in the hell would a Doctor wann'a get up at zero three-hundred, drive through a monsoon and cruise five hours each way in rough seas just to ride a routine Medevac?"

"Insomnia? Cheap thrills? Ran out'a booze?" Lee suggested.

"Besides, how the hell did he even **know** about this

Politically Erect

Medevac? The message came straight to sickbay from the message center. I took it and I only woke you."

"Perhaps lieutenant-san have anterior motive?" San being the Japanese name suffix for respect.

"He ain't no 'san' and you got that right." Billy thought to himself how it just didn't fit. Roscoe was no kind of hero. This would require Rod's advise at a later date.

*

Paddy Kelly

THAT'S THE TROUBLE WITH
POLITICAL JOKES.
THEY GET ELECTED.

CHAPTER NINE

The United States never was and highly likely never will be able to break the strangle hold the God Almighty dollar has on her people particularly where medical care is concerned

A good example is the American medical system which can be considered an immutable example of Darwin's principle of survival of the fittest. Only those who can afford good medical care should have access to it and therefore should be allowed to survive. And those who can't . . . tough shit. Or so the prevailing theory goes.

There's a reason the AMA strictly control how many aspiring young altruists can become doctors each year. The fewer doctors out there the more money for everybody and the more reasonable it appears to disallow a woman in the later stages of labor, entrance to a hospital until she produces a verifiable credit card. This Billy knew to be the case from personal expererience.

There is however one splinter of humanity in American medicine where the AMA haven't sunk their talons into; the U.S. Navy Hospital Corps.

To be treated at a Naval Medical facility, from hangnail to open heart surgery, you show up, flash your I.D. card and get treated. Everyone's wages are set, everyone is there because they want to be there and they want the job. By removing the competative financial factor, you distil the work force down to those who really are in it for the medicine not for the money.

The Navy Medical Corps is, ironically, a socialist island in the vast sea of rampant, mutated capitalism which is The United States of America.

Without exception the members of the U.S.N. Hospital Corps, the only enlisted corps in the entire United States military, are trained to treat and stabilize any emergency trauma situation until evacuation to a competent medical facility can be provided.

It is for this reason alone that it is common to find personnel of all ranks at ease taking instructions from enlisted medical personnel. Consequently both the enlisted and commissioned population have come to hold a special trust in corpsmen and members of the U.S.N. medical corps. Of course any system this vast has its flaws.

Lieutenant Leroy Andrew Jackson Roscoe was one of those flaws.

Leroy slid into the United States Navy Medical corps thanks to the Barry Plan. Another in the long line of inspired ideas which came out of the Washington think tank just as it began to dawn on them they were fighting a war they couldn't possibly win. It was like the 'hurry-up offence' the New York Jets used to employ in the final minutes of the game. Only "The Plan" was used to persuade medical students that their talents would be wasted on ungrateful American civilians and their pain-in-the-ass kids and so should be utilized to better ends. That is keeping soldiers and sailors fit, healthy and in peak mental and physical condition so they could go out and get their arms, legs and balls blown off.

The Barry Plan was a scheme to draft doctors, (without using the "D" word), none of whom were breaking down Uncle Sam's door to get in on the Big Show, as the WWII styled patriotic-rally-to-arms Lyndon Johnson et al foresaw never materialized. Banking on the 'We are your government, you must trust us and go to war!' argument the politicians were basically too sequestered from the reality of life in modern America to realize they had used up their last 'trust us' card back in the Fifties when they dropped the ball during the Korean War. Uh . . . I mean Police Action. The first one. Before the Viet Nam War . . . ahh . . . sorry, Police Action.

So the strategy shifted to ambush the medical students before they were established physicians and had been around more than a day and thereby knew the rules of the game, and more importantly had money to hire lawyers to fight the government.

The Barry Plan itself was kind'a like the horny college guy who really wanted to get as many young co-eds up to his dorm room as possible, so he would offer anything. Including to respect them in the morning after he had fucked them.

Theoretically the program went something like this:

First the lucky third year med student received a letter to the effect of;

Dear Doctor Smith;

You have been chosen to help lead your country in the struggle against world-wide Communist domination. Your last years of medical school will be paid for by the U.S. government, pending qualification of course, after which you will be invited to serve your country for a minimum of four years.

Naturally as you are a valued resource, every attempt will be made to keep you as far from the fighting as possible.

Thank you very much for your enthusiastic cooperation.

A representative will be in touch.

Sincerely,
Richard Head
Mr. Richard Head, Director
United States Armed Forces Induction Center,
Washington, D.C.

Translation;

Dear third year student whom we know is not a doctor yet but whom we are stroking off by addressing you as 'doctor' and who is fully aware that we have the power to keep you from realizing your life-long dream of becoming a doctor by burying you so deep in legal costs that a team of German engineers backed by a brigade of Harvard archaeologists would not be able to excavate you in a hundred years and so you will never be able to afford your last years of med school unless your full cooperation is forthcoming.

Now that all the official looking stamps and signatures accompanying this letter have captured your full attention, and you realize you are actually being drafted you are about to experience the following;

1. A drastic change in wardrobe.

2. Forced dietary habits which go against everything you've been taught in medical school regarding proper nutrition.

3. A piss-poor semblance of a physical training program.

4. Poor to no access to quality medical equipment or treatment.

5. Housing conditions reserved for those so far below the poverty line that they would need a hot air balloon and a Saturn Five booster rocket just to reach the poverty line.

Politically Erect

6. A pay scale so far below the prescribed norm, that pan handling on Main Street would probably put you in a higher tax bracket.

7. The opportunity to "practice" unsupervised medicine on as many warm bodies as you wish, and who will, under threat of physical punishment, give you their full and undivided cooperation. The up side? No matter what you do to them they can't sue you.

We will try and give you some kind of tuition help, providing our worthless, bureaucratic Veteran's Administration can get its head out of its ass long enough to realize how fucked up it is and find somebody who knows how to write a check.

Naturally since we're getting our weenies smacked over there, by a bunch of little yellow bastards, who we will probably eventually kick the shit out of, (as soon as we can find them), you will be sent to the front as soon as we can designate some poor farmer's rice patty as a front line. Or as soon as we can get the little slant-eyed bastards to hold still long enough so that we can shoot at them.

As this is the greatest country on the planet there are of course three alternatives to your forced conscription;

A. Go out and buy a shit load of make-up, a dress and learn to walk in stilettos.

B. Go to school in some third world country like Canada, Mexico or England. (It's working for all the rich kids and senator's sons!)

or,

C. Prove you are the son of a senator or congressman

or have enough money to buy your way out. (Bastard sons also applicable with appropriate form BS-101-a).

We'll be in touch. And remember, we're from the government, we're here to help you.

Signed,
Richard Head
Mr. Richard Head, Director
United States Armed Forces Induction Center,
Washington, D.C.

What a brilliant concept! Take someone highly trained in the use of sharp instruments and pharmaceuticals, piss him off by taking his life away, give him unlimited access to sharp instruments and pharmaceuticals, then tell him to have at it!

Roscoe came in on the Barry Plan. He enlisted in his third year of med school, received a deferment until graduation then showed up on the Navy's doorstep with his broom stick and bag over his shoulder.

Able to treat most minor medical aliments, he was tolerated by the chain-of-command due to the lack of competent help. However, if someone were seriously injured, and he were in charge, start the funeral arrangements as soon as possible to beat the rush.

In fairness, there was one thing at which Leroy did excel. His never ending fight against self-improvement.

Below decks on the tug the crew's quarters were cramped, only two sets of bunks and a centre-board, but the racks had extra linen and handmade pillows sent by the moms, wives and/or girlfriends and so were quite comfortable. Chance had zeroed in on the rack with the embroidered satin pillow.

He popped a Librium and lay down. Rod! Stand the

Politically Erect

fuck by!

A shaky, hand stitched map of the San Diego Zoo greeted his head as a voice echoed through his brain.

You are entering a dimension of sight and sound . . .

The twin Briggs and Stratton engines kicked in and they were underway.

***

As the eye of the storm had passed it left behind fifteen to twenty foot swells, driving rain and winds gusting up to 60 knots per hour.

The *Erin* was underway less than five minutes after the corpsmen were aboard and twenty minutes later, the noticeable jostling of the cabin below decks signaled they were clear of the break water. Even with the Librium Billy found he couldn't sleep and so wearing a streamlined life vest he got from one of the crew he snuck up on deck and into the rain to enjoy the ride.

The pitch of the boat was tolerable but the rolls were challenging and he was compelled to clamp onto the handrail which ran the length of the cabin's interior structure, with both hands.

He foolishly ventured out on deck and from the port quarter Billy got to enjoy the sight he had only seen in films; the dark of the open sea being gradually lit by the encroaching illumination of the dawn as it was about to break over the largest body of water on the planet.

The relative size of the boat in contrast to the giant waves, which seemed to rise from nowhere, creep up on the vessel and suddenly pounce, made him think that perhaps the small deck of a tiny boat in the middle of this awesome display of nature was not a good place for something as insignificant and diminutive as a human to be just then.

"HEY, DOC! GET THE HELL IN OUT'A THE RAIN!" A voice from above called down. Billy looked up to see Emerson shouting down from the rail of the pilot house.

Inside the dry and warmth of the bridge BM3 Emerson stood by a BM2 at the helm who was focused on reading each wave as it came then guiding the vessel to engage the sets at the optimum angle.

"This is BM2 Walton. I'm Emerson."

"Call me Ken." The young helmsman suggested as he ran the helm hard to starboard as they slid down a forty footer into the next trough.

"Billy Chance. HM2. Jersey City."

"Seattle." Walton shot back.

"Where's the Master Chief?" Billy cautiously inquired.

"Racked out below in his quarters. Up all night plotting and prepping."

The pilot house had the helm, which was set on a four and a half foot high stalk of polished brass set dead center of the space. In front of the helm sat the faceted windows which also stood four foot off the deck and encircled 180 degrees of the space. Save for the telegraph off to the port side of the helm for signaling the engine room, the binnicle containing the floating compass card on the starboard side and a small chart table next to that, there were no other fixtures, not even a chair. The surprisingly few electronic instruments, radar and VHF/HF radio were both mounted on the overhead directly above the helm. The table held some charts and a hand compass.

This boat was old school.

Emerson watched Billy perusing the brass fixture

casing of the binnicle.

"Beautiful boat ain't she?" It was more of statement then an interrogative.

"Yeah."

"Master Chief lets us do the plotting but always double checks." He explained. Billy perused the sea.

"Are we on a steady azimuth or do we deviate, I mean are there course corrections enroute?"

Emerson gestured Billy across the rolling deck to the narrow chart table on the starboard side.

"We left off here, these are the 32nd Street Piers across from Coronado Island."

"What's on Coronado Island?"

"All that crazy special ops shit, SEALS, UDT, Marine Force Recon. Mad fuckers out there! The *Mary Elizabeth's* out here, somewhere in this sector." He indicated a red grease mark on the acetate overlay of the chart.

"SOMEWHERE?" Billy asked. The guy on the helm smiled as he guided them down a fifty footer.

"Tides, drifts and in case you haven't noticed, there's the tail end of a typhoon in progress."

"So if your guy's plots are off by a few degrees, we could be steaming off to the Spratly Islnds?!"

"No, no! Not at all."

"That's a relief!"

"If we're off by a **few** degress we wind up in the Philipines. If we're only off by a one degree we miss the fleet and wind up in the Spratleys."

"The reason the fleet went out was to bypass the storm?" Billy confirmed.

"You don't bypass a weather system this large. They're just out far enough that the eye of the storm and the really shitty winds won't bang them around too much. It's calmer waters out in the perimeter but it ain't exactly Miami Beach in June."

"So it's not exactly going to be a cake walk once we find them and tie up alongside. So how do we safely transfer the patient in one piece form a deck forty feet above us in rolling seas?"

Both BM's smiled. "You're the corpsman! We're just the taxi drivers." Emerson smiled and slapped Chance on the back.

"What about magnetic deviation?" Sailor Chance asked.

"Bottom left hand corner of the chart, in the key. Fifteen and a half degrees in these waters." Chance read the key. "Of course old Dead Eye here thinks he can find the fleet by setting a heading then trusting it to dead reckoning." Emerson prodded.

"Get your twenty bucks ready Junior." Walton shot back as he worked the helm.

The next three and a half hours were a monotonous rhythm of standing around the wheel house chatting, going below pretending to rest then returning topside again, when finally . . .

"Ahh hey, Junior, can you help me out here?" Walton handed off the bios and Emerson, waiting until they rose from the next trough, perused the horizon. "Is them some boats out there? Really big boats. You know, like maybe some ships?" Walton taunted. "Ain't there a name for a bunch of ships all gathered together like that? Oh yeah, 'fleet', ain't that right Junior?"

Emerson strolled over to the window and spied the dark grey specs spread halfway acros the horizon.

"Fuck you John Boy!" Emerson grumbled.

"You'd better go below and roust the Master Chief." Walton suggested and Emerson, passing a twenty to Walton went to it. Chance quietly laughed. The Master

Politically Erect

Chief sent word he'd be topside in ten and Lee, with no desire to watch the show, elected to stay in his bunk.

They were now only a mile out from the fleet and nothing much had happened, that is until Lt. Roscoe appeared in the cabin. He stepped to the window pane just to the right of the helm and like a little kid in a car on his first cross-country trip, pressed his head straight up against the glass.

"Wow! Ain't that a beautiful sight?!" The fleet was spread out before them in battle formation and Emerson manned the radio while Walton slowed to one third to bring them in at a slower pace until the *Mary Elizabeth* could be located. They expertly maneuvered around the picket of destroyers holding the outer perimeter and found the two tenders just on their side of the two flat tops the Kennedy and the Lexington. The water was less turbulent but still choppy as they came along side.

Roscoe stared straight up the window at the forty foot high wall of battleship grey steel that appeared on the starboard bow as they slowly drifted alongside. Several mooring lines dropped down from above as the port side personnel ladder was winched down as well.

"Ahh, lieutenant, you might wanna –" Walton's warning was too late. As a twenty foot swell slammed them into the tender broadside, Roscoe's forehead ventilated the space by smashing the eighteen inch wide glass pane which used to occupy that window panel in the wheel house.

Glass crashed to the floor along with a rush of icy cold sea water which flooded the cabin, washed over the deck and soaked the shoes and trousers of Roscoe, the two BM's, Chance and the other person who had just entered the room. The Master Chief.

"WHAT IN GOD DAMNED HELL IS YOU DOIN',

BOY?!" In two splashy strides the Master Chief was in Roscoe's face looking down at him as if he had caught the L.T. finger banging his cat. The dead silence of the space seemed seconds from being broken by the snapping of bones and the wailing of a dying officer when they were hailed by the ship's 1-MC.

"AHOY TUG, AHOY TUG! STAND BY UNTIL THE SHIP'S PARTY DECEND'S THE LADDER!"

Walton gave two blasts on the fog horn to acknowledge they understood and they waited. Scurrying backwrads to avoid the Master Chief Roscoe slipped on the wet deck and fell on his ass. Now lying supine a second wave gushed through the open panel and soaked Roscoe to the bone with more cold sea water.

*

The ship's Independent Duty Corpsman had requested to be notified when the tug was in sight and so had the patient wrapped in a blanket, waterproof poncho and tucked into a Stokes stretcher with a normal saline IV hung. Corpsman and patient were hunkered down in the shelter of the superstructure when a runner appeared and passed the word the tug had been secured alongside.

It took some manuevering but with the ship's I.D.C. supervising, a pair of deck hands and Billy with the two BM's pitching in, the patient was manualy handled down the ladder and on board the *Erin*.

Paper work was signed and exchanged and thirty minutes later the Master Chief was back in his rack, Roscoe was confined to the engine room where he sat shivering uncontrollably while Lee and Chance were below with the patient and the large dark specs of the fleet were fading to aft as the crew and passengers of the tug were on the first leg of their return trip.

Politically Erect

It was full day light now and the storm had largely passed over the area and aside from some residual swells which settled to 15 foot high, the return trip was uneventful.

Wet, but uneventful. Uneventful save for the private medical conference Chance and Lee had in the tiny head of the crew's quarters. Face to face, inches apart, with Lee squatting up on the bowl, they argued the case. Chance argued the case, Lee didn't really give a shit he just wanted to be back on dry land as soon as possible.

"That fucker no more had a fuckin' heart attack than you or I! The EKG strip in his chart is as clean a fuckin' whistle. Except for a short, very mild bout of hypertension his vitals have been normal since the so called 'episode' plus he's giving contradictory symptomology on his medical history!" Chance quietly ranted inches form Lee's face.

"So? What'a you care?"

"I care because we just risked five lives to come all the way out here and get his ass!"

"Six lives! You're forgettin' Roscoe."

"Okay, we risked five good men and Roscoe."

"So,what's you gonna do 'bout it? The lieutenant doctor says he had a 'significant cardiac event'! You gonna tell him he's wrong, Petty Officer?!" Chance seethed but was temporarily speechless. "Besides that the I.D.C. wrote it up as a cardiac event!"

"He had to in order to cover his ass! That so-called patient AKA asshole, is out there right now sittin' up, smokin' and jokin' fer fuck's sake!"

Practically pressed up against one another, neither man, but Lee in particular, had any desire to prolong the ad hoc consultation any longer than required.

"Maybe he spontaneously recovered. Like that guy

we had with the arrow in his head! Remember that guy? Walked into the fuckin' ER on his own. We thought it was one of them Steve Martin joke arrows, remember? He was out'a surgery and on his feet in less than a week!"

"Oh yeah? If that bastard had a real episode then why is he braggin' about what he's gonna do to his old lady once he gets home? I was 34 years old and I just had a fuckin' heart attack I wouldn't be braggin' about gettin' pussy! I'd be drillin' the docs at what I need to do in future to make sure I don't buy the God damned farm next time!"

"Man you know blacks have a greater incidence of heart disease! All that fuckin' fried foods n' shit we eat all the time!"

"I never seen you eat that shit!"

"See if you can guess why, Sherlock!"

"Okay. . . point taken."

"Look, you the senior corpsman! Write your chart entry the way you see it and let it go. When we get his ass to the cardio ward at the NRMC they'll know inside an hour if he's malingering or not!"

Billy looked down and then finally nodded his head in agreement. He wasn't ready to stop venting but needed to change the subject.

"How's your mom?"

"Going down hill slow but sure." Lee answered.

"She on meds?"

"Shit loads, but we can't afford 'em. I send her three quarters of my pay but it ain't enough."

"That's fucked!" Billy supported.

"The bitch is, she got a son's a corpsmen with all the access to drugs in the world and I can't do shit to help her!"

Remembering his father, with no private medical

insurance, who couldn't get emergency surgery on a calcified shoulder, Chance had no reply but stongly empathized.

"Get a list of what she needs."

"What for?"

"I might be able to help. I know some people in Jersey."

"What, you gonna use your 'connections' to hook me up, Mr. Mafia?"

"Hey asshole, you want help or not?" Chance challenged. Lee realized Billy was serious and dialled it back a notch.

"I appreciate it." He dug into his bag and produced a small flask of whiskey. "I brung it in casin' we sink!"

Billy shook his head and smirked.

A short time later sitting across from each other, still down in the crew's quarters they had killed the small flask. Lee had given up and fell over into the bed to sleep.

About an hour into the otherwise completely uneventful return mission Billy decided it was a good time to bring up something he had been kicking around since reporting aboard Balboa.

"Lee!" He barked.

With a perfectly matched pair of brown/red bloodshot eyes Lee slowly shifted from his laying position and faced Chance.

"What?"

"I got something bouncing around in my head. I wanna run it by you."

"Are we gonna need another drink after you 'run it by me'?" He slowly mumbled.

"Could be."

"Seriously man! Can't that shit wait?! I'm sleepin'!"

He pulled the covers back over his head.

"No you're not, you're talkin' to me."

"Man, I don't know why I put up with your ass!" He bitched as he propped himself up on his elbow.

"Because when the Black Panthers, Angela Davis and Huey Newton launch the revolution, lose and white America admits that slavery wasn't a mistake, outlaws blacks as a species and starts shippin' your asses back to Africa you'll have somebody to stand as character witness for you, that's why! Reluctantly, but that's why. Now listen to me. I got a plan." Lee sat up and pretended to listen.

"You know how most of the corpsmen are always bitchin' that they signed up to save lives not take them?"

"Help women and children, blah, blah blah! So what?!" Lee interrupted.

"I heard a story about a G.I. from a small town in Illinois somewhere, went out to Idaho after he got out. Fought in the Second War, was a medic in the Army. It was after the war when all the G.I.'s were coming home and the labor market was flooded."

"Just like it's gonna be when this shit's all over! Yeah, I read something about that. Guy saw action in like every major theater!" Lee affirmed.

"Yeah, sounds like the same guy."

"So what happened?"

"According to legend, he packed up, headed out and settled in a small town out West. Idaho, Montana or somewhere like that."

"Wow! Compelling story Billy. Maybe they'll make a movie!"

"Fuck you. What is compelling is what he did once he showed up in Bum-Fuck, Arizona or where ever he settled."

"Thought you said Idaho?!"

Politically Erect

"Okay, fuckin' Idaho, one's those big, hot, flat states." A dramatic pause was called for. "He hung up a shingle."

"HUNG UP A SHINGLE AS IN MAGICALLY MADE HIMSELF A DOCTOR?!"

"Give that man a Cupie Doll! You're not as dumb as you look!"

"Uh huh."

"Guy's still practising today, so I'm told."

"Uh huh." Lee again grunted.

"We go over there to help those people-" Billy continued referencing Viet Nam.

"Bullshit! You don't believe that crap any more than I do! We're over there to protect the interests of U.S. Steel, Dow Chemical and the Chrysler Corporation!"

"I was gettin' to that! This is gonna be over one day-"

"One day soon by the looks of it." Lee added.

Chance sat back and sighed.

"I forgot you're a motor mouth when you drink!"

Lee flipped him off.

"I got no future back in Jersey Shitty, same as you got no future back in the Bronx."

"Can I get an AMEN to that!" Lee spewed.

"Part of the bullshit they sell us before we sign up is that the military affords you the opportunity to secure your future."

"Yeah, after 20 years you get a whole $276.00 a month or half your base pay whichever is less. Providin' you live to collect it." Lee griped.

"So let's do an end run on the bastards!"

"What the fuck you talkin' about?"

"Those people in Nam were in the shits before we showed up and promised them the world. They're gonna be in a lot worse shit after we pull out. If we can secure enough gear to get us started, instruments, maybe 'coupl'a oxygen tanks, nitrous, stretchers, a GP Large, enough to set up a small ER and relocate out in some remote area, we can start up our own clinic! What'a ya think?"

"I think this heat is getting' to your ass."

"I'm serious!"

"And you reckon the Nav is gonna schedule us regular resupply airdrops once they get hip to what you're doin'?"

"Probably not, that's why we set up a deal with the Yards!!"

"The whats?"

"The Yards! The Montagnards. Technically they're the Degars but everybody calls them Yards for short. Montagnard, it means 'montain' in French I think. Anyway, them and their chiefs and maybe some of the other mountain tribes. Food and supplies for medical treatment for them and their families!" Lee looked even more skeptical. "The S.F. guys have already won their hearts and minds by treating and protecting them for the last ten years. Vaccinations, vitamins, surgery, dental care! Hell some of those S.F. fuckers even got tattoos and have been inducted into the tribes!"

"I ain't getting' no muther fuckin' tattoos and I ain't sure as hell ain't becomin' no muther fuckn' Yard! I got my own tribe thank you very much" Lee was emphatic.

"I'm using them as an example. Yards are loyal little fuckers with loads of spirit! It's in their genes! They been defending their territory for five thousand years!"

"What makes you think the Yards still gonna be our friends after we pull up stakes and leave the poor bastards to the mercy of the Commies?"

"Because they're yards!"

"And riddle me this Batman! Where you suppose you gonna get your resupply from after the show's over and everybody packs up and goes home?"

"Shit! That's easy! You been around long enough, ours is currently the biggest, most diverse black economy in Asia! Hell in the world! Even bigger than the Soviet Union's! And you can be damn sure it ain't gonna dry up when the U.S. pulls out! Hell, probably even increase! Double maybe!" In his enthusiasm Billy flung his arm out and knocked over a coffee cup which smashed to the floor. Lee just stared. Part of the broken shards read; 'Master Chief . . .'

"Uh huh." Lee was not warming up to the idea. Billy continued to push.

"Besides, you think these tens of thousands of tons of supplies produced and shipped over here to stimulate the limp U.S. economy when this thing started is gonna make the trip back after this little shindig is over?" Billy offered.

"What'a **you** think, Uncle Sam's gonna have a giant assed yard sale?" Lee pushed.

"Probably, possibly not but once we're set up they'll still be enough black market supplies floating around the whole peninsula to supply us for a couple of years. By that time we'll have set up legitimate supply lines through the Chinese trade routes or whatever."

"Uh huh, 'or whatever'." Lee sat up on the bunk. "And you know what's it's even gonna take to get started on your Dr. Doolittle adventure?"

"That's the beauty of it Bro! I already got more than I need! Look," Chance came around to sit next to Lee on the bunk and produced a one to ten thousand military issue map. Lee quickly slid over to keep his distance. "Look! A convoy of medical supplies was reported hit by an NVA mortar barrage two weeks ago."

"Man you really do follow what's going on over

there!"

"Yeah, yeah I do. So mortar barrage two weeks ago only thing is, some Nav jet jocks just happened to be on station and, with the help of a trusty SF forward L.P./O.P got a fix on them and napalmed the mortar position!"

"The drivers?"

"Abandoned the vehicles at the first sign of the attack and except for two who were found wandering down Highway One. Haven't been heard from since. They're all now officialy listed as MIA."

"What about the trucks full of gear?"

"That's the clincher! I know a guy with the Seabees! He told me about a warren of cave's up near the DMZ -"

"What-the-fuck's a warren? Only Warren I ever heard of is Earl."

"A bunch'a caves! Point is, for the right price this guy'll get some buds, go over there and secure all that shit in the caves. Waterproof it etc . . ., you know make it so's we can use it in a couple'a years or so after the dust settles."

Lee sat up straight and stared at Billy.

"How ou know all this shit?"

"I got connections!"

"You serious about this shit ain't you? I mean you're crazy, white ass is really willing to go and get yerself locked in the brig, ass shot off, locked in the brig, killed or worse yet get locked in the brig, over helpin' some indig you don't even know, ain't never met and ain't gonna do shit for you except give you some pigs and a goat?"

"And hopefully a chicken or two."

Still unable to agree with where Lee was coming from, Billy assumed his shipmate was out, and so just stared back.

Shaking his head like a disgusted parent at a stupid

child, Lee grabbed the flask and stuffed it back into his bag. Caught up in the passion of his argument Billy hadn't touched the last bit of his drink.

"Count me out my pale brother from another mother!"

And so the great, one man Naval Medical conspiracy was hatched, discussed and died before being stillborn.

The boat continued heading into the rising sun and just over four hours later the patient was delivered to the care of the Admissions Officer of the Naval Regional Medical Center and Corpsmen Chance and Lee were off one of the longest shifts of their lives.

***

The following day they got word that the head of Cardiology gave the sailor they had gone through such straights to medivac out, a clean bill of health.

A day after that it was in the hallway of Ward 2 of the NRMC where Billy, after long hours of internal debate, found the man he had been looking for.

"Doctor Vonnegut, do you have a minute, sir?"

"Just one. What is it?" The full bird captain answered through the cap of a pen in his mouth as he scribbled something in a patient's chart.

"A patient came in a couple of days ago and was referred to Cardiology. A Machinists Mate named Jameson."

"So? That's a nursing function." The cardiologist brushed past him.

"I need some information on his condition."

"Why come to me? You have access to the charts, ask at the nurse's station up on Cardiology!" Remaining aloof the doctor pressed on down the hall.

"I saw your name on the chart sir." Billy called after him.

Billy had run up against the G. C.'s before, the God Complexers, the M.D.'s who thought they were above the rest of the staff. Anybody in any NRMC had, and so he restrairned his anger but not his frustration. "I need **YOUR** opinion, sir, not just the data off his chart." The officer froze, turned back to look at Billy, hesitated then re-approached him. He glanced at Billy's name plate.

"May I ask what business of it is yours, Petty Officer Chance?"

"A shipmate and myself, as well as several others, risked a lot to medivac him off the *Mary Elizabeth*, a tender. We'd just like to know how he's doing. Sir."

"You took time out of your busy day to track me down, confront me with what might be interpreted as borderline insubordination, when you could've just as easily referenced his chart, all out of a case of altruistic, patient follow-up?"

"That's about right sir."

The surgeon, slightly taller than Chance, cocked his head to the side.

"That's your story and you're sticking to it, eh?" The doctor pushed. Billy's non-response was answer enough. "What are you getting at?"

"I need to know if he was really sick. If he actually suffered an episode." The Captain looked him up and down.

"Ahh! No. Not only was there nothing wrong with him, there was no evidence of him ever having suffered any cardiac related event at all. Not even hypertension."

"Thank you Captain."

"You're welcome, Petty Officer." The G. C. called over his shoulder as he scurried off down the hall.

Politically Erect

"Next time use the chain of command, Corpsman!"

"Aye aye sir." Billy answered and walked away. "Dick!"

*

Just back from a lunch run off base Lee plopped himself down at the staff table of the break room in the dispensary and pulled out a chair to dig into his 1 inch Blimpie sub.

"You want some'a this?" He offered.

"Nah, not hungry." Billy grunted, slouched on the couch in front of the muted T.V.

"What's up your ass? Shot down by that blond in pediatrics? Again."

"That pilot, from the medivac, couldn't get us off the ground?"

"Yeah, what about him?" Lee placed his Dr. Pepper on the table and proceeded to unwrap his hoagie.

"I ran into his co-pilot at the Naval Exchange."

"And?"

"He didn't make it back."

"That's fucked." His empathy was genuine. "Hazard of the game. He knew what he signed up for. Don't make it right, but that's the game. You said it yourself. 'We're all expendable'. That's what makes us different. We choose the part of this war where we save people, not waste them."

"You're missing the point!" Billy snapped. Lee was about to take his first bite but way laid the hoagie back on the table.

"Okay Aristotle, what's your point?!" Lee prodded.

"That scumbag nig-" Using the word nigger in jest or

in the context of camaraderie was one thing, but invoking the word in anger was another. A lesson he learned from Lee.

"Go ahead, you can say it! I know you're pissed off. So say it!"

"That low life asshole played us! He was no more having a fucking cardiac event then you or I were getting laid! That asshole takes malingering to a whole new fucking level!"

"I get it. I agree he's the worst kind of nigger." Lee affirmed.

"I mean, we've both seen malingerers, every day at sick call, but never where it cost a good officer his life, not to mention that could have been you or I at the bottom of the ocean that night!"

"That's what you're pissed off about, a low life coon maligering? Or is it about you and I almost getting our asses waxed on a medivac?"

"Fuck no!" Billy snapped. "Well not you so much. But I got plans for my life!"

Lee readjusted his chair and stared over at Chance.

"I know what you're thinkin' about doin'. Don't! Look at me asshole!" Lee cautioned. Billy mechanically turned towards Lee. "That big-lipped baboon fucked a dozen people over that night and cost one man his life. Even though the guy who died was an officer, a good man, might'a had a family too, or at least some body that loved him, but goin' to The Man over this shit ain't gonna do nothing but get your ass fucked up, that dumb assed, red-necked Lieutenant Roscoe a letter of reprimand and that ARF'll still walk. Probably just wind up gettin' his bobbled headed ass discharged which is what he wants anyway!" Lee argued.

"Graphic description. So how do you really feel?"

"Just because we're black don't mean we ain't got our

issue of fucked-up mutha' fuckers." Billy, distracted by Lee's perspective, calmed a bit. "Not as many as you white boys, but we still got our share." Lee turned his attention back to the patiently waiting sandwich.

"I just can't deal with the fact that fucker's gonna get away with it! If he slides this time he'll do it again and maybe the next two HM's won't be as lucky as you and me!"

"Let me correct your grammar. You mean as **good** as you and me."

"Point taken."

"Let it go bro. Besides, you respect the bars not the person!" Lee urged.

"If that's the kind of person they give bars to, then I'll stick with stripes!" A long silence followed. With a passing pat on the shoulder to Lee, Billy left the staff duty room but popped his head right back in the door again.

"What the fuck's an ARF?" He asked.

"I forgot, you from Jersey, no culture. It's a Coney Island reference. African Rock Fish."

"Because blacks can't swim very well?"

"Because we got greater bone density!" Lee mocked.

"Oh yeah! You guys think everything is bigger!"

"It is, white boy!" Lee held up the 12 inch sandwich.

"Maybe but, it ain't the size of the vessel." Chance said. Lee raised the hoagie to his mouth and bit into it. "It's the motion of the ocean! You guys need to eat more pussy!"

Lee spit his food out. "Great talk." Billy called over as he left the room.

"Fuck you Chance!" Lee looked at the mayo oozing from his hoagie and tossed it in the garbage next to the table.

Paddy Kelly

*

Against Lee's better judgment Chance did take it on himself to file a report to Command. A day later Chance was called in to relate his version of events, the Head of Cardiology was requested a report, submitted a medical evaluation and Roscoe was notified.

Following a closed board hearing Lt. Roscoe, M.D. was given a warning but cleared of any wrong doing. He was back on the wards doing more damage the next day.

Machinist's Mate First Class Jameson was not prosecuted for dereliction of duty or malingering, both severely punishable in time of war. The reluctance to prosecute was because he was black and, as everyone knew, the base C.O. was intimidated by the 'racial issue' and so wanted to avoid any potential racial repercussions.

Jameson was however transferred to the East coast fleet putting 3,000 miles between him and his girlfriend.

The lost chopper pilot's family received the customary line of duty death payment. The pilot was denied a medal for bravery which was submitted by his C.O. The reason given for the denial by the base commander was because he considered it was the pilot's duty to fly a chopper and so he didn't deserve any special recognition just for dying.

But his twenty-three old wife did get a little scrap of purple ribbon with a cameo of George Washington it.

As a great writer once said: "And so it goes."

*

The hand lettering on the glass panel of the Quonset

Politically Erect

hut door was shaky and the word 'Command' was spelled with one 'M'.

> Naval Regional Medical Center
> MMC B. L. Dunsten
> Comand Master Chief

Chance knocked smartly on the knock block screwed to the bulkhead to the right of the office entrance.

"ENTER!" Someone yelled from behind the door.

Billy pushed through the door and took up a position and stood tall in front of the overweight senior sailor who sat overshadowing the tiny wooden desk. The soles of the Master Chief's size ten Corfam shoes greeted him.

"Master Chief I was told to report on the double." The Master Chief looked up from his reclined position as he excavated deeper into his left ear with a bent over paper clip.

"Oh yeah. Chance!"

"Yes, HM2 William Chance, Master Chief."

"No, I meant chance as in you like taking chances? As in with your career."

"I don't follow Master Chief." Billy said. The chief let his tubular legs fall off the desk.

"You're one lucky son-of-a-bitch Chance, ya know that?" Billy stared. "Here." He tossed a sheaf of papers across the desk. Billy retrieved the thin pack of type written papers and thumbed through them. "Pretty ballsy move chasin' that malingerer all the way up the chain. Now you got a pissed off full bird cardiologist pissed off at ya, an O-3 M.D. gunniing for ya and all ya get out'a the deal is ta get some coon asshole transferred to the Atlantic Fleet."

Chance was at a complete loss as to where the Master

Chief was heading. "Lemme ask ya a question. What'a you give a shit if some chopper pilot bought it?"

"As long as it was in combat, I don't Master Chief. But chasing some asshole malingerer who put six other people at risk gets up my ass."

"Very noble. Well I got some more news probably gonna piss you off pretty good. San Diego Air Command's decided to go around the base commander and go ahead and put them two chopper pilots in for awards anyways. The tug sailors as well." The Master Cheif purposely paused to let it soak in.

"That's good news Master Chief. The corpsmen?"

"Nope! Nuthin! Day-nada! C.O. says youse two don't get squat on account'a it's your job to save people. That's what the Nav pays you for. They got a point too! E-magine if'n I got a award every time I fixed the fucked up paperwork of some ward corpsman or some dumb assed tech. Hell, I'd havet'a hire me a coolie just to follow around behind me and wearin' a extra jacket to carry all my extra medals!"

"I can see how that's a bit ludicrous Matser Chief."

"Well here's your punishment Chance." The Master Chief brandished set of orders.

The sheaf of papers he tossed across the desk was a set of orders to the Marine Air Wing, in Tan Son Nhut Air Base. Viet Nam.

Billy smiled.

The orders were not just to Nam, but to an air wing that had seen more action than any other in the last two months. An air wing where all the action was with incoming-out going medivacs and incoming busted up planes and choppers. Oh yeah, wounded and KIA's too.

Billy slid the papers back into the manilla envelope and tucked it underneath his arm.

"One question Chief. If we risk our lives on a regular

basis, but don't deserve any awards what happens if we die in the course of a call? We get demoted before they bury us?"

"Get the hell out'a my office before I lose my sense of humor Chance!" Refusing to let the situation get the better of him, Billy did not allow his military bearing to degenerate as he about faced and exited the office.

"I'm doin' you a favor Chance!" The Master Chief called out after Billy cleared the door.

Paddy Kelly

YOU CAN ALWAYS TELL A ZOOMIE BY HIS HANDS.

THEY'RE USUALLY IN HIS POCKETS.

CHAPTER TEN

Tan Son Nhut Air Base
Saigon

Regardless of where you are or where you wind up after that, nowhere or anything is ever as you pictured it before you got there.

The Hawaiian Islands-like atmosphere portrayed in the pre-flight orientation video opened with a slow pan of waving palm trees, happy villagers going about their daily business in the local market places and closed with a montage of long, aerial shots of pristine rice paddies and rolling, green mountains all overdubbed by a pleasant female voice with an indecernable Asian accent.

Chance had lifted off from Lindbergh Airfield in San Diego, twenty-some-odd hours ago and by way of Midway Island, (AKA Midway), then on to the Philippines, (AKA The P.I.), then by way of Guam, (AKA Give Up And Masturbate), his flight touched down in Saigon at around noon the next day.

Stepping off the ramp of the C-130 and out onto the scalding hot tarmac Chance was quickly relieved of the delusion he knew what the word 'heat' meant. By the time he set foot back on the ground he felt as light headed as a bleached blond, was panting like a dog and sweating like a fifty year old insurance salesman at a strip club.

A white, hand painted sign off to the side of the tarmac read:

> Welcme to Tan Son Nhut
> Base Operations
> Elevation 33 Feet

"No wonder I felt light headed. Must be the altitude!" Billy mumbled to the sign.

A half hour later he made it to the check-in desk at the terminal 300 yards away.

"Name?" The clerk asked.

"HM2 . . . Chance, William . . . J."

"Got any combat experience?"

"Does datin' a . . . Puerto Rican from the Bronx . . . . then breakin' up with . . . her in Queens . . . count?" He puffed out.

"I'm from Astoria so, if you went through that, you'll have no problem over here, but I'm gonna give you a slot in the main dispensary first, see how you get along. FMF training?"

"Negative. One year of college, basic training at San Diego, a one year stint in Iceland – "

"ICELAND! Who the fuck did you piss off?!"

"With a year of college I guess . . . they reckoned I'd make a good weather guesser so instead of one of the six combat slots I requested . . . they sent me to Lakehurst, New Jersey to stare at fucking clouds and read . . . thermometers. So I quit. They had no sense of humor about that so . . . Like I was saying, a one year stint in Iceland then Pecker Checker School, now here I am. Ready to fight syphillis, trench foot and the Clap . . . to keep the world safe for democracy."

"You requested to come here?!"

"Yes, yes I did."

"Doc you got a terminal disease? You get a girl pregnant or something?"

"None of the above. Now if you'll please finish in-processing me, . . . I'd like to get over to the chow hall before 15:00."

"Doc, this ain't state side. There ain't no chow hall

Politically Erect

hours here."

"You mean. . . ?"

"24-7 Doc. You got an I.D. card and a hand to hold it up with, you eat. All you want too."

Chance smiled.

"What's the skinny over here? Any real differece from Stateside?" Billy inquired of the Marine behind the counter.

"You mean other than all the foriegners, bad food and somebody shooting at you all the time trying to kill ya?"

"Back in Jersey City if it wasn't the Italians trying to kill the blacks or the cops trying to beat the draft dodgers it was the Hispanics trying to kill each other." Billy snickered.

"Well, over here the Flips have the chow hall and the barracks services. By agreement with the Philippine government, after we kicked the Spanish out of the P.I. and the Flips started bitchin' about us not getting' the fuck out of their country, Uncle Sam gave them a deal. If a Flip completes a four year enlistment in the Nav, regardless of rank, he can go back the P.I. and get a commission in their navy."

"So if he does four years as a cook here he goes back and becomes a Zero over there?!"

"And ten years later he's a commander!"

"Sounds fair." Billy laughed.

"The supply depots and distribution lines and, as always, the personnell offices are owned by the spades."

"Pretty much the same Stateside."

"One Saturday night back in Jacksonville Florida the 'Brothers', following an all out punch-up in the Enlisted Club thought it'd be a good idea to set the place on fire. Riots broke out in other enlisted clubs as all the racial shit escalated."

"I remember! That shit went Navy wide. We were given direct orders not to talk about it outside the gate!"

"Yeah, a mechanic I served with in Pendalton got brig time when he talked to a reporter. But I got a brother in the Big Red One says it was way worse in the Army." He passed a bundle of gear over the counter to Billy. "They caught the arsonists but kept the club closed own for a month. We got word that at one point the Big Boys in the Pentagon were kicking around the idea of closing the E-clubs all together."

"The racial situation back home ain't much better." Billy confirmed.

"Anyway over here, generally speaking, anything that's behind the lines is considered REMF territory."

"REMF?"

"Rear Eschelon Mother Fuckers. In the Army and the Corps thet call them POGES; Persons Other than Grunts. Meaning essentially useless. That's the difference with the Corps. We don't have POGES, REMFS or BLACKSHOES. Everyone here is a Marine. Even the navy cooks have to qualify on the range."

"Huh! Maybe I should'a joined the Corps."

"You're a corpsman, right?"

"Yeah?"

"You're the only rate can switch directly over. Four weeks at 29 Stumps and you're one of us Doc!"

"Huh!" Billy gathered his gear. "What else do I need to do here?"

"I'll stamp your arrival time one hour late, give you time to eat then you can finish checkin' in." The corporal shuffled some more papers, signed and stamped several copies and gave the remainder to Chance then pointed across the compound. "That's the Quartermaster's shack." He pointed to the other end of the airfield. "You're supposed to go there as soon as you leave here.

Politically Erect

But go eat then check in over there for your combat gear issue."

"Much appreciated."

*

Officers, or O's derogatorily called 'zeros' by most enlisted men, are an interesting breed. They wear bars in contrast to enlisted men's stripes. They have their bars by virtue of the fact that they have a college degree however, by that time so did a signifcant sector of the enlisted ranks in the Navy, so it didn't mean they were necassarily any smarter.

Billy's first run in with an officer was just after graduation from Corps School when he was awaitng orders and was temporarily assigned as the demolition range corpsmen at 29 Palms, the Corps' largest base, for the day.

A range is essentially a big open area where you can blow shit up or shoot the hell out of some paper targets which you could pretend were actually your ex-boss, your ex-company commander or your just your ex who dumped you when you found out she was doing the school jock or your best friend.

Like the other 364 in Southern California it was a bright sunny day when a Lt. Colonel Army type had his battlion out at range #7 was sitting with Billy in the shade to avoid the thousand degree heat of the Mojave desert. The troops were out there practicing all the neat ways they had learned in the classroom to blow shit up.

A young butter bar Lt. had a squad, about ten men, down range showing them how to set and arm a 40 pound shape charge. Contrary to what he was taught in demo school, that is to take the dtonator down range with you so you know where it is at all times, he decided to leave the detonator with a private up range near the safety bunker. The words 'private' and 'detonator' should scare anyone just as much as the terms 'holy roller', 'this will only hurt a little' and 'government promise'. Throw in butter bar, a 2nd Lieutenant, and everyone should be running for cover.

Billy and the colonel, a Korean War vet who had done two tours of Nam, sat shooting the shit as the Lt., his men gatheted closely around, carefully set the wired blasting cap into the nose cone of the conical shape charge, screwed home the cap and gave the thumbs up to the private up range to indicte the bomb was live. The same private who apparently took the thumbs up to mean, "Go ahead and wire the detonator". Obedient little troop that he was that's what he did.

Billy noticed what was going on and interupted the colonel and, as he slowly stood and stared in amazement, he realized that the private held the palm-sized detonator and squeezed it. You know, just to be sure it was working.

It was.

The Colonel's continued comment about the time he was pinned down by a sniper was cut short as pulpy pieces of privates, seasoned with generous portions of lieutenant punctuated the afternoon sky for the next 10 to twenty seconds.

The colonel jumped to his feet and yelled at Chance.

"GET THE HELL DOWN THERE CORPSMAN, GOD DAMN IT!"

"What for Colonel?" Chance, who just stared down range at the big black hole and at the randomly dispersed infantry squad, fought back a smirk at the absurdity of the situation. *Officers!* He thought to himself. *Leaders.*

Politically Erect

"I'll contact Graves Registration sir."

So much for college degrees and holders of said sheep skins being smarter then your average grunt or squid.

The colonel put him on report but it was a feel good gesture on the officer's part. Nothing would ever come of it.

Of course when it comes down to where the rubber meets the road, the bullet with your name on it doesn't really give a flying fuck about your educational background.

But most officers do assume an aire of superiority and don't take it very well when they have to deal with an enlisted troop who is more educated then they are in any given area. Areas such as emergency medicine.

Billy had always been facinated by women officers who he reasoned were a particularly interesting, peculiar, strange, different and odd breed. Generally they fell into two catagories; intelligent women who joined to pay off their college loans and seek a little adventure and those who were the son their daddy never had. Most of those in this latter catagory, after a short peiod of dating trying to find the 'right guy', (a guy just like dad), turned gay.

Like the myth of the Viking Shield Maidens, women have a not so long history in the military. Not as long as some promos and politicians would have you believe at any rate and certainly not long in the overall scheme of things.

They do however, have a very interesting history.

The WWII myth that they can multi-task better then men, propagated by the Allied governments to cajole more women into the forces and into factory service to contribute to the war effort, persists to date. Nothing wrong with that. In fact they can multitask pretty good;

so long as it's cooking, cleaning and talking on the phone at the same time. The fact is there is little or no empirical evidence to support this however, it is generally agreed that women are generally exposed to environs where they are required to multitask more often then men. But not in life threatening scenarios, like setting bombs properly.

As fighting is only one of a myriad of things to be done in military service, at war or not, women have especially adopted well to the medical arm of the combat forces. Save for the live fire combat course, the obstacle course and the one mile litter carry the women back at corps school were subject to all the required training standards the men were. And usually did very well at those tasks.

Billy often conjected there were any number of corpswaves he'd be comfortable working with in a life-or-death, trauma situation.

*

By 1974 race relations in the military had reached the point that there were, in essence, two sepearte armies in the U.S. military. One black and one White.

By-and-large-the whites still joined the service to pay off loans, get the G.I. Bill after they got out or to learn a specific skill set they could later use and so signed up for what they could, job wise that is, and then went where they were told.

Blacks by-and-large signed on the dotted line to get the hell out of the shit holes of the slums and escape the dire poverty they had inherited thanks to the economic system in the U.S. which is so woefully out of balance that it is never likely to change. The rich continue to get richer and the poor continue to get poorer. The fact that the country was at war only seemed to accelerate the process.

Aggravated by the fact that the states below the Mason-Dixon Line, from the Carolinas all the way west to Nevada, had an education system which was still slowly crawling into the 19th Century, many blacks entered military service woefully unprepared for the reality of a superpower at war and which was getting its ass kicked in a country few Americans could find on a map while being aided by the American's greatest nemisis - the Communists!

And so it goes.

****

July, 1974, Main Dispensary
Marine Air Wing
Tan Son Nhut Air Base

One of the first things you learn about being around the military during war time, especially if you're in the combat zone, is that time equals mortality. The amount of time you spend hanging around such a place is inversely proportional to the odds of you walking away with all five appendages you were born with still attached to your body. But once outside of a place like this, the unparalleled surrealism doesn't necessarily cease to exist as most all of the returnees would attest to.

After struggling to get back to the rear or even home, a place where things make sense and are 'normal', that is 'as they were before', like they used to be, things aren't and never will be 'like they were before'.

The people back in Civ Land are the same, mom, dad,

sis etc. . . . the neighborhood and everything back on the block remains the same. What changes is your perspective. Although changed doesn't really describe it. Irreversibly altered and skewed is more accurate. Changed for the rest of your life, like herpes. Forever.

One of the things that changes you forever is the realization that there is a point, not far from where you are right now, where nobody gives a shit. About anything. You come to realize there is no god, no heaven or hell and in reality, unless somebody wants to take personal revenge on you, there are no consequences for your actions. Especially based on the shit you witnessed or experienced in the war time military.

Another sad fact of military life is that not all the casualties of war are sustained in theatre. Billy learned that the very first time he volunteered for E.R. duty at the air base dispensary for a few days to fill in for a troop on leave. After all his ultimate goal, the reason he was over here in the first place when tens of thousands of others were running to Canada, was to get experience in trauma management.

During the war Zoomies, (Air Force personnel), had it pretty easy especially back on the state-side duty stations. Good chow, minimal physical fitness requirements and, like some kind of Motel-6 set up, only two to a room. This however, did not render the boys in the bus drivers' uniforms immune from the shit.

*

Airman First Class Sheffield was a good troop. He wasn't drafted, he signed up to do his patriotic duty right out of Deerfield High back in Illinois. He did well in basic airman's school. Scored high in his Aircraft Mechanic's course and lucked out when his first set of

Politically Erect

orders sent him to the Great Lakes Naval Air Station where the only fighting occurred off station at one of the sleaze joints outside the base on The Strip or in the Enlisted Club when racial tensions flared.

About three weeks ago, his worst nightmare came true. He got orders to The Nam. Now he was stationed just outside Saigon at the airbase.

Following morning chow he and his bunkmate Reese, an easy going black kid from Pomona, California, were assigned to assist in routine flight checks and re-fueling of a squad of 104's out on the flight line.

Jet Propulsion fuel mixture #4, JP4 for short, technically doesn't burn. It explodes. When you control that explosion you can propel a 10 ton aircraft through the skies faster than the speed of sound.

About two hours into the morning Sheffield and Reese were on their third aircraft. Reese was doing a canopy check and Sheffield, down on one knee up on the wing, had just started filling the port side tanks with JP4 being pumped from a fuel truck they had pulled up along side.

Sheffield looked over at Reese, smiled and then released the trigger on the fuel nozzle halting the flow of fuel into the wing. Reese thought maybe he wanted to tell him something so he stopped wiping down his wrench and listened up. What Sheffield had to say was that he was terrified of having been shipped out to The Nam and was sure he was coming home in a body bag, or worse yet, missing body parts. Only he didn't say it in so many words. He just put the fuel nozzle in his mouth and pulled down on the trigger and the 80 pounds per square inch the engineers built into that fuel pump saved Airman Sheffield from having to stay in Viet Nam. Forever.

Paddy Kelly

Reese scrambled down to him to pull the nozzle from his mouth but it was a wasted gesture. In three to four seconds Sheffield's insides filled with three or four gallons of JP4 as the fuel filled his esophagus and shot through his intestines while about a second after that, it shot out his nose and mouth forcing him to drop the hose.

Two seconds later Airman First Class Sheffield was a crumpled, convulsing, fuel soaked heap which rolled off the wing, smacked onto the concrete tarmac and after several bouts of projectile vomiting was unconscious.

By the time Chance and Hernandez, the first corpsmen to arrive on the scene, jumped from the 1961 Cadillac ambulance Sheffield had stopped vomiting but was leaking an appreciable amount of JP4 from his anus.

Since he still had a heartbeat and was breathing, albeit with a lot of effort, they couldn't institute CPR. Chance realized this one was going to take a bit of effort and worked frantically to get the kid's coveralls stripped off, get an IV in him to the keep his veins open for medication and began monitoring his vital signs. The Marine driver in the ambulance was a sharp troop and had already radioed ahead to the ER with all the details they needed to stand-by and receive the patient even as he was being treated on the scene.

About ten minutes after Airman Sheffield mistook his mouth for an F-104 fuel port, he was in the Regional Dispensary with a team of crack corpsmen, nurses and M.D.'s crawlin' all over him like a gang of L.A. cops on a black J-walker.

Two and a half weeks and 27 abdominal operations later official word came down that a daeth party had to be sent to notify the next of kin about Sheffield's demise.

A young, state-side corpsman drew the short straw and got to go tell Mrs. Sheffield that her only child, the only one she would ever have, could ever have, was dead.

For the young corpsman it was the first time he had pulled the 'Dead Duty', but was able to detach himself enough to be minimally affected. However, he wasn't too thrilled about the fact that due to a fuck-up in paper work, Mrs. Sheffield never even knew her kid had been hospitalized much less that he had no chance of pullling through. Which was just as well because had he recovered from his self-inflicted injury, some disillusioned JAG officer, (milatary lawyer type), would have probably charged him with dereliction of duty or more likely willful destruction of government property and thrown him in the stockcade.

Maybe it was better off that he was in the ground.

★

Paddy Kelly

FORCE YOUR CONGRESSMAN TO
WORK FOR A LIVING.

DON'T RE-ELECT HIM!

CHAPTER ELEVEN

As he slouched on the couch back in the duty room of the dispensary in front of the small B&W T.V. there was more bad news for Chance's ambitions to stick around the Big Show and possibly see some action. Now, after nearly a three year trek punctuated by an uphill administrative battle, there was a chance he might be headed back state-side already.

From all angles it appeared the war was rapidly winding down. NBC news currently reported that activity around the DMZ had been stepped up, troop withdrawals had increased, more P.O.W's started home in dribs and drabs and Tricky Dick was increasingly talking about 'peace with honor' which everyone on both sides knew meant, "Let's get the fuck out'a Dodge before we get spanked anymore."

To reinforce the bad ju-ju it just so happened that there was a new command directive on allowance for medical discharges upon request, subsequent to the C.O.'s approval. As the C.O. was a medical officer and a Jesus lover who didn't hold with the unholy practice of killing, which was of course why he was in a war zone, he judiciously gave considerable leeway to his medical staff to write any candidate up for dischrge, submit the discharge request and he would give it the once over. Providing there were extenuating circumstances it would likely get the Good Housekeeping Seal of Approval and said candidate would be on the next bird home.

Billy got up, walked over and turned off the telly then scanned the end table for reading material. His mind wrestled between the latest issue of National Geographic and a five month old copy of Playboy. Having already learned about the life cycle of the Tse Tse fly he chose Miss February and ducked into the head. Just as he was getting settled in he heard the lounge door bang open.

"CHANCE, SADDLE UP!" It was HM3 Hernandez yelling from the doorway.

"WHAT'S UP?" He yelled back.

"Section Eight out on Tin Can Alley!"

Tin cans were destroyers, DD's and DE's and along with frigates were the smallest ships in the inventory. They earned their name by how they behaved in rough seas - exactly like a tin can in a storm. Unlike bigger vessels when in port they could be moored strung out side-by-side up to five deep.

A minute later Chance and Hernandez were out the door and in the 1967 Cadillac ambulance. Billy hit the lights and siren as they pulled out.

"Why didn't they call over to the *Sanctuary*, she's right there?"

"*Sanctuary* declined."

"DECLINED? What is this, a fucking game show?"

"Most of the time brother! They declined, we got the call. Said the time it would take to launch a skiff with a shrink on it made us the closest available. Besides, after he beat off the S.P.'s -"

"BEAT OFF THE S.P.'s?! Has he got a fucking weapon?!"

"Dunno but, jew gonna find out, gringo!"

"Asshole!" Billy commented. "Where to?"

"The Mainside piers."

"By the way, I wasn't available either." Chance said. "I was working on a really good shit!"

Ten minutes later they pulled up alongside the line of three strung out destroyers and drove into the emergency vehicle reserved slot on the pier adjacent to the main gangplank.

Politically Erect

"Grab the litter!" Billy said as he manned the M5 med bag. He and Hernandez jogged up the midships gangplank of the inboard DD, saluted the ship's ensign on the fantail and then the OOD. The young officer on duty returned their salutes.

"Chance and Hernandez from the dispensary. We got a call to the *U.S.S. Edson*. Something about a Section Eight?"

"Yeah Doc, seems like one of their snipes lost it and went bananas. The *Edson*'s most outboard, two over, I'll call over on the sound powered phone, let 'em know you're coming."

"Much appreciated sir." They exchanged salutes again and the two were plank hopping over to the *U.S.S. Edson* where several of the ship's crew were up on deck to watch the show. The duo were directed by the OOD to the fantail where a burley boatswain's mate stood sentry over an open deck hatch on the port side fantail as Billy approached.

"What's ya got Boats?"

"Crazy fucker! Came aboard about a year ago. Gets along with most of the crew but he's from the South, Georgia. Seems to have a problem with blacks."

"Anybody hurt?"

"Not that we can tell so far, but he's got a Warrant Officer Two trapped down in the bilge. Says he's gonna kill him he get's the chance."

"Where's your docs?"

"One on emergency leave and one on liberty."

"The warrant down there with him, his supervisor?"

"Yeah. Nice enough fella, teacher out'a Minnesota."

"Black?" Billy asked.

"Yep."

"Is he hurt?"

"Not that we can tell from here."

Billy looked at Hernandez and smiled. Although Cuban, Hernandez too was a bit dark.

"You're out'a your fucking white boy mind! Don't even think about it!" Hernandez spouted.

"Awright, I'm elected. Boats, you got a Neil Robertson handy?" The BM1 nodded to a seaman standing by and the kid took off to fetch the stretcher. "Is he armed?" Billy asked.

"We don't know Doc, but he sure as hell scared the piss out'a them Shore Patrol pukes!" The BM laughed. "They double timed outta here like Ann Margret was doin' a nudie show at the club! Said they was going for more help."

"Okay, standby here Boats. I'll recon the situation and get back to you."

Even having seen it in films it's hard to get a true picture of what it's like down in the guts of a war ship, even a small one like a destroyer. The fantail deck hatch, commonly known as a scull, was narrower than a standard street manhole and allowed one sailor at a time to descend, via a vertical ladder, to little less than halfway down into the lower decks. At that point the light was less than half what it had been directly under the deck hatch and walking was only possible via a narrow, grated catwalk.

At the base of the ladder Billy listened, heard nothing and so cautiouly proceeded along the catwalk into the dark towards the forward sector of the ship. The pungent stench of diesel fuel permeated the entire space and a slight headache began to set in.

As he descended a second vertical ladder deeper into the bowels of the destroyer Billy heard a heavy tool of some description bouncing off the bulkheads at some unknown location forward of the midships.

Politically Erect

"I'M GONNA KILL ME A NIGGA BEFORE THE DAY'S DONE! YA'LL CAN COUNT ON THAT SHIT!" A rabid drawl-tainted voice echoed through the hold.

As he came to the end of the long catwalk, Billy was now only four or five yards above the bilge, and nearly amidships. He peered down over the side rail of the catwalk and strained through the dim light to see a figure huddled behind a cluster of some 10 inch steam pipes. He recognized the khaki uniform of the warrant officer. The voice once again called out this time to the tune of *Workin' On The Railroad.*

"I BEEN KIL-LIN' ME A NIG-GA, ALL THE LIVE LONG DAY!" A metal tool rhythmically banged in time on a pipe.

I know that fucked up drawl! Billy thought to himself. He was able to get the Warrant's attention and signalled for him to stand fast which garnered a thumbs up from the terrified engineering officer.

"RIDGERUNNER! THAT YOU?!" Billy called out. The banging stopped.

"WHO'S THERE? YOU ANOTHER FUCKIN' SHORE PATROL PUKE? CONTESTENT NUMBER THREE, COM'ON DOWN! I'M GOWNA FUCK YOU UP!"

"HEY, TERRY, WHAT SAY WE FORGET THIS FUCKIN' OFFICER AND GO GET US A ROAST BEEF SANDWICH with extra ketchup? I'M BUYIN!" The word roast beef triggered the crazy man's memory.

"BILLY? BILLY CHANCE?!"

"TERRY, IT'S ME!" Realizing they were old chums the WO2 relaxed and figured it was safe to come out from behind the pipe array. Billy immediately waved him back just in time to avoid a flying monkey wrench which twanged off a steam pipe just above his head.

"Fuck!" Chance cursed.

They may have been old friends from Corps School, but Chance had no idea how far gone Terry was and was in no great hurry to become a casualty himself, at least not at the hands of a bilge snipe who in all likelihood was suffering from heavy metal poisoning form sucking on diesel fumes for a year.

"I COME OVER THERE AND TALK WITH YOU, WE GONNA GET OUR UNIFORMS ALL FUCKED UP WHEN YOU TRY AND GO ALL DELIVERENCE ON MY ASS?"

"NAW, I GOT NOTHIN' 'GAINST YOU. JUST THAT NIGGA WARRANT OFFICER."

"WHAT'S THE BEEF?" As Billy kept Ridgerunner talking he signalled to the officer to quietly make his way towards the fantail and up through the topside hatch.

"FUCKER WOULDN'T LET ME PUT IN FOR AN EARLY OUT!"

"YOU DON'T SAY?! WELL MY OLD HILLBILLY SHIPMATE, I MIGHT JUST BE ABLE TO HELP YOU WITH THAT." He watched the warrant disappear into the darkness of the fantail and slowly made his way towards Terry's voice.

"KEEP TALKING SO I CAN FIND YOU." Through the forest of fixtures and dense undergrowth of pipes Chance made his way past the mid-ships and over to the starboard side where he spotted an obviously depressed Ridgerunner planted on a large drainage pipe valve. He decended yet antother verticle ladder and, avoiding the plethora of trip hazards moved to where Terry could see him.

"Hey!" Chance greeted from a couple of meters away.

"Hey." Terry looked like shit. Even in the limited

light Chance could see the sheen had completely gone from his eyes which were sunken and listless. His face was gaunt and drawn and he appeared to be half the weight he had been back at corps school. Staring down he balanced a two foot length of pipe in both hands.

Terry's dress whites were hardly white any more and heavily smeared with grease.

"How the fuck do you people work down here?"

"Fucked up like a soup sandwich in the rain ain't it?" The space reminded Chance of something out of a Hammer horror film. "Spend a year down here and suddenly prison don't look so bad." Terry added.

"Where the fuck is everybody? The crew I mean, and why are you in dress whites?"

"Liberty. Everybody's got liberty."

"Not you?"

"FUCK NO! Fuckin' nigg'a bastard put me on the duty roster at the last minute! Again!" Chance quickly noted to avoid the warrant officer as a subject.

"You think you got a case of reverse racism here?"

Terry didn't answer he just looked away and slowly perused the bilge. Fluid slowly dripped from an overhead pipe and splashed into the six inches of sea water in the bilge.

"Mind if I cop a squat?"

"Hell no, pull up a pipe. Sorry about the state of the place." He gestured around the filthy, oil and grease drenched space. "Wasn't expectin' company."

"You tellin' me you got no Alabama tea in the cupboards?"

"No, but . . ." Reaching in his front hip pocket Terry produced a rolled up sandwich bag containing about half an ounce of weed. "I got some Panama Red."

"Guess that'll have to do." There were several joints

already rolled up and Terry fished one out and fired it up. He toked up and passed it to Billy.

"So, talk to me bro." Billy started off. Ridgerunner didn't reply until they were half way through the doobie, it was obvious he had been holding back for some time.

"My granddaddy fought at Appomattox. Had two grand uncles killed in the First War. My daddy, his brother and my mother's brother all served in World War II. We got another uncle never come back from Korea." He took another toke and passed the J. "I turned 18 figured it was my turn to serve. Always knew I would, it was my duty." He shrugged. "Like on all the recruiting commercials. 'You have a duty to your country!' Hell, only cowards duck out and I wasn't gonna be no coward! Besides, Canada's got that fucked up bacon!" He stared back down into the bilge water. "But now, after four years of this shit . . ."

"It's right to question what's going on Ridge-"

"Instead'a sending me ta fight all I am is a glorified wrench monkey!"

"It's not like you haven't made a contrib-" Billy's interuptions didn't seem to register.

"On top'a everything else, now everybody's sayin' the war can't be won! That it's all over, and we lost!" He took a deep drag on the doobie. "They's not a god damned one of them senator's sons-a-bitchs gonna serve one god damned day behind bars for dodgin' the draft Billy! Not a one! Clintons' kid, Bush's kid, none of 'em! Which means in the final analysis, years from now, people's gonna be sayin' we was the one's who was wrong. Wrong for comin' over here and getting' involved in somebody else's fight!"

"Fuck 'em! Politicians are the same everywhere Terry." Billy reassured.

"Yeah but we're supposed to be different Billy!

Politically Erect

America's suppossed to be different! We're supposed to be settin' the example! I mean Watergate, the L.A. riots . . . Kent State fer fuck's sake! Unarmed college kids gunned down like wild animals! Them eggheads got a right to go to school if they want to without getting' bullets put em! Followed by the cops going in there and beatin' the shit outta the rest of 'em! Shit Doc, I got no use fer college but, this is supposed to be the fuckin' United States of America!"

Billy, focused on allowing Ridgerunner to sedate himself, passed the joint back. After taking a toke.

"Hell, there was a time back when all I wanted to do was get over here and fight the Reds! Now I wouldn't fight even if the bastards gave me orders and a gun!"

Billy listened as Terry polished off the spliff and flicked it out into the blackness.

"I read in the paper back home some judge give a lady 30 days in the tank on account'a she wouldn't find some guy guilty of possession of an ounce of dope! A fuckin' ounce and it's a felony! She thought 10 years was excessive so didn't find the kid guilty, so the judge put her in jail! Mother of two! What the fuck is happin' out there in Civ Land Doc?!"

"It's turbulent times Terry. Everybody sees it, but nobody seems to have the balls to do anything about it. I read where some Yale professor wrote a paper saying America has strayed so far from what the founding fathers intended that it's no longer represented by the laws which govern it."

"Guys like that fuckin' judge are the fuckers we're over here fightin' to defend! So they can shit on the system?! Stop the communists here so they don't come over there, that's what all the papers, radio, politicians and priests are tellin' us every day!"

Paddy Kelly

Ridgerunner held up the sandwich bag and smiled. "Dangerous narcotic! Ten years in the Federal pen!" With the help of the dope they both laughed at the absurdity of their situation. "Sometimes I feel like it's all developed its own dynamic and nobody's drivin' the train. Ya know-what-I-mean Doc?"

"I think I do Terry, I think I do."

They sat silent for a moment tuning in to the rythm of the dripping pipe. Suddenly they heard a commotion back towards the fantail.

"CHANCE?! WHERE THE FUCK YOU AT?" It was Hernandez come looking for him.

"I'M HERE!" He looked back and spied Hernandez peering around an overhead fixture about fifty yards back. "GO BACK AND TELL THE BOATS TO HAVE THE NEILS-ROBERTSON STANDING BY AND A STOKES AS WELL! I'M COMIN' UP." Footsteps faded in the distance.

"Whatt'a ya think Doc?" Ridgerunner asked.

"Well, ball's in your court, brother. Whatt'a **you** wanna do?"

"It ain't what I thought it would be Billy! I wanted to go do my patriotic duty, fight sum com'nists, free the world of oppression like in World War II ya know! Instead . . . now . . . I just want the fuck out." Although he didn't think it was the right time to say anything, Chance began to understand what Terry was talking about. Billy's former indifference towards the war began to wear a little thinner. "What'a ya think Doc? You think the Great Experiment has failed?" Ridgerunner seemed to be pleading.

Billy figured wiggin' out and trying to brain your immediate supervisor with a 12 pound monkey wrench qualified you as being bat shit crazy which in turn probably qualified as the symptom of extenuating

Politically Erect

circumstances.

"I'm 90% sure I can get you a medical, but I need you to work with me."

"Tell me what I need to do and it's done."

"I'm gonna take care of you. You sure there's nobody else around down here?"

"Nobody ceptin' that fuckin' warrant officer."

"Not any more bro, he slipped out while we were chattin'." Terry laughed to himself.

"You're a sneaky bastard! Guess that's why I trust you!" Terry confided.

"Good, then stay here, I'll be right back." Chance made his way back up topside where he grabbed a few things out of the M5 med bag. Off to the side he gave some directions to Hernandez and ten minutes later he was back down in the hole with Ridgerunner.

"My partner's coming down in a few with a Neil Robertson stretcher. Here's the plan. You're gonna act like a madman, I'm talkin' hillbilly crazy, ya got that?"

"Shit! That all?! Don't you sweat it none! Back home I drink moonshine by the quart!"

"Good man, but I'm also gonna give ya a little something to help you out."

"I don't want none'a them heavy drugs now, ya hear?! I don't take drugs!"

"Trust me!"

"I do Billy, I do." Terry got quiet then spoke up. "Hey."

"Yeah?" Chance acknowledged as he retrieved a syringe, a vial of valium and two Alka-Seltzer tablets from his M-1.

"You still got somethin' going with that pretty little corpswave, the one you met back in school?" Chance had no way to know it wasn't idle chit chat.

"Connie. Yeah. I haven't heard from her in awhile, but we still talk, yeah. We talked about getting together for Christmas. Why'd ya ask?" Billy worked as they talked injecting Terry with five cc's of valium.

"Doc . . ." Terry took him by the arm.

"Hold still till I get this in ya!"

"Doc I got some bad news." Chance suddenly felt light headed. "She bought it in a car accident." Ridgerunner waited for Billy's reaction. "Home on leave, in Illinois. Some asshole in a tractor trailer side swiped her and ran her of the road into an embankment. She slammed into a tree."

Billy fell back on his knees and stared straight ahead. Death. Again.

"Jimmy Del La Reece heard it while he was going through Fleet Marine Force at Twenty-nine Palms." Terry immediately regretted giving Chance the news but figured he may never see him again after this. "If it matters, they said it was painless. She never knew what happened."

Billy looked over at him.

"When was the funeral?"

"HEY!? WHERE THE HELL YA'LL AT?" At the sound of Hernandez's voice Billy snapped back to reality and he re-swabbed the injection site on Terry's arm as he handed him the two Alka-Seltzer tablets.

"HE'S MEDICATED AND STABLE. COME ON DOWN AND GIVE ME A HAND GETTING HIM TOP SIDE." Billy yelled back then turned his attention back to Ridgerunner.

"These things dissolve instantly, so don't pop them till we're just up near the hatch. Better yet," He reached for the tabs and Terry passed them back. "When we get you to the topside ladder we'll have to get you onto a Stokes litter. I'll distract everybody and fake like I'm checking your pupils. When they're looking away I'll feed them to you. Got it?"

"Doc I'm sorry for . . ."

"Forget it. I appreciate you tellin' me. Shit news is always better coming from a friend." Billy composed himself and got back to work packing up his gear. "Guess I'm free for Christmas."

A few ninutes later, strapped into the mummy-like, O.D. green Neil Robertson, Billy and Hernandez carried Terry back to the fantail then handed him up the ladder to the guys top side who hoisted him up through the hatch, up into the daylight and onto the deck where he was laid on a standard navy litter.

Terry's Academy Award winning performance as he thrashed and growled, Alka Selza foam spewing from his tightly clenched jaws, was convincing enough that even though wrapped tighter than a slab of fresh Hahei tuna in a sushi roll, the black warrant officer and several of the by standers took three steps backwards.

An hour later Terry had been shot full of some more valium, was out of the mummy bag and restrained in one of the dispensary treatment rooms. Chance sat nearby at a small desk typing up a medical report to accompany Ridgerunner's request for immediate discharge on medical grounds.

At the bootom of the page was a last pair of boxes labled: 'Line Of Duty?'

Chance checked the 'Yes' box.

**

Paddy Kelly

LET HISTORY RECORD THAT WE WERE THE UNWILLING LED BY THE UNQUALIFIED TO DO THE IMPOSSIBLE FOR THE UNGRATEFUL.

CHAPTER TWELVE

Despite his mental agility at diagnosis and prescription and the fact that he got through corps school with good grades, once it was discovered that Bob Achmen hated people and therefore couldn't stand seeing patients, something had to give.

The situation resolved itself when eventually, by his own request Bob was re-assigned to Medical Repairs. This request for reassignment was not arbitrary.

For Uncle Sam sending him to hospital corps school instead of aircraft mechanic's school as he had requested and been promised on enlistment, so he could make a bundle of money fixing rich people's airplanes when he got out, Bob had concocted an alternative plan for his long term retirement.

The Med Repairs shack was just that, a shack. Located, unmarked, out behind the dispensary in the far corner of the parking lot detached from the main clinic a hundred yards or so from the rear entrance of the dispensary it was, as far as HM3 Achmen was concerned, ideally fit for purpose.

Just inside the door of the 10 foot by 15 foot wooden shed, dominating the left wall was a full length wooden work bench with an overhead tool rack. The left side of the wall above the bench was a series of open bins cluttered with electrical parts as well as some large hunks of various diagnostic machines of various sizes. The portable X-Ray machine wedged into the right rear corner was labled 'part needed'. The date on the single sheet of 81/2 x 11 loose leaf paper taped to the casing was dated three and a half years ago.

The entire electrical source for the two sockets in the

shack was a single 50 foot extension cord strung along the rafters and wired into an old transformer which in turn was rigged up to a nearby telephone pole with a single 220 line hanging from it.

Bob could tinker all day at the few pieces of medical gear, stethoscopes, scales and things of this sort, in his self-imposed and isolated exile, while allowing him to remain unencumbered by the company of other human beings. Any of the more complicated repairs had to be sent out to the U.S.S. Ajax, the fleet's repair ship, which meant a one to three week wait and so bought him more time to pursue his own personal interest.

There was never a time when there was complete silence in the garage sized MR shack. Once when leaving with Bob, Billy had attempted to turn off the beat-up, old boom box/radio/eight track perched on a shelf above the workbench which constantly wafted tunes through the space.

"No! Leave it on!" Bob ordered.

"Why, we're leaving?"

"Because, it fills the room with music while we're gone! When we get back the room'll be full of tunes, keeps out the bad vibes man!" Bob enlightened Chance.

"Makes sense." Billy shrugged.

"And close the door quick so the tunes don't leak out." Bob further instructed. Thereafter Chance was careful to avoid anything spiritual, esoteric or religious when he talked with Achmen.

There was a reason Bob A. kept to himself all the time and only ventured beyond the plywood and metal boundaries of his love shack twice a day. Once for morning muster and once again for quitting time.

Bob was more than happy to wait out the remainder of his military sentence tucked away in the MR shack, particularly since his brother state-side in San Louis

Politically Erect

Obispo back in California, had sent him a back issue of *The Whole Earth Catalogue* where-in there happened to be a detailed article one month on how to synthesize LSD from certain basic ingredients. Certain ingredients which, for most civilians were controlled substances, but for your friendly neighborhood corpsman, could readily be had in your local, neighborhood dispensary.

Although the Boys in the black shiny FBI shoes had busted Ken Kesey and the Merry Pranksters out in Haight Ashbury a few years before, they had yet to discover the massive underground movement which Ken and the lads had spawned and all the folks they had helped to 'Tune in, turn on and drop out'.

Being a medical facility there were any number of things useful to a budding, pharmaceutically oriented scientist. As a consequence, a couple of weeks after setting up in the MR shack, Bob had heself a little lab where-by he could produce upwards of 100 milliliters of pure Lysergic Acid Diethylamide a week. By the second week he had honed the process to produce just over 200 mils. However, Bob's chemical endevors soon grew beyond the boundaries of recreational activities.

At the going rate, one to two dollars a hit, and requiring only one drop per tab for blotter acid, and given that 100 mils would yield up to 2000 drops. . . you get the picture.

Although this appreciably exceeded the $327 a month Bob was raking in from Uncle Sam, trying to move and unload upwards of $4,000 worth of acid per week would certainly send up some red flags. So Bob was wise enough to store his supply and only move it once every couple of months or so out of county. As freshly distilled LSD manifested as a clear, water-like solution he did this via a standard lunch Thermos so as not to raise any suspicions. For the first couple of trips, this worked well for all concerned.

Achmen's regular civilian contact, a freelance reporter for *Rolling Stone Magazine*, who took it out of Saigon via the regularly scheduled return flights, inconsiderably went and got himself wounded trying to win a Pulitzer during a fire fight up near the DMZ. With no one to act as fill in for the next run, and stocks of his Lucy in the Sky with Diamonds commodity quickly backing up, Achmen decided to take some well earned leave and make the run to L.A. himself.

By the end of the month all was worked out and Bob made the trip.

All was worked out that is except for a certain Military Policeman wanna-be type who had been rejected twice for military service due to a long standing personality disorder. Namely being given to unprovoked fits of violent rage. Said L.A.P.D. type decided he liked carrying a gun with a badge which allowed him to shoot people without answering for it and who had only a year ago gave up on the Army and became a California State Trooper. A state trooper who patrolled the L.A. area highways. Easy pickin's, so to speak.

Early that sunny Saturday morning, the day after landing back in the States, Bob was on liberty driving north to meet his brother's contacts in the Hell's Angels.

The aforementioned super trooper had eaten a particularly large bowl of Mr. Macho corn flakes for breakfast that morning and decided Bob cruising up the 401 in his orange Dodge Dart wearing custom reflective sun glasses was a prime soft target for that most popular game of state police called, "Let's play fuck-fuck with a random driver and see if we can insite him to become belligerent enough to justify an arrest".

After doing the lights and siren thing, officer Mike

Politically Erect

Macho, in his custom tailored, heavily starched and pressed, khaki uniform with the brown leather body harness and jack boots, (the kind Nazi's used to wear), strode, hand on holster, also brown, up to Bob's alleged vehicle and ordered the alleged suspect, (Bob), to disembark out of the alleged orange vehicle.

After Petty Officer Achmen had obediently dismounted the suspect vehicle Terminator cop eyed him up and down and displayed obvious offence at his appearance.

"Take of your glasses!" He demanded.

Apparently Bob hadn't gotten the memo that said only California State Troopers were allowed to wear refletive Ray Bans so Bob complied. Terminator didn't remove his.

"Where you goin' in such a hurry sailor boy?" Bob having grown up in California knew the Fuck With Random Drivers game and so responded calmly.

"Officer? Speed limit's 65. I was more than 10 miles under the speed limit."

"Licence and registration." Bob complied. "A California boy, you ought'a know better son. I got you on radar doin' 90."

"I was ten miles under the speed limit. Officer."

"What's your job in the Navy, boy?"

"I'm a corpsmen."

"What the hell's that?"

"Like a paramedic, but we also perform minor surgery and administer drugs."

DRUGS! The cop's dull eyes lit up like the baubles on the Christmas tree at Rockefeller Center on Thanksgiving eve.

"Oh yeah, non-combatant types!" Terminator, amongst innumerable other facts, was ignorant of the statistic where Navy Corpsmen have garnered nearly 3,000 special combat awards since the rate was established. Not counting hundreds of Purple Hearts.

"What kind'a drugs?!" At this point Super Trooper started poking around behind Bob peering inside the car.

"Whatever's required for the patient." Bob stepped to the side to avoid allowing the cop to get behind him.

"I never went in the service! I serve my country by risking my life to protect people from criminals!" Now off to the side of the cop, Bob fought back a smirk at the remark as the officer poked into the car and rummaged through the few things on the front seat. He pulled a blue, Tupperware food container from the floor.

"What's you got in here?" He brandished it at Bob.

"Coupl'a cheese and bologna sandwiches, some Cheetoes and a drink. My lunch."

The cop unclipped the top and perused the items. He tossed the Cheetoes bag at Bob and barked.

"Open it!" Again Bob complied. The cop was determined and saw his last chance. "What's in here?" He held up the Thermos.

"Water."

"We'll see. Better not be booze!" He said as he prayed to the cop gods it was booze. He unscrewed the red plastic cup from the top, smelled it then unscrewed the lid. Once that was off he sniffed the liquid which came nearly to the brim. "Looks like water. We better be sure."

"It's been in the car officer, it's kind'a warm, you might not wanna -"

Bob's gesticulation of a warning came too late as without hesitation the cop lifted the container to his lips and helped himself to a deep swig.

Who knows what broken sporadic and disconnected thoughts sputter through the minds of people of this caliber. The kind who reinforce their own egos by

Politically Erect

bullying others. The kind who hold the power of life and death in their hands and use that power to lord over others because some people have the audacity to wear the wrong sunglasses.

Whatever the origins of his mentality the California Highway Patrolman was in for, what was known in the military, as a significant emotional event.

No one in the annals of medicine had ever written or otherwise ventured a scientific opinion on how the human brain might be affected by suddenly ingesting up to a thousand hits of pure Lysergic Acid Diethylamide at a one to 3,500 microgram concentration but, unbeknownst and unannounced to all of mankind, the first guinea pig had been found.

Bob did the only thing he could do. As the cop swallowed he stoically fought back any overt reaction and waited for the officer's head to explode like an over ripe, pressurized melon. It did not. Not yet.

Instead the cop made a 'yukkie' face and replaced the lid on the Thermos.

"I think your water's gone bad, son!"

"It's been in the car all morning officer, that's probably why."

The cop moved to hand the container back to Bob and it was with extreme relief that Achmen reached for it but the cop had second thoughts. He pulled it back.

"We'd better keep this! Just in case. Might be gin. Gin din't have no taste." Bob stared. "You can go. And watch the speed."

Bob purposely took his time getting into his car and getting back on the road. His strategy worked. By the time he pulled out onto the highway the cop had waited for him to pull out first which put the squad car just behind him.

Paddy Kelly

He watched carefully in the rear view mirror slowly creeping forward putting distance between himself and the squad car without breaking the speed limit. Five to ten minutes later, a little under ten miles up the road, the squad car began to drop back and gently swerve.

Within minutes the car attempted to pull off the highway but suddenly shot back on, jumped the median and fired across into the southbound lanes. It seemed to stabilize but the next course correction was more dramatic and following a long slow 'S' manouever it drifted off the road altogether, rolled through the shallow drainage ditch and gently bumped into a Howard Johnson's billboard on the other side.

Bob slowly changed lanes, drove across the median and headed back south to the crash site.

He drove a mile or so further south before he found a crossing point, turned around and drove back north, slowing when he could see what looked like the parked cop car up ahead waiting to trap a speeder.

Carefully scanning for any signs of oncoming traffic he saw none and pulled off onto the shoulder of the north bound lanes.

Bob again quickly glanced up and down the highway, saw no one and scurried across the three lanes to the lightly crumpled car.

Inside an uninjured Macho cop, protected by his seat belt, was babbling incoherently to himself in between laughing fits.

Bob reached in through the broken window on the passenger's side, snatched up the Thermos, tucked it under his shirt and calmly made for his car.

Once out on the median of the deserted road he had second thoughts and hesitated, removed his sunglasses and looked down.

"What the hell? I am a corpsman." He said to

Politically Erect

himself.

Back at the cop car Achmen reached in through the window and gently slid the Ray Bans off the puzzled trooper's face as he pocketed his own.

"If you needed a red capped Thermos to complete your lunch box . . . you should'a just bought one." He then quickly but calmly walked back across to his car. "Besides, you should know better, stealing's against the law." He commented when he reached his car. He got in and drove off.

A half a day later Bob and his brother's contact were in a lush private residence just outside Hollywood disposing of the load and completing their deal.

"Keep the Thermos." Bob quipped to leather draped biker as he left the house for the airport that afternoon.

****

Paddy Kelly

OEDIPUS WAS THE FIRST MAN TO BRIDGE THE GENERATION GAP.

CHAPTER THIRTEEN

It was three and half hours into the 23:00 shift and, save for a sprained wrist and a torn finger nail sustained while doing battle with a beer bottle, things were quiet. Not a patient to be had.

Billy was sitting outside the emergency room enjoying the cool clear night when a taxi pulled up and three blacks in civilian casual clothes, who had obviously been out for the night, tumbled out of the car, rushed past him, kicked the door open and struggled into the ER. Two of them had the arms of the third draped over their shoulders. He was being dragged more than he was walking.

Well, looks like our first customer of the evening has arrived. Billy informed himself as he followed them in.

As he came around behind the reception desk to log the patient in he noticed the patient's chest was soaked in blood to the waist, his expensive flowered, silk shirt was in tatters and he was delirious. The second thing Billy noticed was he was a dead ringer for the martial arts movie star Jim Kelly.

"Is that-?"

"No, he just looks like him!" One of them answered.

"Get him into treatment room one. What happened?" Billy asked as he was right behind them.

"Fight over in the EM club." The big one responded.

"How much alcohol has he had and don't bullshit me!"

"Hardly any Doc, he normally don't drink! He just went to get his second drink when the shit started."

"Drugs?" Chance donned a pair of surgical gloves as they exchanged information.

"He's a fuckin' boy scout Doc, no shit!" The big one insisted.

"Not even weed!" The other added. Chance made eye contact with the short one as if seeking confirmation. "Serious!" Shorty verified.

"How many others involved?" The last thing Billy needed was a full scale donnybrook at the E.M. club, a regular occurrence in the military lately it seemed, when he was alone in the ER.

"Only one."

"Anybody got his I.D. card?"

"Yeah, me."

"Sign him in. The log's out on the desk."

Billy scurried across the treatment room to the exam table where the young man lie and began his initial exam. He grabbed a pair of one point sharps on his way and cut away the shredded dress shirt the tall, slender sailor wore. He immediately grabbed a two liter bottle of alcohol and an extra package of surgical sponges, tore it open on the roller table and opened the alcohol. He made eye contact with the big guy and nodded.

"What's his name?"

"Leonard."

"LEONARD, THIS IS GONNA BURN A LITTLE."

"Hold his arms." Chance said quietly. They complied.

With a handful of the sponges in his right hand he gently poured the ethanol over the patient's chest and dabbed away, carefully observing the wounds as he went. Leonard hardly reacted.

Blood loss had been minimal but the patient remained semi-conscious.

"This guy a diabetic?"

"Yeah, why?"

"Was he drinking sugary drinks?"

"Not sure. That important?"

Politically Erect

"Kind'a." Chance shot back.

Over a dozen slices varying in length from three to four inches to over a foot long marred his chest exposing mostly subcutaneous but also some muscle tissue, especially around the pecs. The relevant thing Billy noticed was that the wounds were all about the same depth.

"Who'd he fight with?"

"A fuckin' Flip!"

Philippino kids growing up on the streets of Manila learned to handle a butterfly knife before they were weaned. Looked like this guy met himself a native.

"Looks like Jim here was introduced to the art of the stinging butterfly!" Billy probed the friends.

"Yeah well what ever that shit is ol' butterfly boy gonna meet up with sumfin' else when we find 'em!" The big bro brandished his fist.

Billy appreciated the fact that there were two kinds of people who came in with trauma patients. Pussies and vampires. Those who passed out when they saw blood or those who starred in fascination at their friend's rearranged anatomical bits. These guys were one of each.

"You guys are welcome to hang around, but ya might want to send out for coffee."

"Why?"

"Because this is gonna take a while."

Billy went to work setting up half a dozen five-O nylon suture packs and a couple of four-O gut packs he retrieved from the cabinet behind him and scrubbed up.

"What happened?" He finally asked after he was set up.

"He went to the bar to get a couple of drinks for him and his girl, that's when the Flip fucker started hittin' on her. Leonard here came back and they went at it."

"The Philippino had a butterfly knife?" Billy sought to confirm

"Yeah, and knew how to use the mutha-fuck'a too." The other one announced as he tossed a pair of nunchucks on the counter behind Chance. Billy noticed the parachute cord which had joined the two octagonal sticks had been sliced clean in half. *Guess that's why the Chinese make nunchucks with chain.* Billy thought to himself.

"Anything we can do to help Doc?" The big guy asked.

"Yeah, either of you guys got an electrical rating?"

"Yeah Doc, I do. What'a ya need?" The short one spoke up.

"You see that autoclave over there, the round oven thingy?"

"Yeah." He made his way around the treatment table to the area Billy had indicated. "What'a I do now Doc?"

"Pop open that cassette player next to it and flip that cassette tape over for me would ya?" Billy directed as he sutured. "Then press play."

The other big guy had a good laugh. Zevon's *Sentimental Hygiene* waifed through the treatment room and the patient began to stir.

"Leonard, welcome back bro. How you doin'?"

"Doin' okay Doc. Doin'. . . okay." He struggled but was able to lift his head and survey the damage. Chance monitored his facial reaction.

"Damn!" Was all Leonard commented.

"You feel any pain, let me know. I got plenty of this pain juice here, compliments of Joe Taxpayer. Green?"

"Green Doc. I appreciate it." He let his head fall back onto the table. "Hey Doc, this gonna scar?" He finally asked.

"Ain't gonna lie to a shipmate. Blacks form the same

Politically Erect

keloid tissue as anybody else. Problem is keloid has no melanin."

"The stuff that gives us color!" Anxious to show he didn't sleep all the way through high school biology the short one chimed in.

"Bingo!" Billy congradulated. "So the colorless, actually white-ish, sorry bro, stands out more than it does on Caucasians."

"Looks like you gonna have some white boy on you Leonard!"

"Hey, Slimboy?"

"Yeah?"

"Shut up!"

"The good news is a couple of Navy dermatologists have been playing around with steroids." Billy spoke as he went into his fourth pack of suture. "Injecting them into the scar tissue after it's fully formed. They've been getting some impressive results."

Billy's explanation was suddenly interrupted as a God awful racket flooded the emergency room outside when a gaggle of bodies burst through the front doors into the waiting room knocking over furniture, upright ashtrays and the coat rack as they did.

Billy cursed, draped the patient's chest with a sterile towel, folded his hands together to maintain sterility and backed through the treatment room door and out into the waiting room to investigate.

Two Rent-A-Cops in their bus driver's uniforms had apparently went on a rampage and, forming a two man drag net had snagged every Philippino, navy or civilian, who was unfortunate enough to be meandering about the base that night. About twenty in all, they were all handcuffed to each other.

The two security geeks had forced all the prisoners

against the far wall and were considering what to do next when Billy came out of the treatment room.

"You fellas lost?"

"Who are you?" Apparently the scrubs, surgical cap and blood stained gloves along with the caduceus on his left arm presented a mystery to the two crack investigators.

"Dr. Kildare, who does it look like?"

"DON'T GET SMART WITH ME YOU LITTLE -"

"THIS AIN'T THE WHOSEKOW! Or haven't ya noticed! Why are you here? The brig's a half mile up the road, you got prisoners who're not hurt take 'em there!"

"We're here to get a positive I.D. on the alleged perp! Where's the victim?" Billy perused the unfortunate collection of Philippinos, the handcuffed sailors and civilians now huddled, backs to the far wall, sitting down.

"What's with the final round-up?" Chance pushed.

"We figure one'a these Flips is probably one of them."

"Or could be several of 'em! These slants never fight alone!" The other cop piped up.

"Unlike rent-a-cops." Billy was forced to comment. "Flipped?" Billy asked. "Did somebody flip? Go crazy I mean?" Billy sarcastically queried.

"NO God damn it! Flip as in these guys!"

"OOOHHH! You mean these Philippino sailors! The ones serving in the same navy as me! My shipmates. The same ones who we fucked out'a their land after we helped them kick the Spanish out of their islands? Those Philippinos?" Several of the prisoners smirked. Billy shook his head and turned to go back into the treatment room to tend his patient.

With a hand on his holstered weapon the short sawed-off cop wanna-be tried pushing past Billy whose mind flashed back to the lobby incident in Florida and how the civilian security guards abused the wounded chief. He was determined not to have a repeat performance here. Quickly losing control he side stepped in front of the guard and blocked him off at the wall.

"HOLD ON THERE WYATT EARP! Where the hell you going?"

"I'm goin' in to talk to the victim!"

"No you're not! He's in surgery. You'll interrogate him when I'm done putting his chest back together and after the dugs wear off! Meanwhile why don't you take a couple of these guys out back and beat a confession out of them!" Billy turned and went back into the treatment room. "Fuckin' Rent-A-Cops!" He mumbled.

As Billy was re-entering the treatment room loud, boisterous shouting erupted back out in the reception area.

Three more rent-a-cops barged through the front doors dragging another Philippino in civilian clothes into the dispensary. The five guards were being verbally harangued by the sailors they had arrested and the three new comers were having a hard time with the immaculately dressed, middle-aged prisoner as he wasn't going willingly and made a prodigious display of his command of the English language as well as his skill at judo. The new detainee was clothed in a three piece suit, silk tie and designer Brogans.

Chance watched the show and smiled. The knife attack patient had been given more local anaesthetic which would be wearing off in the next twenty to thirty minutes but for the moment Chance couldn't tear himself away and stood, riveted with anticipation at what **he** was about to unleash.

"Hey, Mr. Wizard!" He called over to one of the other

guards who nodded over at him. "You guys get unemployment compensation when you get your asses sacked?"

"What the fuck you talking about?" The belligerent cop approached him.

"Your new suspect-" The soon-to-be-civilian glanced over at the ranting freshly arrested prisoner. "That guy look like he's been out on the tear tonight much less in a bar fight?"

"What the hell you care? You know him?"

"Yeah. As a matter of fact I do." The guard's expression metamorphosed into a frown, Billy smiled. "Ahhh! There it is, the Kodak moment I'd been waiting for." Chance quipped as he crossed the room to where two of the rent-a-cops were picking themselves up off the floor in front of the doctor. "His name's Rodriguez."

Billy stood where their latest prisoner was rising from the floor, Billy leaned down and addressed him. "Commander Rodriguez, how are you sir?"

"Alot better then these two when I file my report to the C.O. in the morning!"! The two guards' eyes were wide as saucers.

"Happy to testify for you too, sir. Gentlemen, Dr. Rodriguez, the duty surgeon. Or as we address him, Commander Rodriguez."

The two were that stupid that they had to be told what to do next, namely to release the prisoner.

Billy headed back to his patient.

"Scratch three rent-a-cops." He said to himself as he returned to re-glove and finish applying the last of the 150 sutures to the retired ninja's chest area.

***

Politically Erect

Tuesday Evening 19:47

Billy picked up the phone.

"Base dispensary, HM2 Billy Chance speaking. How may I help you?"

Shouting into the transceiver a panic-stricken woman attempted to relay her situation.

"HE'S ACTING REALLY STRANGE! I'M REALLY AFRAID HE'E BEEN POISONED OR SOMETHING! PLEASE SEND SOMEONE, SEND SOMEONE RIGHT AWAY!"

"Ma'am, calm down please, calm down. Who's acting strange?"

"MY SON! IT'S-"

"Is he injured?"

"No, NO! Just that-" Someone apparently ripped the phone from her hand.

"WHO IS THIS?!" The male voice demanded.

"HM2 Chance, who is this?"

"Chief Electrician's Mate Corville! Get me a god damned corpsman over here on the double! Something's wrong with my kid god damn it!"

"Chief, is there any trauma? Wounds et cetra?"

"No god damn it! Whatever it is it's in his head! He's locked himself in his room and playing that rock shit for the last three hours!"

"Can you talk with him Chief?"

"Yeah but he talks all crazy like. No fuckin' idea what the hell he's sayin'! He just keeps playin' that god damned music! *The Windows* or some stupid shit!" Billy fought back a smirk. *The Doors.*

"What's your address Chief?"

"Hunterwasser on Tarawa circle. 118, green door."

"If he's sitting quietly in his room keep him there.

We're rolling an ambulance on the double Chief. And don't attempt any more communication with him until we get there." Billy hung up. "Just let the kid enjoy his fucking trip before he comes down and you kick his ass!" Billy mumbled to himself as he dialled the in-house line to the back repair shed. With Pink Floyd blaring in the back ground Bob Achmen looked up at the fashing light he'd rigged over the front door, grumbled and pushed up off his overstuffed easy chair. He picked up on the sixth ring.

"Achmen, saddle up. We got a call over to enlisted housing."

"FUCK!" And the phone slammed down. Less than a minute later, lights flashing and siren screaming through the night they were enroute to housing.

"It's definitely an hallucinogenic." Billy relayed to Bob.

"Probably not shrooms or anything from the psilocybin family. Sounds like acid." Bob the chemist relayed.

"How can you tell it's not shrooms, we don't have any other symptoms yet?"

"Nothing on the street for the last couple of weeks, ever since that big bust last month State-side."

"What kind'a acid's been circulating?"

"Mostly watered down shit. Fucking dealers are getting greedy. That's why I don't step on my shit. I let the secondaries do it."

"Very considerate."

As they slowly snaked their way through the snarl of the convoluted streets in the enlisted housing complex Billy manned the exterior high powered spot light mounted on the driver's side of the ambulance. In the passenger's seat Bob just sat gently swaying to the residual vapors of Pink Floyd still wafting around in his

Politically Erect

head.

Five minutes after pulling out of the parking lot of the dispensary they were where they needed to be.

"118 Hunterwasse. We're here." He said to Bob. "The parents are freaking more than someone on their first trip." Billy warned. "So we'll have to deal with them first." Bob was two steps ahead.

"I'm guessing he dropped blotter. If that's the case, and there was nothing in his stomach, he'll top out in 40 to 60 minutes after dropping, should peak for two to three hours and start to come down between four to six hours after blast off."

"Anything else?"

"Well, there was a batch of Mickey Mouse circulating around last week. If that's the case he'll drift down, not drop and should have a pretty soft landing. Of course he won't be worth a fuck tomorrow." Bob giggled.

"You okay?"

Bob slowly turned towards Billy with an evil smiled.
SHIT! Billy thought.

The mother was standing in the doorway as they made their way up the path.

"How long's he been in the room ma'am?" Billy asked. Her husband sat in his easy chair in the middle of the living room in front of the blacked out TV.

"Christ! In my day worst you could do was fuckin' cigarettes for fuck's sake!" The Chief bitched as they entered the house.

Back in the ER, Nadine, the pretty, black dental tech, left to babysit the ER, was lost in *The Four Tops, Live* as her Sony Walkman permeated her brain through her ears and she nervously paced the floor. She had never been left to babysit The entire dispensary before and didn't hear the phone until the fourth or fifth ring.

"Billy, thank God you called! We just got another call and no one's here!"

"What'a ya mean no one's there? Where the hell's Annie and Reggie?"

"I don't know! He said they was just going across to the EM club to get a burger, that was a half hour ago!"

SHIT!

"Okay, don't panic. Give me the address of the new call."

"It's 112 West Midway, in the Yellow Loop."

"We're in the Yello Loop! Move to the wall map."

"Okay." Back in the dispensary as Nadine moved to the oversized base map on the wall left of the reception desk. Billy peered up through the dark and located a tall multi-purpose industrial radio aerial.

"Locate the shore patrol radio tower and give me the coords."

"Got it! 2306. 1872."

"Good! Now find Tarawa Street and give me the coords to the apex of the loop in the road."

"Ah . . . 2307, 1866."

"So the aerial is northwest of the call?"

"Yeah, that's right!"

"Okay, I got it. Go and find those assholes and get them back in the ER!"

"Got it!"

"And radio back when you find them! Mobile One out."

"Base out."

Chance figured the first priority was to tell Bob he was leaving the scene to attend another call. He made his way back into the house where the chief was holding his sobbing wife. Fortunately the bedroom door containing the son wasn't locked so Billy went in.

The sight which greeted him made him wish he had

Politically Erect

just went on the other call. Bob and the teen sat back to back in the darkened room, staring at the rhythmic flashing of the strobe as it bounced off the ceiling in time with the down beat of *White Rabbit*.

Billy made his way over and squatted next to Achmen.

Bob greeted him with a wide smile. "I was right! It was blotter!"

"What the fuck Achmen?! We're on duty!"

"Hey, what the hell man?! It's the best way to talk him down!"

Chance reached over and closed the door to muffle the conversation.

"When did you drop?"

"About an hour before we got the call. Chill man! It's okay!"

"How the fuck is it okay?!"

"He didn't drop *Mickey Mouse*. It was *Pink Princess*. Not as strong."

"STAY THE FUCK HERE! I'm going on another call, I'll be back for you. You got that?"

"Not an issue, bro! My ass is planted here in front of these tunes and with my little bro here!" Bob gave the kid a high five.

Chance left to attend the other call but on the way out he was intercepted by the chief.

"Well? What's goin on?"

"I thought it better to leave Petty Officer Achmen in there with your son for a little while Chief. He's got much more experience in this area then I do. We got another call." Billy was conscious of the urgency of the other call and so kept moving as they spoke.

"Trust me Chief, your son's gonna be a little dysfunctional in the morning but –"

Paddy Kelly

"You mean like a hangover?" The Chief asked.

"Exactly, like a hangover. But he's going to be okay."

"The fuck he is! He's gonna be a little more than dysfunctional! You can bet your fucking flat hat on that!" The Chief stormed off back to the parlor, his easy chair and to the end of AFN rerun of *The Johnny Carson Show*.

"What should we do in the meantime?" The wife pleaded. Billy was back at the front door but stopped to make eye contact with the obviously distraught mother.

"Nothing Mrs. Corville. There's nothing you need to do save to let him rest. He's not in any danger. He is with our resident pharmaceutical expert."

"What can he do?"

"Well, the medical books say we're supposed to get into the mind set f the patient as much as possible."

"And the other corpsman he's-"

"He's got hours of experience ma'am, trust me."

Billy dashed out, but yelled back in as he moved down the path. "Above all, DON'T go back in there! I'll be back right after this other call."

Minutes later when he pulled up at the second call address he found the base security had cordoned off the entire area and Rent-Cop squads were crawling all over the scene.

Billy, med bag over his shoulder hopped out of the rig and started off around the barriers to the house. On cue a pot bellied, civilian security guard in his bus driver's uniform ran towards Chance and despite there being no one visible in or around the house, grabbed Billy as if he were performing life saving maneuver while six others popped out from behind cars, trees and a garbage cans and trained their .45's and M16's on the front door.

Once off to the side Billy slapped the pasta loving cop away from him.

Politically Erect

"What the hell'a you doin'?!" Billy demanded.

"Who the hell are you?" The guard demanded.

"Is everybody in that new God damned cop shop stupid? I'm the God damned corpsman! What does that shiny white van with the red cross on the side look like! A fucking Good Humor ice cream truck or am I in my dress whites because I'm here to get married?"

"Why are you here?!"

"Because somebody called the dispensary and said send an ambulance! You got a casualty or what?"

"No but we got-" Just then, from inside the house, a shot rang out followed by a second.

"Looks like you better stick around Doc!"

"You wanna bring me up to speed?"

"Senior Chief lives here. PBR driver. Been away on his third tour of Nam. Two Purple Hearts, Bronze Star and a bunch of other commendations. Came home earlier this evening found the wife in bed with another guy. Apparently chased 'em both out of the house with his side arm."

"Not good."

"Worse, it was a nineteen year old seaman apprentice."

"An E-2?!" Billy affirmed.

"Yeah, any wonder the poor bastard's pissed off?" The rent-a-cop quipped.

"Welcome home Joe!" Billy said as he peered around the security van they were now sheltered behind to see the house."What'a you guys gonna do?"

"Looks like we might have to storm the place."

"That's a good idea. This way somebody gets shot for sure."

"You second guessing us doing our job?!"

"No, no no. Just happy that I'm not losing a good

night's sleep for nothing. At least I get to treat somebody. That is if they're not shot dead. Nothing I can do for a corpse, know-what-I-mean?"

One of the guards on the far side of the cordon manned a bullhorn.

"CHEIF BENSON, WE KNOW YOU'RE IN THERE ALONE! COME OUT WITH YOUR HANDS UP AND NOBODY HAS TO GET HURT!"

In response a woman's voice called out from the house.

"DON'T TRY AND COME IN! HE'S NOT GOING TO HURT ME!" Chance looked over at the man he now knew to be the head guard.

"Guess he didn't drive them both out of the house. What if the E2 is still in there with a bullet in him?" Billy protested.

"He's shot, but he's not in there. We got him in custody for the last hour."

"He's shot and you locked him up?!"

"He's alright! We patched him up. It's only a flesh wound."

These assholes never quit! Billy mused.

"Lemme try and talk to him." Chance ventured again.

"You crazy?! He's got a gun!"

"He kill anybody yet? Or you wanna go in and try and talk him down." There was no response. "Maybe he doesn't really want to use it against anybody. Maybe he's just blowing steam." Billy suggested, not fully believing hmself.

"And maybe he is lookin' to kill somebody! What the hell you gonna do if you go in there? Use psychology? You a shrink or you got some magic potion in that bag of tricks?" The head rent-a-cop argued.

Billy had by this point in his enlistment developed an airtight opinion of the mentality of the newly formed

Politically Erect

civilian security service which had replaced the shore patrol units made up of active duty ship's crews. Men who had not only more common sense on how to handle drunk and disorderly sailors but a bit of empathy as well.

Chance took the cue and unzipped his bag.

"You got any physical stats on this guy?"

"What?!"

"Physical stats! Height, weight etc . . .?"

"Where the hell would I get that?"

"You got a name, a full name?"

"Senior Chief Boatswain's Mate Benson, Eric Benson."

"Gimme five minutes. Keep him talking."

"Why should I?!"

"Because your alternative is get somebody shot and I know how much you guys like paper work. Work with me will ya?" Billy jogged back over to his ambulance and manned the radio.

"Base, Base, this is mobile One. Do you copy?"

"Mobile One, Base here. We copy."

"Nadine, those two assholes show up yet?"

"Not yet Billy."

"Okay. Listen up, we got a situation here. I need some stats on a sailor right away."

"You need what?"

"Physical stats! A Senior Chief BM by the name of Benson, Eric Benson. You got that?"

"Yeah. What'a you need?"

"His weight, I need to know how much he weights."

"Why? You gonna put him on a diet? Where the hell I'm gonna find his weight?"

"Try his medical chart sweetheart!"

"But I don't-"

"Just go back to medical records and do it!"

"Okay, oaky! Don't get testy! I need the last four of his social security."

Security had already pulled it from their rcords and so Billy gotit from the head cop and passed it on to Nadine.

"Hold on." Nadine went off the air and Billy waited.

A few minutes later she came back up on the radio.

"Base to Mobile One. Billy you there?"

"Yeah Nadine. You find his chart?"

"Yeah. He's six foot two, one hundred and sixty pounds."

"Just need the weight Nadine." Billy reaffirmed. "Any known allergies?"

"No, chart is stamped NKA. But he's got blond hair and baby blues, so when you're done with him send him over the dental clinic. You know, for a check-up!"

"Put it back in your pants Nadine. He's about to be a patient. Mobile One out."

Taking the long way around, Chance headed back over where the head guard was still sheltered behind his pick-up.

"Okay, here's the plan. . ."

After listening to Billy's strategy the cop stared at him with a blank look.

"You actually gonna do this?" The security guard pushed.

"No guts no air medals, eh? Just make sure none of your guys gets trigger happy!"

A few minutes later, crouched behind two flak-vested cops with pistols, Billy approached the front door while two others stood ready at the back door of the house.

The two rent-a-cops flanked the door and on a prearranged signal, Billy held his breath, rang the doorbell and waited. To everyone's amazement, his .45 Colt lowered at his side, the chief himself opened the door.

Politically Erect

Without warning the rent-a-cops rushed the door.

The two guards with a late arrival from the third tackled the chief inside and as they struggled to control him Billy stabbed him in the left thigh with a syringe full of diazepam hydrochloride. The 16 gauge needle easily penetrated the chief's trousers, skin and thigh muscle flooding the valium into his leg.

"Just hold him, just hold him!" Billy instructed, the whole time fearing one of the guards would suddenly develop an itchy trigger finger. He leaned forward on the floor and spoke into the struggling chief's ear.

"Just a sedative Chief! Something to calm you down. You'll sleep for awhile and when you wake up this'll be all over." The senior sailor stopped struggling as the weapon was pried from his hand. He smiled and turned to Chance.

"Thanks Doc." His eyes half closed over and his entire body seemed to relax. A minute later his glassed over eyes slowly closed.

"That's some hole you made in his thigh Doc!" One of the guards commented as Billy ripped open the patient's trousers and applied a bandage.

While the rent-a-cops handcuffed him and stretchered him out of the house Chance approached the wife now sitting at the kitchen table, zombie-eyed as hse atred off into the distance, a burning cigarette in her hand.

"You okay?" Billy asked.

"I can't believe I caused this." She appeared on the verge of breaking down.

"You want me to give you something? Something to relax." She looked up at him. Her face was gaunt and vacant as the magnitude of her new life set in.

"No. Thank you."

Paddy Kelly

✯

It was nearly zero six thirty by the time they were ready to leave the regional medical center after transporting Chief Benson o the mainside hospital. They were due to be off shift in less than an hour. Billy glanced at his watch as they walked down th ehall on their way back to the ambulance bay in back of the hospital.

"Shit!" He declared.

Still in a paranoid delusional state Bob screeched to a halt and slowly moved to the nearest wall, frantically looking around for the problem.

"It's nearly time for sick call!" Billy said as Achmen relaxed.

"Don't fuckin' do that shit man! I nearly shit myself!"

"You still trippin'?"

"Fuck yeah man! I told you this is some good shit, real good batch! You gotta drop with me sometime."

"Yeah maybe . . ." Billy trailed off as they turned a corner and they came through a doorway into the passageway to the rear of the building leading back to where they had left the ambulance.

Chance slowed his pace and stared ahead down the long hallway. He was staring at an old man in a wheel chair, the sole occupant of the desolate corridor. Billy, now oblivious to Achmen's presence, moved closer.

He moved closer and recognized the decrepit old man. It was Chief Stump who sat outside the Psych Ward in the wheel chair dressed in hospital slippers and the standard U.S. Navy issue hospital gown.

The seemingly hundred year old man was hardly recognizable as a human. With heavily glassed-over, grey eyes his emotionless face stared out and down in the hallmark '1000 yard stare' normally reserved for shell

Politically Erect

shocked combat veterans. His emaciated state was reminiscent of anything seen after the liberation of Dachau and, aside from the occasional breath, he displayed no discernable movement.

"He retiring?" Billy asked the civilian orderly who had just appeared from an adjacent room.

"This cat? Oh this cat's retirin' alright." He stuffed the chart he was holding into the pouch in the back of the chair. "Straight to the funny farm!" Pushing the wheel chair the orderly faded down the corridor and through the polished metal double doors. Bob came up alongside Chance.

"You know that guy?" Billy stared as all the theological arguments concerning good and evil, karma and come-uppance he had ever been presented with blitzed through his mind.

Was this a result of what happened in Iceland more than two years ago or was Stump just so hateful a little man that he had been consumed by his hatred of everything different then the backwards, primitive world he had left in Arkansas as a young man?

Billy Chance could find no fertile ground for the relevancy of his speculation to grow upon. The land was clear. The last Stump had been removed.

"No. Just curious." He shrugged.

*

Paddy Kelly

JOIN THE NAVY, SEE THE WORLD AND INTERVENE IN THE COUNTRY OF YOUR CHOICE.

CHAPTER FOURTEEN

U.S.S. Hancock **Flight Deck**
April, 1975 13:10

Now hear this! Now hear this! Medical triage team report to the fantail on the double! Report to the fantail helo pad on the double! Wounded inbound! Wounded inbound! That is all!

Flat tops are what sailors in the Navy call aircraft carriers. The ships which influenced the imagnations of writers to concoct all the big space ships from *Buck Rogers* to *Star Trek* to *Star Wars*.

The largest ships in the fleet they vary in many ways such as classes, sizes and crew compliment. But one thing they all have in common is that they are essentially floating cities. It's not uncommon for two sailors to be stationed on the same flat top for two or three years and never meet. The compliments range from 3,000 to 5,000 officers and men. The *U.S.S. Lexington*, for example, has the population of Sioux City Iowa.

The bosses of these brobdingnagian boats aren't even considered for the job unless thay have three qualifications; a minimum of twenty years in service, when most sailors retire, an exemplary service record and they must have an overwhelming desire to be the mayor of a city that has no permanent foundations, travels the world and might one day get blown up and sunk killing all aboard.

Why would somebody apply for a job like that? Precisly because of the job description.

When he first arrived Billy, as was the rest of the U.S.

public, unaware of the actual extent of the wind down by the U.S. in Vietnam and was less than satisfied with the amount of action he was experiencing. By now accepting that he would never actually get to work out in 'the bush', he had hoped to see at least a little action. However, by the end of the year the greater majority of casualties were being directly evacuated to the fleet, which left little work at the small dispensary.

Luck for most is good. For some not so good.

Billy had, less than two months ago accepted an offer, to take a temporary assigned duty slot out in the Pacific fleet. The TAD assigment came about when another corpsman with the same rank aboard the *Hancock* had been compassionately transferred back to The States after losing his wife and kid to a drunk driver in a car accident.

*

As he had the morning off after pulling the 23:00 to 07:00 shift Chance was currently stretched out on the flight deck off to the side of the fantail helo landing pad enjoying a sun bathing session. Just as he was about to catch a little shut-eye he heard a chopper approaching and was simultaneously awakened by the 1MC's alert for the trauma team.

Now hear this! Now hear this! Medical triage team report to the fantail on the double! Report to the fantail helo pad on the double! Wounded inbound! Wounded inbound! That is all!

"SHIT!" He sat up and spotted the bird a half a klick out and leisurely climbed into his Navy issue swim trunks and nearly had his second boot laced up as the

Politically Erect

CH-46 flared in for touchdown.

When Billy peered in and up over the ramp into the passenger compartment as the bird floated down to the deck his attention level rose markedly.

In the middle of the helo's cargo bay was a young FMF corpsmen from a grunt company, working with more vigor than a one legged man in an ass-kicking contest.

It was rare for company corpsmen to accompany their casualties in from the evac LZ as there was almost always an HM on board the Medevac chopper plus it was considered bad form to leave your unit without medical coverage in the bush.

At a quick glance Billy understood why tis Doc was with his marines. Chance counted eleven casualties almost all of which were lying down or struggling to sit up.

The crew chief was still lowering the ramp when Billy hopped aboard and surveyed the damage.

These poor bastards got their asses handed to them!

At least two of the marines were missing legs, another an arm and one well-built corporal was missing most of the left side of his face. The rest appeared to be puncture wounds waist level and below. *AP mines*, Chance thought to himself.

Billy grabbed the crew chief and yelled into his exposed ear as he ripped a med bag from the bulkhead of the aircraft and yanked it open.

"Trauma team's on the way up. Radio over to the FOO that the helo pad's gonna be in use for the better part of half an hour till we get these guys ready to transport below!"

"Roger that Doc!" The crew chief manned his head and relayed the info to his pilot who in turn sent it up to the pike to the flight Ops Officer in the C&C.

"CHARLIE FOXTROT ONE, looks like your aft section's gonna be tied up for thirty minutes or so with the triage docs going at it. Suggest you reroute any other traffic for the duration.

The two man trauma team, who had gotten word there were only two or three casualties, arrived and were taken off guard however quickly rallied and went to work getting everybody off the bird so it could clear the vessel and get airborne again.

Out on the deck Chance was already at work on the nearest casualty, a partial amputee who's right leg was held on by parts of some of the muscles of the thigh and splinters of bone, when he spied an errant deck hand rubber-necking the inside of the aircraft.

"YO! GIMME A HAND OVER HERE NOW!" The dumbfounded deck hand stared back then looked around as if there was somebody else in the area. There wasn't.

"I ain't no medic!" The deckhand protested.

"Neither am I! I'm a fuckin' corpsman! Now get the fuck over here and hold this!"

"Man I ain't gots no medicu trainin'!"

"I DON'T GIVE A FUCK, I NEED YOU!" Chance yelled over never looking up from where he knelt next to the wounded marine changing out a compress. The deck hand, pumped full of attitude, strutted over to the helo deck, took one look at the casualties in the chopper and strewn about the deck turned his head and retched all over himself.

"DO NOT PUKE ON MY PATIENTS YOU FUCKING DECK MONKEY!"

Billy finished the compress which halted the hemorrhage and moved to another marine who had been peppered by mine pellets up his side and across his face.

Politically Erect

As he worked he noticed the young FMF corpsman a few yards away administering CPR to a sergeant. Unfortunately, in the scattered field of blood, IV fluid and medical debris the deck area had become, the young sailor missed the narrow neck wound which oozed dribbles of arterial blood in time with his chest compressions.

"HEY!" Billy yelled over. The young doc looked over to see Chance running his hand across his neck to signal ceasing his efforts. Billy pointed to his own neck and then to the dead casualty. The kid looked down and saw the wound, turned white and fell back on folded legs. "THERE!" Chance pointed to a moaning corporal behind the kid who quickly shifted to another marine with an abdominal wound.

Chance spoke as he started his head to toe exam on his own casualty.

"Where you hit?!" The Gunny pointed to his abdomen. His dark cami blouse obscured most of the blood which had soaked in but as Billy quickly peeled back the slit of the cami top he was shocked by the 10 inch slice running horizontally across the marine's stomach. The implication was clear. This marine had been wounded in hand-to-hand.

The wound wasn't deep but deep enough that if he wasn't on the table in the next ten to fifteen minutes somebody would be getting a telegram that would ruin their day. Billy dressed the wound and grabbed for a litter and directed the new arrivals of the trauma team to take the Gunny away first.

From the time the CH-46 offload was set in motion a young Flight Ops officer, standing off at a distance, had also swung into action redirecting F-104's which had been scheduled to start touch and go's just before the

Medevac came in. His flight duties temporarily on hold he suddenly spoke into his head set and double timed over to where Billy was now re-setting a tourniquet on another casualty, just above where his leg used to be.

"What can I do to help Doc?" The young officer asked.

"You got commo with the C&C?"

"Yeah why?"

"Radio in and get some deck hands to get us three or four more litters up here so we can get these marines below! This Gunny has priority!"

"Already called it in."

"Good, now give me a hand getting' this guy on a litter."

Half a dozen stretcher bearers arrived as they spoke.

"You got it Doc!" The FOO went to work as instructed and a few minutes later, twenty-two minutes after they had been hit while on patrol in the bush, the nine casualties who were still alive were below decks in surgery or in the sickbay being administered definitive treatment.

Unbeknownst to Chance or nearly anyone else on board an SF team had been T.A.D.'d to the ship for a five day R&R. A short, stocky but well-built Philippino in casual civilian attire had stepped through the hatch on the island structure and was taking notice of the action out on the deck just as the chopper sat down.

Now as the last two marines were being littered through the hatch and down the ladder to sickbay, Billy followed suit intent on going below and showering up.

"You're a hound dog's wet dream son!" The Army guy blurted out as Billy came within earshot.

"Excuse me?"

"First time I ever smelled Hawaiian Tropic and fresh blood mixed."

Politically Erect

"I was engaged in mandatory skin conditioning when the shit hit the fan." Wiping his hands with his skivvy shirt Billy stared at the guy. "We met somewhere?"

"First Sergeant Tangualeg, Fifth Special Forces." He extended a hand.

"First Sergeant." Billy nodded. "Sorry if we don't shake hands." Chance displayed his blood covered hands.

"Not a problem. You a . . . you happy here? On the boat I mean." Billy stepped in out of the blazing sun.

"I'm a corpsman, I'm doing trauma medicine. Earning money for med school. Yeah, I'm happy. Why?"

"So making a contribution is important to you?"

"My dad always said, if you can't get out'a something, get into it. I signed up for this and as long as I'm here . . . You from the Happy Police or what?

"What if you could do more?" Billy eyed him with suspicion.

"If you're lookin' to tell me about the Lord, talk to my mother. If you're from the Red Cross, I gave at the office, so unless you're here to offer me an early out with full benefits, so I can get back to school I gotta go." Billy started to push past him.

"Ever thought about COPs?" The stout man asked. Billy kept moving.

"First Sergeant, I grew up in Jersey City! You go to sleep thinkin' about cops and you wake up thinking about cops!"

"The Pentagon's Cross-Over Program."

"Never heard of it! Besides I kind'a like the blue side."

"You get through our training program and life'll never be the same."

Chance stopped halfway down the ladder.

"At one time I was kickin' around the idea of Force Recon."

"Special Ops is Special Ops, green side, blue side or otherwise. Besides, you do a stint with us and you're practically guaranteed an in anywhere else." The Special Operations soldier could see the wheels in Chance's head starting to turn. "You're a pretty good medic."

"I'm an incredible, out-fucking-standing medic first sergeant! I'm a pretty good hospital corpsman."

"Modest too."

"Runs in the family." Billy shrugged.

"Get yourself cleaned up and meet me down in the ops room. We got a legal briefing. Afterwards we'll have a talk."

The First Sergeant nodded and, as fast as he had appeaed, disappeared up the ladder.

****

The Top Sergeant had notified his Team Leader to meet Billy below and to escort him to the Operational Planning Room down on the 02 level where the rest of the team were to aassemble. An hour later they met up below decks.

"Welcome to Ethics 101. SF Style." The unknown team memeber quipped as they came through the hatchway into the small ten man compartment. The rest of Tangualeg's team sat around a long table. Billy took a seat next to the First Sergeant.

"Every time we're on a stand down of a week or more, which means you just train for missions instead of actually running them, some scumbag lawyer, apologies for the repetition in terminology-"

"Apology accepted" Chance quipped.

"Some asshole decides that we need a class in ethics.

Politically Erect

No doubt an epiphany suffered in the midst of a drunken stupor halfway between Dutch courage and unconsciousness brought on by the realization that he, as a lawyer is only about two steps below a child molester."

Billy smirked at the metaphor. The operator sitting across from Chance leaned in and whispered over to him.

"Ethics for Special Operations. Something else the useless piece of shit could put on his eval sheet."

As a youngish looking legal officer stepped into the space and moved to the front of the compartment Billy mused to himself.

This should be pretty good! Perry Mason is gonna play make believe with a team of guys who eat, breath and shit hard core reality 24/7.

"Let us suppose you have just taken a prisoner . . ."

"S.O.P. Sir. We don't take prisoners." The Team Sergeant informed him.

"Who decided that S.O.P., Sergeant?"

"Some officer." With no sense of humor Perry Mson didn't laugh. He just resumed his TV, legal show posture, pacing the front of the room, hands behind his back accented by the occasional, forced, nonchalant glance down at the deck.

"Let us suppose you have just taken a prisoner. During transport said prisoner secures a weapon and attempts an escape."

Two chances of that happening, slim and none and Slim just left town. Chance thought to himself.

"Said prisoner kills one of your team mates during the escape attempt. What do you do with him?"

"You mean what do we do with the body, sir?" One of them enquired.

"Yes, what's your S.O.P. for transport of deceased

team members while on a mission, Sergeant Kennedy?" He direted to the operator next to Chance. "Surely as a former Navy Corpsman and Marine Recon Combat Swimmer you should know what to do!"

"Not my team mate, Sir. I'm taking about the poor dumb bastard I just sent to his god."

"So you're telling me you wpuld shoot him?!"

"No alternative sir."

"A HA! That's exactly what I wanted you to say!" Perry was certain he scored a goal. "Under the Geneva Convention, if you kill a prisoner while in your custody you will be imprisoned for up to 20 years, dishonorably discharged and fined up to $20,000!"

The team members all smirked at just how far removed from reality this clown was.

Being all college guys, they all had copies and had read the articles of the Convention. The fact that the GC doesn't say that and actually **does** provide for retaliatory action under such circumstances aside, who gave a fuck? The GC, as with all conventions, agreed with the basic principle of, 'shoot at me and I'm gonna shoot back!'

Billy grabbed a pen and slip of paper from the center board on the table top and quickly scribbled a note.

'Did the V.C sign the G.C?'

The Team Sergeant glanced at it and shook his head no.

The Clarence Darrow wanna-be was visibly disappointed that none of them was phased in the least by his tainted revelation. The Team Sergeant, Steve Morales, former CIA type, spoke up next.

"Sir, if a prisoner attacks us in any capacity we have the right to defend ourselves."

"To an extent Sergeant, however . . ."

"Sir . . ." It was Birdo, the radioman who interruppted. "Out of curiosity, who's going to prosecute

Politically Erect

us?" There was a moment of silence as the penny slowly dropped. The lawyer's normally dull eyes displayed a faint glow.

"I would! It would be my sworn duty."

Kennedy couldn't resist saying what the rest of the team were thinking.

"Then, Sir, it would be our sworn duty to shoot you." Two wide, shit brown unbelieving eyes stared back at them.

"And who **exactly** would shoot me?!" Nearly everyone's mouths were cocked and ready but Kennedy happened to get it out first.

"I would sir. As a corpsman, I'd know exactly where to place the bullet for a sure kill." He replied.

"And, as the back-up medic, I'd shoot you too, sir. Just to make sure the mission was accomplished. Sir." Added Tony Hernandez.

"Now now Hernandez, you know the motto. 'One shot, one kill!'" Birdo interrupted.

The lawyer wasn't amused by their little game.

"Perhaps we'd better take a break! Sergeant Kennedy, I'd like to talk to you in my office."

The lawyer stormed out and Tangueleg nodded for Kennedy to follow. They went into his 'office', the tiny partitioned area off to the left, where the officer made a common mistake. He did the very thing they do to you from day one in SF training and for the next year and a half of your life.

Aside from tugging on Superman's cape, pullin' a bone from a bulldog's mouth and pissin' in the wind, using intimidation tactics against an SF operative is the other thing Jim Crochey didn't but should have mentioned in his song.

Being the REMF, (Rear Echelon Mother Fucker), he

was the lawyer resorted to his most lethal weapon - the dreaded Incident Report! Perry would no doubt want to know what the medical sergeant's commander was going to do, in terms of disciplinary action, about this 'audacious threat to a superior officer'.

Superior to what wasn't addressed in the charges as he scribbled them across a sheet of paper.

Following the 'class' Kennedy was standing tall in front of the Team Leader down the passageway in a side compartment.

"Kennedy, did you actually threaten to kill an officer from the JAG's office?" With animated disbelief the First Lieutenant asked. Kennedy knew he had already interviewed the rest of the team starting with the Team Sergeant, Morales as these 'investigations' always went by rank.

"Sir, the Major proposed a suppositional problem and I presented the likely suppositional solution."

"According to his report, you said if he prosecuted one of your team mates, you'd take revenge by killing him."

"My exact words were, that . . . 'it would be our sworn duty to shoot you, Sir'."

"You used the word 'sir' when you addressed him?"

"At all times, Lieutenant."

"At least you were respectful." The L.T. looked down to gather his words. "Kennedy, what the hell's wrong with you? You been around this dog and pony show more than a day! You shoot that dumb bastard and everybody within 300 meters is gonna hear the shot! Use your god damn Sykes dagger! Why the hell you think we give 'em to you?"

"Sorry Lieutenant. I wasn't thinking."

"See that it doesn't happen again."

"Roger that Lieutenant."

Politically Erect

"Now you realize I have to meter out punishment for this flagrant display of insubordination?"

"Yes sir."

"I'll need time to think about this."

"Roger that sir, and I'm prepared to take whatever punishment you see fit sir."

"Very well. Step outside into the passageway and I'll call you in when I've reached a decision."

"Aye aye sir." He saluted as he responded and stepped out through the hatchway. As soon as he was outside he heard the lieutenant call.

"SERGEANT KENNEDY, REPORT!" Kennedy undogged the hatch and stepped back through.

"Sergeant Kennedy reporting as ordered sir!" Once again he saluted.

"You're a damn fine operator and are a valuable asset too this team, but I've reached a difficult decision sergeant."

"Yes sir, thank you sir." Kennedy replied standing tall in front of his C.O.'s desk. The Lieutenant looked up, scratched his head and cleared his throat.

"You are to retire back to the briefing room where the offence occurred, assume the position, drop to the deck and execute one miliatery styled push-up."

"Yes sir, one push-up!" For the third time in as many minutes Kennedy saluted then turned to leave.

"Sergeant Kennedy?"

"Lieutenant?"

"You were at morning P.T.?"

"I was sir."

"You successfully executed the standard Special Forces regime?"

"I did sir to include the standard 100 push-ups."

"Very well. Punishment suspended. I officially

declare this investigation closed and this hearing concluded. Dismissed!"

"Thank you sir!"

Kennedy and the L.T. made their way back down to the briefing room where the rest of the team was standing by. As they entered the space Tangualeg leaned over and spoke to Billy.

"Doc, stand fast after I dismiss the team."

"Aye aye First Sergeant." The lieutenant stepped up to the front of the table.

"Well men, the bad news is the rest of the week's morality classes have been cancelled." Smirks all around sufficed to convey the mood. "Good news is we've been offered a mission." Chance was puzzled by the verb 'offered'. "That being the case, I need you people to form up on the fantail in thirty minutes with weapons and 200-300 rounds each, one meal and water. Birdo, no 203's, save the ammo for the HK mission next week."

"What about the CREW served five-five-six?"

"We're gonna pack the 12 gauge instead." Tangualeg responded. Even Billy realized this meant some possible close quarters work. "Move out."

As they filed out Chance was duly impressed by the level of professionalism with which the team interacted. They appeared to be a 'team' in every sense of the word. Unlike the Black Shoes, non-SF qualified individuals, he had served with until now, these men were the true embodiment of the professional military as it was being sold to America by the government back home.

Following a few more instructions to the team Tangualeg pulled Chance aside and sat with him at one of the small tables in the briefing room. Tangualeg smiled as he read Chance's face.

"You sound like a team of contractors packing your tool bags for a call out at a construction site." Billy commented.

"That's exactly what we are. Only we're not just a contractors. We're specialists, specialists at what we do."

"Okay, First Sergeant, now the sixty-four thousand dollar question."

"Why you?"

"Bingo!"

"It's no state secret that we're not doin' too good in this war at the moment."

"So I've heard from Walter Cronkite and the other experts."

"But it's not all bad news. The SF units, across the board, are inflicting disproportionately heavy casualties." Billy smiled at the comment. "Problem is there's never enough of us. Especially medics." He let it sink in. Billy got the picture. "Nothing wins the hearts and minds of the indig like quality medical care, especially for their kids and old ones."

"So you want me to sign up, join the team, and come in for the big win?"

"Don't delude yourself. There's not gonna be any big win. There never was. Westmoreland and his collection of Bozo's in Washington are thirty years behind the times. They still think they're fighting WW II! With Tricky Dick's loss of credibility, the Joint Chief's bickering like school boy's over a game of jacks in a school yard and the Press already consulting their crystal balls –"

"Top, you don't believe all that Walter Cronkite bullshit do ya? About the war being 'unwinable'?"

"Let me tell you something young troop, motivated by the knowledge that with few exceptions these people, the Vietnamese, don't give a shit which government tells them what to do as long as they don't have to fight, the commies are massing for a big push. Add to that the fact that the U.S. lacks the political will to fight back and this war is all but over. The V.C. and the N.V.A. accompanied by the Chi Coms and supplied by the Russians will be in Saigon by the end of the year."

"I'm confused! If you really believe that then why . . . why are you and your guys still fighting so hard? Risking life and limb to fight back to win this 'lost' war?"

"Given that we inflected the highest and so the most effective enemy casualty rate, Special Operations will be an integral part of warfare from now on." Billy nodded. Tangualeg stood to leave. "We ain't fightin' for this war, son! We're getting our live fire training in for the next one."

"The next one?!"

"This country has been at war to one extent or another since it was founded by waging war. There's always gonna be a next one. It's only a matter of where and when."

Billy couldn't fault Tangualeg's logic as the epiphany dawned.

"And we'll always need good medics!"

"Corpsman First Sergeant! Corpsmen."

"We'd like to have you on board. Talk when we get back."

Tangualeg left and Billy's mind reeled. He wasn't sure what just happened but he was also too occupied trying to decide if he was more impressed or put off by Tangualeg's confidence in himself and what he was doing. Now in his last year of enlistment Billy had more than once heard stories of how hard and long some troops fought to get a slot in Special Forces. Here was a senior veteran of SF extending him an open invite.

"'Talk when we get back." Billy mumbled to himself

Politically Erect

as he sat alone in the small briefing room preoccupied by the fact that the First Sergeant was cock sure he was coming back.

*

Below decks in the sickbay, a few days after the evac incident, Billy Chance was putting in his 100th suture for the day when Master Chief Hospitalman Emory, a stout, muscular forty year old that Billy had come to respect in the five days they had been working together, strode into surgery space number three and perused the compartment.

"CHANCE!?"

"Yes Master Chief?"

"Drop what you're doing, report to the armory and draw some combat gear!"

"WHAT?"

"Am I not speaking English boy? Get your ass over to the armory then report aft to the helo deck! Tell the Traffic Control Officer you're the replacement corpsman for flight 17-Kilo! You've been assigned to evac duty for runs into Tan Son Nhut." Billy was both thrilled and scared by the news. After three and a half years on a four year hitch he had finally made it to The Shit!

With the Master Chief still watching he trimmed the last suture on the Marine's massive thigh and, as he quickly scribbled a prescription he ordered the apprentice corpsman to clean and bandage the shrapnel wound.

"This is a script for 250 Pen-V-K, q4, times seven days. Make sure he gets it, give him the usual instructions and take care of the nursing notes! Think you can handle that?"

"Yes Petty Officer!"

"Never mind that shit! Just call me 'Doc'."

"Aye aye, Doc Chance." The rookie smiled.

"Aye aye Doc!"

"Chance?" It was the Master Chief standing in the hatchway.

"Yeah Master Chief?!" Billy made eye contact as the chief plucked the unlit cigar stub from his mouth and spit into the kick bucket under the treatment table.

"Thanks for volunteerin'! The Navy needs more men like you!"

"Why thank you Chief! It's nice to be recognized." Chance saluted a sarcastic salute and moved out.

Chief turned to the apprentice and scowled.

"WHY THE FUCK AIN'T YOU ALREADY IN THE PHARMACY BOY!" He yelled at the kid who immediately stumbled through the hatch and double timed it down the passageway.

***

Up on the flight deck Chance was held back by the TCO as a UH-1 lifted off from the fantail.

"HM2 Chance reporting." He informed the TCO. "Replacement for 17-Kilo."

"You Chance, first name William?"

"Yes sir, that's right."

"Stand by." Billy watched as the Lt. scurried across the deck and back to the island structure. The sky swarmed with aircraft. Hueys, Loaches and various model Bells and at higher altitudes there were fast movers standing by for air cover if needed.

A few minutes later the TCO returned with a salty

Politically Erect

looking Marine who wore no rank. The Lt. pulled Billy just inside the island structure next to the marine.

"This is Acting Captain Coats, Team 3-7-5, Force Recon."

"Sir." Although he was new in theater Billy knew enough not to salute in the open. They shook hands.

"Your chief tells me you're one of those gung-ho mutha-fuckers wants to get into the shit, that right?"

"Seem a shame to have made the trip for nothin' don't ya think sir?!" The TCO smirked and continued to brief Billy.

"Their Corpsman got waxed on the last mission. Instead of goin' out with 17 and just running a shuttle service for the Tan Son Nhut medivacs I can get you on the Force Recon bird. You want in?" The TCO asked. Billy looked at the TCO then back to the Captain.

"Would Nixon make a good used car salesman?" He asked.

"I'll take that as a yes." The TCO entered the action in the daily log on the podium next to him then addressed Coats. "Petty Officer Chance has answered in the affirmative. I'll have some temporary orders typed up meanwhile get over to gear issue draw some cami's and 782 gear and report to the green side of the boat by16:00."

"Aye aye sir!" Halfway down the ladder Billy thought to ask. "Captain, who's my POC?"

"Gunny Sergeant Deuth." The Captain replied. "Tall guy, dark hair, blue eyes. His guys call him 'Movie Star'. It's his team you'll be going out with."

"Roger that Sir."

*

Paddy Kelly

An hour and a half later, Chance, now decked out in newly issued cami gear and floppy hat, ruck sack and med bag at his feet, sat directly across from the Gunny as the CH-46 cleared U.S. controlled territory. He leaned over and shouted to Deuth.

"Sergeant Deuth, what's the mission?" The Gunny looked him up and down.

"Where's your weapon?"

"I'm a corpsman. We're only supposed to carry sidearms." Billy tapped the holster of his Colt. Deuth shook his head and never relinquishing his weapon, strode to the front of the aircraft. Billy leaned forward and spied up the aisle as Deuth had a word with the co-pilot. A minute later the team leader was back in his seat and handing Chance a Car-15 and a couple of fully loaded mags.

"Officers and corpsmen are the first ones they go for."

"Good to know." Billy nodded as he pointed the weapon muzzle down on the deck following suit from the other four Recon Marines.

The Gunny pulled a folded up map from his left cargo pocket and indicated an area just north of Hue city.

"Coupl'a missionary doctor types from Mèdecins Sans Frontiérs, tried hooffin' it south as the commies rolled in from the north in force. Apparently God was watchin' over them, because they made it through the DMZ night before last. They're trapped just north of Hue. Took a detour and dug in outside the city when they came on the fighting."

"We got a good fix on where they are?"

"Nope!" Billy sat back and stared. "We're not 100% sure but it appears one of 'em snagged a radio from a dead Chi Com advisor and stumbled across one of our freqs. Orders are to touch down, launch a patrol, find 'em and escort them to this inlet here." He pointed to a small dent in the shore of the river south of Hue.

"Is that the intended exfil point?"

"Yeah. Nav says they'll have PBR's on station from tomorrow night at 23:00. They can loiter around the area until day after tomorrow. After that they'll hae to rotate in and out. Too risky to hang any longer."

"Is there a secondary method of exfil?"

"Uh huh."

"What is it?" Billy asked. By way of answer Deuth raised one foot and pointed at his jungle boot. Billy had no more questions. He turned and gazed out the circular port hole on the side of the bird.

They floated, seemingly over another planet light years away from the war back on earth, for the better part of two hours sticking close to the coast to maximise the air superiority the U.S. had so far enjoyed. Checkered rice paddies, irrigation canals and at times the sea itself glinted and winked up at the chopper as if the land knew something they didn't. The vibrant greens were tempered with golden yellows contrasting hard against the mud brown and black of the beautiful landscape.

Hard to believe war is within 100 miles of this place. Small wonder people are fighting over this piece of real estate.

Chance's meandering mind was snapped back to reality when Deuth reached over and slapped him on the leg. Billy looked over to see him holding up five fingers to him and the rest of the team. All responded with a thumbs up and went to work donning their packs, readying their weapons and moving to the tail of the aircraft where they squatted down.

The bird slowed, flared and dropped quickly from its hover. Chance moved to exit but was held back by the team leader.

"Hold on to somethin'!" Deuth ordered.

Chance understood when, after about thirty seconds the bird quickly lifted off again, flared hard to the left and rose to a couple of thousand feet. Three minutes later the process was repeated and at the third fake infil they quickly double timed off the ramp and headed for the heavy bush to left of the tiny LZ and hit the deck forming a tight circle and facing outboard with their weapons poised scanning their respective arcs for potential contact.

A minute later the bird was gone and they were nearly 100 miles behind enemy lines with only what they had on their backs to survive and rescue a small mass of missing, misguided missionaries.

*

Politically Erect

**WAR DOESN'T DECIDE WHO'S RIGHT.
ONLY WHO'S LEFT.**

CHAPTER FIFTEEN

**19:10: Seven Klicks NE of Hue City
Night One of Operation Button Hook Retrieve**

Billy couldn't recall a time since the infil six hours ago when he couldn't hear small arms fire and occasional artillery in the distance. For over an hour after the chopper faded from sight the team lay, spread out in the prone position, perfectly still facing outboard in a tight circle waiting until first evening nautical twilight. This SOP also allowed them to ambush or evade any enemy snooping around the area.

Now, as they slowly rose and moved through the evening brush in single file, all senses were on high alert. The distant artillery and small arms fire had diminished to sporadic rifle bursts, mostly without return fire.

"Take your finger off the trigger." The operator behind Billy quietly instructed. "Instead keep the safety off but keep your trigger finger on the trigger guard."

By midnight of the first night they had made it to and through the best guess, last reported position of the missionaries, a burned out Buddhist monastery flanked by a small river. They had spent the better part of an hour searching for traces of recent habitation but found none.

It was near three in the morning when they heard a column of tracked vehicles up ahead and decided to take cover until it passed. Unfortunately the armor was protected by infantry and the column had flanking recon out.

A young NVA soldier with his rifle flung over his shoulder ambled down the narrow animal trail

Politically Erect

paralleling the main road and as he approached, a black faced Sergant Greer silently emerged from the brush, K-bar in hand. From across the trail Deuth signalled for him to stand down and he acknowledged by slowly fading back into the shadows. The lucky young soldier passed within a yard and continued down the trail.

That night Billy's finger never left the trigger guard of his Car-15.

By dawn they had covered nearly four kilometres of their intended search area and elected to rest for a few hours while Greer and Deuth did a short forward recon.

*

The stealth, survival and navigational skills of the SF operative are the finest, most well honed in the world. He is trained and tested to negotiate 25+ kilometers of rough, unknown terrain in twenty-four hours, carrying a pack, usually weighing as much, or in combat, more than he does on little or no food, virtually undetected, locating various checkpoints, in all weather with pin point precision along the way.

Nearing the end of the third day of the patrol food and time were running low and it was the general consensus that if by dawn the next morning no promising trail had been located they would have to abandon the search and report the misguided do-gooders lost to enemy action.

However after nearly three days in the bush, behind enemy lines with no solid intel to rely on, it was by a twist of fate that Gunny Deuth's recon team stumbled across a lead.

Late that afternoon, just as their commo man, Daniel

Paddy Kelly

Byrd, sent in the day's SIT-TEP, they heard the rustle of bushes ahead. The team quickly disbursed deeper into the brush on the sides of the road, manned weapons and took cover.

A minute later a small, barefoot boy in a loincloth and ragged Coca-Cola tee shirt, dragging a stick along behind him, meandered down the one lane, dirt road.

As everyone eased their weapons off safe and froze, Chance raised his head for a better look. The child passed right in front of him. He smiled, rose to his feet and lowered his weapon.

"DOC! Get the hell down!" Somebody loudly whispered. Chance moved to the road.

"DOC! Get the hell back here, it could be a trap!" Deuth reiterated. Chance waved him off as he drew a C-rat chocolate bar from his cargo pocket, checked up and down the road and approached the kid. Billy smiled and without resistance the child allowed him to trade the John Wayne bar for the expensive looking trinket which hung from his scrawny neck to well below his swollen belly. Billy held it up for the others to see.

It was a black enamel crucifix trimmed in silver with a sterling silver figure of Christ. The kind that as any Catholic knew, priests and nuns traditionally wore.

Greer was closest and so the first onto the road.

"Good thing we got all that training in navigation, huh?" He quipped. Deuth came up from behind and took the rosary.

"Yeah but sometimes ya just get lucky anyway." Deuth replied. "Well done Doc!"

"Thanks. If he's not from the refugees fleeing the fighting there's gotta be a settlement near-by. I suggest two of us locate his people, probe and if they're not occupied by commies, we snoop around for leads."

"Guys?" Deuth sought a consensus and, receiving

Politically Erect

nods, issued his orders. "Okay, but the day light deadline stands. No Bible thumpers by dawn, we head for the exfil point."

There was no disagreement. "Doc, stay here with the kid and the rest of the team. Jimmy, probe for the village, observe for twenty to thirty then report back."

"Aye aye chief."

"We'll be 100 meters in that direction, other side of that rise." Greer moved out until he was about 50 meters off the road then turned left and vanished into the bush.

"Doc bring the kid."

✦

Nearly an hour later Deuth and Greer were both peering through the dense undergrowth observing a small clearing occupied by a small group of indigenous people. There were two pairs of adults, three single adults and a couple of teens. All the adults were well into their sixties or older and the teens, like the adults, were in the advanced stages of malnutrition. There was one small child, a year or two at the most hanging off the hip of one of the female teens. All were huddled around a small fire holding green sticks skewed through some kind of partially charred meat.

"What'a ya think?" Jimmy whispered.

"Cover me. Watch the huts." Greer dropped the bipod on his weapon, fell to the prone, adjusted his sights and set a bead on the hut in the center of the camp. Deuth broke cover and with his weapon in hand but lowered, he approached the gathering of Montagnards.

They hardly stirred when the marine came into sight. When he was within ten or fifteen feet he smiled and could discern the meal they were preparing as pieces of rat meat.

Deuth guessed the devastation of the entire Montagnard village was probably due to the NVA's scorched earth policy. That and the NVA hated the Yards as much as they hated the Americans.

There were no real habitable structures left standing but several temporary, improvised huts had been stitched together out of the ruins of several others.

The eldest of the small clan looked up and squinted. Deuth held out his hand and allowed the crucifix to drop and dangle from between his fingers.

The youngest female spoke first then, following a brief silence there was some terse and heated discussion amongst the group which ended when the eldest man snapped at them and ordered one of the teens to fetch something.

A minute later, from one of the burnt out huts the small teen returned holding the hand of a late middle-aged, gaunt-faced priest. He smiled when he spotted Deuth. The natives quietly continued their meal.

"You okay?" He asked the priest.

"Yes, yes I'm fine. Thank God you found us!"

"Thank Colt Armalite and the Marine Corps. The others?"

The priest sighed and nodded.

"They're in the hut."

Deuth signalled for Greer to double back and retrieve Doc and the others.

By the time Billy and the rest of the team came up to meet Deuth several more missionaries, four nuns, three more peiests and another younger civilian, had been uncovered.

"Whose in charge?" He asked the motly group of clergy.

Politically Erect

They all looked at each other as if the Gunney was speaking Mandain. Finally the first priest owned up.

"I guess I am."

"I was briefed there'd be 12 of you."

The priest drew a long face as he rummaged through his emotions for a response.

"Now we are nine." He quietly answered.

"Doc give these guys the once over, then get me a status on their fitness to travel. If they're good to go we move out before dark."

"Roger that." Chance answered as he pulled Deuth aside.

"Gunney, given we don't run into any serious shit, how long to the exfil point?" Deuth narrowed his eyes as he tried to figure out what Chance was getting at.

"Better part of a day at patrol speed. But with this bunch. . . Why?"

"I don't know about you Jarheads, but I can go without food for a day or so."

"That a challenge Doc?"

"Just sayin', ya know?" He nodded over towards the half starved civilians. What Billy was proposing went against all the survival techniques Deuth had been taught. But he knew Chance was right.

"Okay asshole." Deuth replied. The Doc smiled. "We'll give up some food, but no cans! The gooks use them to make AP mines. And tell Greer to get a collection going and give some to the Bible thumpers."

"Got it."

"And tell the priests to tell the Yards to burn and bury the wrappers."

Thirty minutes later the team was huddled together about 100 meters outside the village in a small cluster of bushes.

"Okay, we've got the lay of the land now we need a plan of action." Jimmy kicked it off.

"There's been a shit load of activity between us and this draw." He indicated the predetermined check point on the map spread out between them. "To go around it we're looking at a day, day and a half. I say we hang out till morning. Give us all a chance to get some sleep and start out fresh just before dawn. Our exfil point is well east of the action at present. If the gooks are moving south there's a good chance they'll be out of the area by the time we show up and we'll be behind the main force."

"Doc what'a you think?" Chance was taken off guard at Deuth's apparent acceptance of him as one of the team.

"We leave now we'll wind up navigating through the bush at night with a bunch of civilians. Civilians who, by the looks of it, haven't seen a decent meal since Lindy saw Paris. Besides a substantial noise signature they'll slow us down even more. I mean, Yards know how to move through the bush, but the missionaries . . . We spend the night, maybe send out a recon a few klicks at dawn, we'll be all rested, have some idea of what's ahead and not have to worry about the missionaries giving us away. Besides, if there is a mass Commie push to the south with a little luck they'll be thinned out by morning which will give us a better chance of getting through." Deuth nodded.

"Byrdo, it's your floor."

"I think Doc's right. Soon as it gets dark we take two hour watches just this side of the road, away from the village. Whoever has the second dog watch has wake up duty, we move out as soon as we can. I'll take the recon patrol out two to three klicks and come back just before dawn."

Politically Erect

"I'll take the first dog." Greer chimed in.

"Right, sounds like we got ourselves a plan. Doc go set the bible thumpers wise to the plan. Watch rotation starts at first evening nautical twilight. I'm on deck, Doc that puts you in second dog. Wake the holy rollers first. They'll take longer to get their shit together."

"Got it."

★

The second dog watch rolled around and in the dead still of night Chance took up a position between the center of camp back from the road about 100 meters.

His position, facing the way they had come in, gave him the advantage of seeing or hearing any heavy equipment which might meander through the dark as the heavy forest on either side would require the enemy to use the road. However, it was unlikely any small units would be in the area after dark.

The old Montagnard, who for some unknown reason had decided to sit up with Billy that night had perched himself on a thousand year old stump off to Billy's right.

"Guess you have no idea what the hell I'm sayin', do ya?" Billy spoke in a hushed tone, just enough so the old man could hear.

The elder brandished the few teeth he still owned, stained purple from a lifetime of chewing beetle nut and nodded.

Billy had planted himself on the felled upper half of a palm tree which had been cut down by an artillery shell.

"You got a name?" There was no response. "How about if I call you Cà? You are the first Vietnamese native I've ever talked to . . . with . . at? And you're an elder." More nodding from the elder followed. "Okay Cà it is!"

Thirty minutes of silence crept by. Eyes glued to the road, Billy decidedto try again.

"Good thing we ain't in Boston! Paak the Cà in the yaad!" Billy laughed at his own joke.

"If it's any consolation, they'll be some good come out of this whole shitty mess. Maybe not enough for you to get anything from it, but -" Suddenly what sounded like a twig cracking in the distance echoed through the trees. Billy quietly fell to the prone and manned his weapon. The old man sat stone still eyes gliued to the vanishing pont down the road. After ten minutes no other sound was heard so Chance returned to observation mode.

"Guess after you've been here four or five thousand years ya get used to those sounds, huh?" The old man once more smiled and nodded. "Course, I guess, if I took you back to Times Square you'd probably shit yerself the first time a taxi driver laid on the horn!" He laughed and the old man laughed along.

Billy considered the irony of his example and of how neither of them belonged in the other's environment.

Chance, accompanied by his new friend Cà, now sitting on the ground besides him, were up until just before dawn began to break over the lush forest.

★

"Father Leary, it's time." Billy, weapon in hand, whispered as he shook the partially dressed missionary leader. The groggy priest cleared his eyes then his head as he looked up at Billy. "We go in five. Anyone's not ready, they stay behind. Meet us out by the road."

Politically Erect

"Huddle up!" Deuth quietly ordered once the missionaries had come out and joined the team. He waved the clergy in close to himself. Doc, Jimmy and Byrdo automatically took up strategic positions facing outboard of the village.

"When we move out women in the middle. Leary you stay behind the point man, junior you stay behind the women, make sure they keep up." The young priest nodded.

"All you folks gotta do for the next twenty-four hours is keep your mouths shut, your eyes open and pay attention to what's going on at all times! And whatever you do, whatever happens, listen for instructions! Any questions?" The elderly priest raised his hand.

"Yeah?"

"What exactly is a point man'?" He asked. Deuth dropped and shook his head.

"Just don't do anything that might attract the attention of the little yellow bastards that are looking to find and kill you because, remember, they don't believe in your god."

Greer, just in earshot of the impromptu meeting smirked at Deuth's disregard of etiquette.

They formed a single file with Byrdo at point and Jimmy Greer at the six. As they moved out Doc approached the old priest.

"He's a bit rough around the edges and a little hard on the outside, but he's got a soft chewy center."

"Good to know." The father replied.

They hardly walked a hundred meters when Chance glanced to the rear and saw the family of Yards about fifty meters behind Jimmy, their meager belongings rolled into bundles slung over their shoulders. One of the teens carried the child. Billy signalled Greer who turned, saw them and shrugged. He then signalled Billy to pass it on.

Billy jogged up to Deuth and pointed to the rear. Gunney glanced back then again at Chance.

"'I don't know about you Jarheads, but I can go without food for a day or so.'" Deuth mocked. "Great idea Doc!"

"At least now you know what it feels like to be human Gunney." Doc smiled as he added an MRE to the one he had just collected from Deuth. Billy patted him on the back. Deuth flipped him the finger.

With a minimum of intermittent stops for water, by noon they had reached their second of five checkpoints.

They seemed to be making good time until they were within eight to ten klicks of the coast when it started to go wrong.

Greer who had the point, signalled to halt then quickly to disperse. Deuth made his way up to the point man, was briefed then quietly jogged back.

"We've got movement up ahead about a hundred and fifty to two hundred meters. Get the thumpers behind that low ridge over there and post LP/OP's by that cluster of palms there and the eastern bend of the ridge there." Deuth signalled up for Greer to take a look-see.

Ten minutes after the group were tucked into the back of the small ridge Greer reappeared through the dense brush. He waited at the top of the ridge, scanning behind him to be sure he hadn't picked up a tail then crested the ridge above the team. He crept back down to their position where they were all huddled.

"It's a combined enemy patrol, NVA with VC reinforcements on their flanks."

"That's new." Deuth commented.

"This is not good." Byrdo added.

"What else did ya see?"

Politically Erect

"They got a couple of ChiCom advisors with them."
"Which means . . . ?" Chance inquired.
"Charlie uses his Chi Coms sparingly so only the brigade sized units and above get the wisdom of Uncle Ho's minions."
"A brigade?!" Doc declared.
"Yeah, but there's a chance-"
"A brigade?!" Doc repeated.
"Could be a brigade."
"Probably is a brigade." Byrd declared.
Suddenly a squad sized unit which was part of battalion sized element tasked with sweeping a five klick wide sector north to south, came within earshot.
Deuth's people fell silent and froze.
The enemy squad were following on behind the main body which meant that Gunney Deuth's patrol was now sandwiched behind the enemy brigade and an NVA squad. A squad who no doubt had radio contact with the main body.
"Probably a part of that squad we danced around back there. We need to-" Just as Deuth was about to layout an emergency plan the decision about what to do was made for him.
An NVA point man broke through the bush about 200 meters to their rear. Everyone froze. He hadn't spotted them. Yet.
"Byrdo! Play 327!" Deuth directed in a loud whisper. Without a word Byrdo vanished into the bush off to the left side of the path as Jimmy Greer simultaneously slung his weapon, double timed up behind Deuth's pack and pulled out a pre-wired Claymore and immediately began to unravel the lead wire which had already been armed with a blasting cap.
"Doc you got the azimuth?" Deuth yelled.

"Yeah!" Billy yelled back.

"Keep pushing them another two klicks, fall off when you find some C&C and wait 30 minutes. If we don't catch up by then get them to the exfil point! Clear?!"

"Roger that Gunney!"

Without a word Greer, Claymore in hand, fell off to the right and disappeared into the jungle. The jibber jabber of the NVA squad behind grew louder, Chance and the civilians quickly pushed on.

As he jogged through the winding path, the terrified and exhausted missionaries close behind, Chance had no idea what the hell was happening but, in between abject fear, uncontrollable excitement and a haze of confusion he felt absolute security in how Deuth was controlling the situation.

A klick back down the path Greer had sheltered behind a tree, the Claymore detonator in hand.

At the rear of the NVA column, which was cautiously but hurriedly negotiating the narrow path, the last two enemy in line quickly turned when they heard someone running up behind them. They turned just in time to see Byrdo charging full speed at them, his Remington 16 gauge at hip height. Three blasts took them both out and as the next NVA in line, 20 meters up, turned and looked down the empty path as an explosion at the front left of the column took out the point man and the two soldiers behind him. The remaining five in the column broke into a panic, dropped to the forest floor and begun firing in all directions.

From Chance's vantage point with the missionaries in the small clearing they had reached, he suddenly heard several bursts of gun fire coming from their former position quickly followed by the explosion. There was an eerie silence and, several more small arms bursts then more silence.

The small irregular circle of NVA fire quickly withered as one by one they were compelled to reload and that's when the four grenades flew unseen out of the dense undergrowth with near perfect accuracy. There were a few screams which quickly died off to leave one lingering, deep moan as the lone survivor of what started out that day as a routine NVA patrol, now decimated, dropped his weapon, broke and ran.

Deuth appeared from nowhere, stood, took careful aim and prepared to fire, but he quickly checked his aim, brought the muzzle of his weapon to and smirked.

The eldest teen Yard sprang out from behind a mango tree and, machete in hand, with one smooth motion slit the NVA's throat to the bone.

"Gotta love them Yards, huh?!" Greer commented as he moved to rummage through the badly mangled bodies. "Glad the little bastards are on our side."

Byrdo came jogging up the trail and had to step over the body parts to reach where his team leader was standing.

"You good?" Deuth asked. Byrdo held the muzzle of his shotgun to his mouth and blew over it cowboy style.

"Scratch two bad guys." He answered as he reloaded. Deuth smiled. Greer was rummaging through one of the bodies.

"Jimmy, never mind the souvenirs. Let's catch up to the Doc." Deuth instructed.

"Hey Gunney, notice anything special about this patrol?"

Deuth scanned the carnage and quickly picked up on Jimmy's clue.

"Well, at least we know they didn't make contact with the main body!"

Byrd also scanned what was left of the bodies.

"Son-of-a-bitch! No radio!"

Greer approached the gunney and handed him a packet of papers with an official looking seal. Gunney, now well into his third tour, had accumulated an appreciable knowledge of Vietnamese and so perused the papers.

"That wasn't a routine patrol we just erased. They were carrying orders to halt outside Saigon and, '. . . in accordance with *Resolution 21* establish a permanent base to used as a launch point'." Deuth made eye contact with Byrdo and Jimmy.

"What the hell is *Resolution 21*?" Jimmy asked. Deuth looked up at him.

"The commies are planning to move on Saigon!"

"Fuck me Alice!"

"Danno?"

"Gunney?"

"Soon as we're a klick out we'll pull over and set up a perimeter. Get on the horn and send: 'Pizza's ready. Then send an addendum. 'Orders intercepted. Reds to move on Saigon.' Clear?"

"Clear."

"Let's Didi mau the A.O.!" They took off at a swift pace with Deuth automatically assuming point.

"Gunney, can I send, pepperoni pizza's ready?"

"You're an asshole."

"Love you too Gunney."

Two and a half hours later Gunney Deuth's team along with their long lost, scared shitless, exhausted and a slightly more world-wise missionaries, were speeding south by south-east towards the South China Sea and to their next step to an airplane home.

They set up on the north bank of a tributary which flowed to the sea. It was deep enough to allow for the shallow draft PBR's to come in from the exposure of the open water. The high reeds of the river provided good concealment.

"Doc, you want the honor?" Greer offered him the smoke canister as Byrdo, manning the radio, talked the PBR captain up the small river.

"I am popping smoke." Byrd relayed. Doc pulled the pin and tossed the canister. "That's a good copy Bird Dog. Watch along your port side."

Chance pulled the pin and popped the smoke canister.

Zero-seven-six, we see yellow smoke. I say again, yellow smoke. How copy?

The reassuring sound of the diesel engines of the two PBR's was heard a moment before they were spotted slowly cruising up the river.

On signal, with one man standing watch to the rear, the team disbursed into the chest high water to form a line from the bank out to the first boat as she steered into their position. Bird Dog One cut engines and floated up to them, throwing a bow line to Deuth as the second boat manned all weapons and the crew scanned perimeter standing as overwatch.

The nuns were escorted out first and the priests followed. Team 076 would be ferried back south on board Bird Dog Two.

Deuth grabbed onto the handrail and called up to the boat's commander.

"Hey Chief, give us whatever chow you got on board will ya?"

"You fools ain't going back in are ya?"

"Negative. There's small clan of Yards back out by the road not doing too good."

The Chief disappeared below decks and came back up with a case of rations.

"How many out there?" He asked.

"'Bout a dozen. They got some young ones with them." He passed the food over the rail to Deuth and brandished a folded over map.

"Get them these. Tell 'em to make their way down to this point and I'll have another pair of PBR's up here in an hour or so to take 'em south."

"I knew all you squids weren't as fucked up as they told us back in Lejeune!" Deuth took the case of rations and tasked Jimmy with running it out to the natives.

With Gunney next to him Doc helped the priest, the last of the missionaries, up to and over the side into the boat. As he tossed the bow line back to the petty officer on board the priest leaned back over the gun'al to speak to him.

"I want you to know you have changed my belief in God." The priest said.

"Padre? Now you doubt there's a God?"

"Oh no! There's a God! You can count on that!"

"So?"

"Now I don't believe in God the way I used to. Before I only knew him as God. Now I believe at one time he must have been a Marine."

Chance and Deuth smiled at the priest.

*

Politically Erect

MASTURBATION IS A WASTE OF FUCKING TIME.

Paddy Kelly

CHAPTER SIXTEEN

William W.Chance Jr.
Apt 1106,Bldg 1
Federal Housing Project
Duncan Ave. Jersey City, N.J.

HM2 William W.Chance
U.S.S. Hancock
U.S. Seventh Fleet
PO Box 3790

Dear Mom;   February 21st, 1975

Well still mostly office work here, records and things like that. Pretty boring actually. Filing charts and stuff, but there are some interesting patients sometimes. Had a couple of clergy who were a bit disoriented, but we got them straightened out okay.

My leave time is building up so I'll be taking some time off soon. You asked about the girl I wrote you abut. Didn't work out. We'll talk more next time I make it home.

Glad to hear Chris got married! Heide's a great girl I liked her when I first met her in The City that time.

You didn't write me about Dad's test results in your last letter. Don't forget this time!

Sorry this will be short but there's only the one working typewriter here in the sick bay annex, but will write again soon.

Politically Erect

Love you guys!

*

A little over a day ago as the PBR he was on drifted up to the dock and the team prepared to disembark, Billy looked back north across the South China Sea and came to the conclusion that he had discovered what he wanted to do for the rest of his life.

In his mind and with no thought to further commitment, Billy began to solidify a plan for his medical education after the Navy.

*

Sick Bay, *U.S.S. Hancock*
11:35 Thursday, March. 3rd, 1975

"Hey Boudine, where's Chance?" Feisty blurted out as he whizzed through the sick bay and past Boudine who was reclined on one of the operating tables reading a *National Geographic*.

"Dunno, why? What's up?"

"None'a yer fuckin' business what's up! That's what's up! Just where is he?"

"He's over in . . . Jees, ya know what?" He let the mag drop to his chest. "I knew but suddenly forgot! Sorry about that!" He returned to his magazine.

"Fuck you very much!" Feisty retorted as he stormed on through and under the "VICI, VENI, VD" sign over the hatchway on the other side of the O.R. He headed back topside. Fifteen minutes and five 'Fuck you's' later he found Chance sunbathing nude out on the aft section of the flight deck.

"Hey Chance. CHANCE!"

"WHAT?!"

"You know The Old Man put out a standing order against being nude on deck!"

"I'm not nude Feisty. I'm wearing sunglasses. If you weren't such a meat gazer you'd'a noticed that."

"Ya got orders!" He held out the single twixt sheet and Billy slowly raised his Ray-Bans.

"Bullshit! I ain't due to rotate back the World for another six months!"

"You ain't rotatin' no wheres asshole! You're goin' south ta pick up some organs or something." Billy sat up and looked at the twixt then at the human skeleton who was Feisty. "Be topside in one hour!" Feisty commanded.

"I am topside or you still too busy checking out my package?"

"Be topside in uniform in one hour! You're getting' a helo ride on a Shit Hook down to the peninsula."

"For how long?"

"How the fuck do I know?! I look like I work in CnC!? Here! Report to the Operations Officer on board the *Washoe County* when you get there." He held out a slip of note paper to accompany the twixt message.

"What the fuck is a *Washoe County*?"

"It's a *fucking* boat! A LST!" He called back as he stormed back towards the island structure.

Feisty was an interesting case study. He was almost drafted, which means he should have been wearing Army green crawling in the mud being eaten alive by insects and being shot at. But, due to a heads up by a mail sorter friend at the local post office, in Beaverlick, Kentucky, he beat the postman to the Navy recruiter's

Politically Erect

office by less than half an hour. He signed on the dotted line to wear Navy blue before he officially received his draft notice the day after graduating high school.

"Hey Feisty, how come you're in such a good mood all the time?" Billy called after him.

"Fuck off!" Feisty disappeared into the island structure.

"No doubt in my mind that boy'll wind up in Public Relations!" Billy said to himself as he got dressed to head out.

Forty-five minutes later he was sittin' with a monkey harness strapped to the ass end of a Marine Chinook CH-47 5,000 feet over the South China Sea, all by his lonesome. In between wonderin' why he had been picked to ferry transplant organs across a war zone he mostly enjoyed the view.

Suddenly Connie the corpswave, the brunette beauty he had been spending time with during and after corps school materialized in his mind.

Except for the nurse at that party state-side Connie was the only sex he had had since signing on the dotted line to join Uncle Sam's boys in white to go over and fight Uncle Ho's boys in black which of course made it dead handy to tell the good guys from the bad guys. Connie, the nurse and that hooker in San Diego just before he shipped out. But what the hell, hookers don't really count. Do they?

As his thoughts wondered to pass the time, the night they spent together in the motel off base shoe horned its way into his fantasies and he climbed up onto a sling seat and faded off to a restful nap.

*****

Paddy Kelly

Billy Chance's alter ego J.K. consciously concentrated on trying to become unconscious, as his mind once again sought to go on permanent vacation to places like Smitfield.

Smitfield, Illinois was actually Smithfield, Illinois, but seeing as how the Smithfield All Powerful Rotary Club was too miserly to hire a real sign painter for $85, Henry Watkins, their Treasurer, did the job for half the price and so the welcome sign at the end of Sherman Street just off the slip road of Route 79 cost the town fathers $125,276.96 in reprinted tourist brochures, ball caps and school book covers, not to mention the re-lettering of the police car and the fire truck which were still owned by the Moriarity Savings and Loan.

Ralph Jenkin's lawsuit over the re-painting of his hardware store sign and delivery van is still pending.

Incorporating late, by mid-western standards, the Smitfield citizenry had experienced World Wars I and II, the post war booms, the Cold War, the Korean War, the labor wars of the Twenties and Thirties, the on-going race wars, the inception of the 'War on Drugs', and William Shatner's war on believable acting.

For half the population of the hamlet and surrounding area things made pretty good sense and were as they should be. Folks got up, went to work, came home to their loved ones and got paid every Friday at five 'clock so they could repay all the money they had spent last week.

For the other half, (those under thirty), a one armed blind man in a dark room trying to shove a pound of hot, melted butter up a wild cat's ass had a better chance of trying to make sense out of what was going on in the U.S. at the time.

Both hoped and prayed for a better life somewhere

Politically Erect

down the road.

From the perspective of the good people of Smitfield, or even from the perspective of a farmer in Jesus Christ-It's-Fuckin-Cold, North Dakota for that matter, the winter of '72 was memorable. It was a harsh winter. The weather was terrible, crop yields were low, and the curse of the eighth plague, Disco, was upon them.

At the same time of course, for the citizens fighting the war, trying like hell not to come home from Viet Nam in a sandwich bag was even more memorable.

The thing was that in August of '72, in order for Tricky Dick to get himself re-elected, he told the world the war was over. What he neglected to mention was the fighting was gonna take another three years or so.

The 11th was the official day all the ground troops were going home. People State-side cheered, Tricky reckoned he was on the government tit for another four years and Uncle Ho lifted a glass of rice wine. Meanwhile the fly boys in the Philippine Islands geared up their B52's to launch the largest Operation Archlight Charles has ever been invited to.

In case you've never heard of Archlight let me put it in perspective for you.

Drop three hits of purple microdot, wait an hour or so then go skydiving naked shagging Miss January from behind on the way down and don't pop your chute until you're at about 300 feet off the ground so you can get the most out of the ground rush. That's probably the rough equivalent of what it feels like when a full squadron of B-52 Stratofortresses drop their shit on you non-stop for 24 hours. Only not as much fun. Curtis J. "bomb them back into the Stone Age" LeMay christened it "carpet bombing".

What a lovely way to redecorate.

Paddy Kelly

Reputedly Curtis never said that, but far be it from Walter and the Good Ole' Boys Clubs over at CBS, ABC & NBC to miss an opportunity to boost viewership and pay homage to William Randolph Hearst and the long standing tradition of journalistic propaganda.

Three cheers for yellow journalism.

In 1970 Tricky Dick et al declared the end of the war was in sight. The moon, the sun and Alpha Centauri were also in sight.

In 1971 Cronkite declared the war was all but "unwinable." Which, to the vast majority of the American public made it so.

In 1972 Tricky et al declared the war over. For the first time.

The boys on the front lines getting' their asses shot off had other opinions about the state of the war. Ahh . . . excuse me, I mean Police Action.

Meanwhile on the southern most boarder of Meriam County, just across the state line from Lincoln County, next door to Smitfield, lies Patriot, Illinois. About fifteen minutes just outside of town there was a small trailer park, which had thrice been wiped out by tornadoes. Slow learners that they were, the residents kept rebuilding their solid plywood, aluminium and glass dwellings never realizing the storms were probably God's way of saying "Get that shit off my earth!"

Herein, on lot #127, of the *U-Need-A-Rest Trailer Park* resided the Derber family.

Chester Derber, aged 18 years, was feeling very proud that afternoon as he prepared the Bar-B-Que for his parent's seventeenth wedding anniversary party, which was scheduled to begin promptly at somewhere between three and six that evening.

The exact time couldn't be set because there was no reliable way to know when Cleatus Derber would get

Politically Erect

home from *The Veteran's Of Foreign Wars Post #339* where he shared a few beers and a Jack Daniels or two at least four times a week with the war buddies he never served with. Also they had to wait for Zelda Derber, alias The Wife, to close up and get off work from the *Beautician Magicians Beauty & Sun Tanning Salon* over on Pershing Avenue.

The guest list was fairly comprehensive so all nine of their friends had been invited. Ten counting Mario Ippolito Sanchez, the sixteen year old, muscular Hispanic delivery boy from the Shop Rite supermarket which Cleatus still couldn't figure out why his wife was so insistent on inviting. He reasoned that maybe it was because Mario was so obliging when it came to delivering even the smallest grocery orders. Like the time Sanchez had taken the time to peddle his ten speed bike all the way out to the trailer park at eleven in the morning just to make sure Zelda got what she needed.

A single pack of Kool filtered cigarettes.

Like a judge who had just successfully manipulated a trial young Chester was pumped full of pride that day. The source of young Chester's new found pride was his Selective Service Registration Document, SA Form 80, (Draft Card), which had arrived in the afternoon mail, thus giving official certification of his manhood. Monday morning Chester Derber, 'Man', would dutifully register at the Hall of Records, over at the county seat, which was really just a post office, (which was just a small room in the back of *J. D.'s Feed and Grain Emporium*).

That afternoon, about an hour before the party, Chester had his masculinity tucked neatly in the top pocket of his baby blue, Dacron Hanes dress shirt with the button down collar, when it happened. While

Paddy Kelly

reaching across the Bar-B-Que for some more Fast-Lite Bricketts the SA Form 80, (Draft Card), made a break for it and gently floated down coming to rest on the glowing coals.

In the blink of a Walter Cronkite CBS eye, Chester was no longer a dutiful, loyal patriot, but a dangerous treasonous felon, who no doubt was a Commie terrorist sympathiser, or worse yet a Socialist, facing 7 to 10 years in the federal pen and/or a $20,000 fine, the standard penalty for burning a draft card agreed upon by the enlightened 'onorable get'lemen of the United States Congress, alias the Boys on the Hill.

On entering the gravel strewn, weed infested yard later that afternoon, Mrs. Derber saw that her son was so distraught that she was compelled to cancel the party. Mustering further concern for her son's disrupted emotional state, over the next week the now unnerved mother took to seeking advice and council from everyone, including Phil the mail man. Oh yeah, and Mario Ippolito Sanchez too.

Sometimes twice a day.

That afternoon Phil the mail man was besides himself as he spread the word down at the C. P. D. & S. C., (Central Postal Distribution and Sorting Center to normal civilians), over on Washington and Lincoln Streets which, coincidentally overlapped into Lincoln county, home of Smitfield whose town council had just last week passed a town ordnance against trailer parks. The reasoning was anyone not able to afford proper housing had no business in Smithfield. Like all those Little Yellow Bastards coming over here from Viet Nam looking to the good and loyal God-fearing citizens of the U.S. of A. to take them in after they went and messed up their own country.

Not coincidentally, seven eighths of the Smithfield

Politically Erect

town council, as well as the mayor, were active members of the All Powerful Rotary Club. So when his Honor Henry Watkins heard from his mail man that the kids over in Meriam county were burning their draft cards he nearly took a heart attack thinking about the impending rioting in the streets and the inevitable occupation of his fair city by National Guard troops who would no doubt be called in by morning to restore peace and make sure all the black kids could still get onto their own buses and into their own schools over on their own side of town.

"We don't want no Kent State, God-damn it!" He dutifully informed the hurriedly assembled Town Council.

Meanwhile, Doris Huntzinger, sitting comfortably under the purple, plastic, bullet-shaped hair dryer, which made her look like Robbie the Robot from *Lost In Space*, had just begun drying her new beehive bouffant when she was startled by Arthur Crowley, President of the A.P.R.C., as he burst through the front door of *Mary Hurley's Curl Up & Dye* on North Patton Street.

Aside from being the personal secretary to the Mayor, The Elks Lodge, The Moose Lodge, and The Royal Order Of The Rainbow Trout, Doris was also the Executive Secretary of the All Powerful Rotary Club.

"DORIS! DORIS! Come quick! We need you over to the court house! There's an emergency meetin' of the Rotary Club!"

"What? Why?" Doris enquired lifting Robbie the Robot's parasitic shell from her own.

"There's an emergency meetin' right away about the riotin' goin' on over in Meriam county!"

"Riotin'? What riotin'?" The other bouffants became nervous, dropped their *Home & Garden* magazines, *Montgomery Wards* and *Sears & Roebucks* catalogues and snapped to attention.

"The riotin' that's goin' on 'cause'a the draft card burnin'!"

"Oh my heavenly father up in heaven!" Doris rarely resorted to profanity but was very upset at this news as she gathered her things. "I told Pete it was only a matter of time till it reached here! But he didn't want to sell the house and move over ta Smithfield! Maybe now he'll listen to reason!"

As Doris removed her plastic bib apron and gathered up her genuine imitation Gucci bag all the other patients in the beauty clinic wasted no time disengaging themselves from their purple, orange and lime green plastic space helmets before dashing through the front door, still being held open by Arthur Crowley and headed out to the Shop Rite grocery store to stock up on emergency supplies of Twizzlers, Tampons and Twinkies. After all, once it started there was no tellin' how long the siege might last!

All the others in the salon, except that is the part-time beauty student Linda Davis, who knew a girl that once dated a guy who used to hang around with a friend of Chester Derber's and therefore was of the opinion that most guys in Meriam county didn't have the balls to burn a joint much less a draft card. Linda just calmly sat behind the reception desk, hand on chin, shaking her head and thumbing through last year's *Cosmopolitan Magazine*. Again.

"Fuckin' morons!" Linda mumbled to the empty beauty parlor

The last two minutes on board Titanic must have seemed uneventful when compared to the melee that passed for the emergency meeting of the A.P.R.C. that day. *Robert's Rules of Order* never saw the likes.

The end result of the gathering of the A.P.R.C. was a

Politically Erect

barrage of ordinances, legally binding articles and laws forbidding the burning, mutilating, tearing, defacing, altering in any way shape or form, (to include use as an improvised toothpick), the United States issue Selective Service Document SA 80, (Draft Card), within the city limits of Smitfield, Illinois.

The council members were gathered in the Town Council Chambers around the 30 seat, French polished, mahogany table, proceeding with the speed of molasses going uphill in the wintertime as the meeting continued . . .

"What about coverin' it in plastic so's it don't get damaged?" A council member at the end of the table on the other side of the room queried.

"That's a good point Frank!   Doris, draft an exemption clause."

"Yes sir."

"Gentlemen, other suggestions for exceptions?"

"That's a good point George! Doris, add 'in the event of loosure' to the exemption clause."

"Yes sir."

"How's about if it gets stolen?!"

"Good point Frank! Good point! Doris –"

"Stealin' clause. Got it."

"What if it gets accidentally burnt?" As one the entire table stopped and stared at Horace Johnson.

"That's ridiculous! How can a man's draft card get **accidentally** burnt?!" Henry Watkins challenged.

"I dunno! Maybe somebody could be leanin' over a camp fire or sumthin' and BANG! It gets knocked into the fire?!"

"Never happen! Any other **realistic** ideas?!"

Along with the fact that the town's name was spelled wrong on the A.P.R.C.'s ordnances and the fact that it

Paddy Kelly

was already a federal offence to burn or alter the Selective Service Document SA 80, (Draft Card) and so superseded and nullified anything the Smithfield A.P.R.C. had to say about it never occurred to any of the stalwart, middle-aged, jaded gentlemen of the local bureaucracy.

**

Just under an hour later a small cluster of ships came into view from the open ramp of the CH-47. Billy felt a nudge on the shoulder, snapped back into the real world and looked up to see the Crew Chief signalling they were coming in to land. Chance glanced over the partially retracted ramp of the Chinook and saw the southern fleet anchored off the coast.

"DIXIE STATION!" He yelled over the roar of the rotors as he pointed to one of the largest vessels in the fleet. *"Washoe County*'s over there." He pointed to an LST anchored on the western perimeter of the fleet then tapped Billy again and signaled they'd be setting down in two minutes.

The *U.S.S. Washoe County*, LST 1165, had been operating close off the coast of the Ca Mau peninsula at the southern tip of Vietnam, where they were tasked with supporting a variety of different units including Swift Boats, Seawolf helos, SEALS, Mike Strike Force and various other units.

They didn't actually set down but did a touch-and-go as the chopper crew were assigned another mission as they descended. Chance grabbed his gear and scrambled down the ramp which was retracting even as he stepped off it. He was intercepted by a petty officer. The Chinook rose, banked left and disapeared.

"Loking for the ops officer." Billy greeted him. The

Politically Erect

deck hand gave him a thumbs up and then proceeded to lead him to the ladder well leading up to the CNC.

The Operations Officer that morning was a Lt. Geoffrey Meade a native Texan. Billy later learned that the L.T., a qualified expert marksman who despite the fact he didn't realize the Navy would give him time off to compete in the '72 Olympics thus missing a shot at a gold medal was, by most accounts, a pretty God-damned good officer.

While in sex the size of your gun may or may not matter, because there are alternatives, in war it can mean the difference between coming home under your own steam or in shoe box. Or worse yet, with or without your gun.

Although the LST only mounted 3" guns, basically designed for anti air craft fire, they drew a very shallow draft and were able to get in much closer to shore than any of the destroyers or frigates which occasionally visited the area.

"HM2 Chance from the Hancock reporting sir." He handed the L.T. his orders as they exchanged salutes and Lt. Meade quickly perused the papers.

"Doc Milford's on his way up from sick bay he'll –" Meade was interrupted by his Radioman.

"Sir we've got traffic."

Getting closer to shore also meant the ship could take naval gunfire requests and had developed a working relationship with the U.S. Air Force's Forward Air Controllers or FACS, who routinely called on them to shoot up something the fly boys spotted in the local rivers or canals.

This was sufficiently annoying to Uncle Ho's finest who responded by, among other things, infiltrating their radio gunfire nets with bogus instructions hoping to make the Nav fire on friendlies, thus forcing them to resort to special authentication codes.

A senior corpsman entered the space and shook hands with Billy as they both listened in on the radio chatter. The shirt stencil over his left breast pocket introduced him as HM1 Milford.

The normal U.S.N. S.O.P. consisted of the F.A.C., after spotting something shootable and coming up on the G.N.G.N., General Naval Gunfire Net, and giving the coordinates for said target to call for naval gunfire. If the guns of any given vessel were within range they'd take the fire mission.

This required a formal procedure that involved giving the spotter a "Gun-target Line", the azimuth the shells would follow from point of origin to the target and a "Max Ord", which means the highest point the shells would reach en-route. This was followed by a "Time of Flight" for the shells.

The procedure was intended to temporarily keep the FAC's wife and/or mistress back home in The World from receiving a KIA notice due to friendly fire.

It usually worked.

Everybody pretty much knew each other so the formal procedures were often omitted especially if the target suspected that Uncle Sam's finest were sniffing around his A.O. looking to dispose of any IBGB's, (Itty Bitty Gook Boats), by expending some of that expensive ordnance all those nice folks back home at Dow Chemical were considerately grinding out in order to help keep the 'yellow commie hoards' from invading the Long Beach area of southern California.

The irony is that not only did some Europeans invade southern California about a century earlier but in just a few short months Uncle Sam's finest would actually be relocating tens of thousands of Vietnamese into the sunny southern California climes of Westminster in Orange County.

But, that's another story.

On this particular day however, the *Washoe County's* spotter was an unarmed Cessna, call sign "Shotgun 49".

The radio crackled to life.

Eagle, Eagle, Shotgun 49 request fire mission. Have several sampans spotted moving out of a camouflaged, known supply area and heading up river. Coordinates to follow.

Lt. Meade manned the hand set and radioed back.

"Shotgun, Shotgun Eagle Actual. Those cords are just outside the effective range of our 3 inchers. Suggest you try general call out to other units in the A.O. Someone might be able to help you. Eagle out."

"Much obliged Eagle." Shotgun took Meade's suggestion and sent the call out. He was quickly answered by someone using the call sign "Onrush," who offered to take the mission.

Lt. Meade, his radioman as well as several other sailors who were on deck exchanged puzzled glances.

"Who the hell is Onrush?" The radioman asked.

"Anybody ever heard of an Onrush?" The L.T. threw out. No one spoke up.

Since they generally knew everyone in the area and had never heard that call sign before Meade ordered commo with the top side watches and asked them to scan the area for any other gun vessels on their side of the peninsula.

Nothing here L.T. The starboard watch reported as did the port side watch.

The L.T. assumed it was that wily old Charlie guy interfering on their net again, and so went through the whole authentication procedure.

Paddy Kelly

Onrush correctly authenticated and still stated he wanted the mission, saying he was on the other side of the peninsula which would put him a good 20-21 miles away from Shotgun's target.

Meade remembered everyone on the bridge having a laugh at the FNG, (Fucking New Guy), gunnery officer who had plotted things incorrectly, but Shotgun 49 dutifully went through his spiel and told Onrush the target was moving upriver fast.

The L.T. and his crew intently listened as the story unfolded and the FAC asked for three rounds of Willy Pete, White Phosphorous, to spot and said he'd correct their fire from where they landed.

"Shotgun 49 be advised, we have only HE available at this time but am prepeared to send you one round." Onrush replied.

"Ahh in this dense foliage I don't think I'm gonna see one round but the bad guys are moving pretty fast upriver and will be out of range shortly. So go ahead and send what you got."

"Shotgun I'm fairly confident you'll see our HE when it spalhes down." There was a short pause and Onrush radioed; "Shot over." Fives seconds before imoact he ws to send the order; Stand by. Out."

Onrush dutifully called "SHOT OVER," and after a reasonable time, Meade and his crew, now out on the bridge with the volume turned down on their Radio Shack combination AM/FM cassette deck and binos raised, could see the Cessna dropping down to look for evidence of the shot. When he apparently didn't see anything, Shotgun 49 came back up on the net and started explaining to

"Onrush this is Shotgun 49, I'm really gonna need either some Willie Pete or several rounds of HE for an adequate spot because I can't see any signs of impact"

Politically Erect

As soon as he un-keyed his mike, Onrush hurridly broke in.

"STAND CLEAR OF THE AO! STAND CLEAR OF THE AO! MY ROUND HAS NOT YET IMPACTED!"

At this point the cheering section aboard the LST could see the Cessna with his ass end nearly 180 degrees to the turf going into a steep climb and not five seconds after he cleared the area a substantaial portion of the grid square below him exploded into a tremendous splash of muddy water, underbrush and as several of the crew remember it, a half dozen rather large palm trees, slowly tumbling up into the air.

Mr. Roberts would'a been proud.

Realizing his wife and or sweetheart nearly qualified for a special visit from the Chaplin, Shotgun 49 came back up, his voice now in a somewhat higher register.

"Onrush, be advised . . . I think . . .you got a secondary with that one. A BIG fucking secondary! Hell, I didn't know there was even a target over there!"

On the other end, a calm voice responded.

"Ahh, be advised Shotgun, that was probably just our HE round, over."

Back on the bridge of the *Washoe County* Meade's crew were intrigued and so the L.T. had his signalman frantically thumb through their copy of JANAP-128 looking to identify this Onrush guy. Meanwhile, the show went on.

"Onrush, this is Shotgun 49. Say again type of round fired?"

"That was a one-six inch HE round. Over."

"Say again, you have one six inch gun? Over."

"Negative. I have nine one-six inch guns, over."

More confused than ever Shotgun came back.

"I understand you have nine, six inch guns, is that

correct, over?"

"Negative, negative! We have nine one-six, I say again, nine 16 inch, guns over!" The spotter became incredulous.

"Is that the bore diameter, over?"

"Affirmative. We have nine guns with 16 inch bores. That round was 2000 lbs of HE, over." Shotgun 49 was sure somebody was fucking with him.

"Onrush, what are you, over?"

"We are a BB, over."

"I'm in the Air Force, God-damn-it! I don't know that Navy stuff! In plain English, what are you? Over."

"We-are-a-Battle-ship. Over."

Back on the LST the Signalman slammed the JANAP-128 shut and stared at the L.T.

"Holy Shit, Sir! It's the *U.S.S. New Jersey!*" In the background they heard the FAC continue to receive his lesson in naval armament.

"You mean battleship like in WWII battleship, Midway, Pearl Harbor, Leyte Gulf type battleship?!"

"Affirmative Shotgun 49. Over." Ten seconds of static filled dead air time.

"Ahh . . . can you guys possibly give me five more for effect? About three hundred meters to the north. Please?"

"Affirmative Shotgun 49. Five rounds HE for effect, 300 meters north. Shot, over." At this point on the LST a couple of beers had been passed out, chairs commandeered and the bridge of the LST temporarily converted into a steel-grey garden patio.

Just as one of the crew lit a cigerrette Lt. Meade spotted Shotgun 49 out in the distance racing straight due East at full throttle. It was a wise move because, following an uncomfortably long pause, Krakatoa erupted in the middle of the jungle.

Politically Erect

The eruption seemed endless. One of the crew counted 15 seconds of explosion, as earth, water, trees and what looked like a small herd of water buffalo, mushroomed into the sky as a couple of grid squares of God's creation ceased to exist. At least in its original form.

Several long minutes later, when it was over, they saw the Cessna return, meandering low over the area to do a Gun Damage Assessment report. When the small plane finally began climbing Shotgun once again came up on the net.

"Un-fucking-believable!" Crackled over the radio.

"Shotgun 49, Onrush. Please advise as to GDA, over." The ship's gunnery officer requested.

"Un-fucking-believable!" Was followed with more silence.

"Shotgun 49 this is Onrush requesting a formal Gun Damage Assessment. Can you say, was target destroyed?"

"Roger . . . that's affirmative. From what I can make out confirm five sampans destroyed, 13 probable KIA's, and one indigenous river WIA."

"Say again, Shotgun?"

"Looks like you created a new canal and . . . the river appears to be changing course due west at point of impact!"

The *Washoe's* Signalman slid back his headphones and laughingly gave his assessment to Lt. Meade.

"SIR, THEY REROUTED THE GOD-DAMNED RIVER?!" Lt. Meade just shook his head and mumbled.

"They rerouted the god-damned river!" Echoing what he had been told by his signalman. The bridge crew gave a standing ovation. Just then the C.O. of the *Washoe* came through on the 1-MC.

"Operations! What the hell was that explosion?"
Meade manned the squawk box and replied.
"One of our spotters called in a fire mission, Sir." Meade replied.
"How'd it go?"
"Apparently they rerouted the God-damned Me Cong, Sir."
"Good for them! Give the bridge a beer."
"Thank you Sir." Six sailors scrambled to the Styrofoam cooler under the control panel.
"Captain out."
Everyone on the bridge froze as the radio again crackled to life.
"Onrush, ahh . . .this is Shotgun 49. Can you guys possibly take another fire mission, coordinates to follow?"
And that was the last time the *U.S.S. Washoe County*, LST-1165, worked with the Air Force FACS.
At least until the *U.S.S. New Jersey* left the area.

**

With A plastic beer cooler prominently marked with a big red cross and labeled: 'HUMAN ORGANS', Chance hitched a ride on a Loach to the hospital ship *U.S.S. Sanctuary*, delivered the kidneys, which were installed in their new owners less than an hour later, and was on his way that afternoon back to the *Hancock*.

**

Politically Erect

YOU COULD WADE THROUGH NIXON'S DEEPEST THOUGHTS AND NOT GET YOUR ANKLES WET.

CHAPTER SEVENTEEN

"MAKE WAY, MAKE WAY! We got a live one here!" The marine orderly yelled as he quickly pushed the guerney through to the triage area. The unconcious patient was coverd with a blood stained sheet. Henandez, who was suturing a leg wound on another patient looked over his shoulder and saw this was likely a surgical case.

"Commander, need you out here sir!" He called out and down the narrow passageway fom the small treatment compartment where he worked. "What's his vitals?" Henandez asked and the orderly, still out in the passageway with the guerney. He quickly referenced the big card tied off to the patient's lapel.

"BP 100 over 90, pulse 130, respirations 18 to 20 and labored!"

Ten meters down the narrow passageway a hatch swung open and a tall, dark haired Lt. Commander darted out and up to the patient.

"Put him in OR2! Get him stripped down, look for holes while I scrub up, and be careful, we don't know the extent of his injuries!"

"Aye aye commander." The marine took the scissors offered and went to work. He didn't get far. As he pulled back the sheet his eyes widened and his jaw dropped. "HOLY SHIT!" He called out as he backed away from the guerney. The scissors hit the deck at his feet.

"Where's he hit?" The doctor called over his shoulder as he scrubbed up.

"Right shoulder sir. The clavicle I think." The surgeon turned to see the marine standing stark still with his eye's glued to the patient. There were four small metal fins protruding from the patient's right shoulder

Politically Erect

just forward of his collar bone.

"Looks like he walked into a mortar barrage." Hernandez donated from his treatment table.

"Sir is this guy a gook?" The marine asked.

"He's not a guy, he's a patient God dmn it! Our patient! And he's a ROK. A Republic of Korea Marine, a brother marine, he's one of you!" Lt. Commander Shelton's mind raced as he realized his anger was not at the marine but sparked by the fear of the situation he found himself faced with. "You're dismissed!" The marine left as Hernandez finished up on the leg patient.

Shelton collected himself and got to work.

It would be the safe bet to evac the patient to the flight deck and stow him off in a corner soemwhere until he eventually expired. Then Shelton noticed the guy's wedding ring.

"Where the hell is everybody?!" He mumbled at the deserted passageway.

"Captain's inspection sir. They scheduled it last week. That marine must not have gotten the word."

"Hernandez?!" The surgeon called over as he finished drawing a second tube of blood.

"Right here sir!"

"Get these to the lab, tell them drop what they're doing and run them. I want a type and cross match, a CBC, a crit, a SMAC 12 and tell them blood gases to follow. Also tell them to prep three pints of O Neg and to follow on with three pints of what ever type they come up with." As he barked the orders the surgeon changed out the two near empty bags of IV fluids dangling from the patient's rack. "Next get me a nurse and an OR Tech scrubbed and ready in the next ten minutes. Nine would be even better! Tell them to meet me here."

"On top of it Commander!"

Hernandez grabbed the Vac-U-tainer tubes and turned to run. The doctor called after him.

"And get me somebody knows about mortars!"

"What?"

"Mortars God damn it! I need to know what we're dealing with here!"

"It's a ChiCom M60!" Hernandez called back.

"You sure?!" The stunned surgeon pressed.

"Bottle of Jose Cuervo says I'm right! M60, ChiCom!"

"Then see if you can find out the blast radius!"

"Depends." Hernandez stopped and turned just up the passageway. "Willie Pete, 30 meters, H.E. 60 meters.Sir."

"How can we tell which one it is?"

"The tips are color coded, white for Willy Pete and red for High Explosive. Sir."

"Well seeing as how they haven't invented colored X-rays and the nose of this thing is buried in his lower lung we can't see the tip now can we?!"

"Then assume it's high explosive! Sir." With that Hernandez disapeared around the corner.

Shelton gently laid the blood stained sheet back over the partially exposed tail fins of the mortar round as he saw a nurse scurring down the hall.

"What's your name?"

"Lieutenant Hadley Commander, Maureen Hadley."

"Lieutenant Hadley, we have a potential situation here."

"Sir?"

He lifted the sheet enough for her to see the protruding fins.

The color drained from her face and, stifling a scream, she backed into the bulkhead.

"Nurse, calmly proceed to OR2 with this patient and

Politically Erect

get anybody within fifty yards out of all the adjoining compartments, understand?"

She continued to stare blankly.

"Lieutenant Hadley?!"

"Yes . . . yes doctor?"

"You can leave if you want to."

"Negative sir!" She pulled it together. "Tell me what you need sir."

As surgical SOP dictated that all incoming casualties were to be stripped down completly to I.D. hidden wounds, and some novice grunts had the annoying habit of pinning grenades inside their pockets to grab and throw, ordanance in the operating room became a problem.

Only three months ago the unthinkable happened. A triage team was stripping a casualty for an emergency exam and inadvertantly detonated a M67 grenade he had in his pocket killing three and wounding two.

"Calmly proceed to OR2. Secure the hatch and wait outside. Let no one in or out. Get his vitals before you lock him in. Got that?"

"Yes sir."

"I'll be back in less than ten minutes. And see if you can get someone to wheel the portable X-ray unit down here we'll need a P.A. and if possible a Lat of his chest and abdomen. We need to see exactly where the tip of that thing is. For now don't move him around! At all!"

"Yes commander." Shelton turned to leave. "May I ask where you're going sir?"

"Up to the CnC. Be right back." Shelton left and Hadley manned the sound powered telephone on the bulkhead to call over to X-Ray.

A minute later Lt. Commander. Shelton was talking via open frequency with the Acting Command Surgeon

General, Admiral Koates who was onboard the fleet's flagship the *U.S.S. Blueridge*

"Sir I'm requesting guidence on how to proceed."

Lieutenant Commander, are we certain there's no chance to medivac this patient?

"**If** he holds on long enough to be medivaced he'll be dead in the next hour Admiral. Not to metion the risk to life and limb if that thing detonates during the airlift in which case we lose a patient, a surgical attendent, a flight crew and a heliocopter." There was a long silence.

This guy being a foriegn national could raise some questions ya know.

"Sir, are you giving me a direct order to abandon this patient? If so sir, that's what I'll do." There was a longer pause. "Admiral?"

No Doctor, I am not. I'm leaving you to your better judgement. You will not be held accountable regardless of your decision on how to proceed with your patient.

"Is there anything else I need to know sir?"

I remember a similar situation back in Korea. If you think you're patient can hold out a few minutes longer, you might consider relocatng your O.R. to the fantail of the ship. Just in case.

"Yes sir. I'll certainly consider that idea. Thank you Admiral. *U.S.S. Hancock* out."

Blueridge out." The Admiral keyed off then quickly re-keyed on again. *Commander Shelton?*

"Sir?"

Good luck!

**

Billy, Bulldyke and the X-ray tech were returning from inspection and were in the mess area when the

Politically Erect

runner sent by Dr. Shelton found them and passed the order for an OR Tech to report to OR2 to scrub in.

"Get some Bulldyke!" Billy, sitting next to her, slapped her on the knee.

"Rugmuncher to the OR! Rugmuncher to the OR please!" The X-ray Tech added to which she flipped him off.

"See all you bush leagueers later! It's show time in the big leagues!" She said as she disapeared around the corner.

"That's what I like about her!" Billy said.

"What's that, she likes eating pussy too?"

"No, her modesty."

★

Lt. Commander Shelton wasn't the only troop under consideable duress at the moment.

At the same time Shelton was on the line with the fleet Surgeon General a black Mercedes was speeding its way through District Five towards the U.S. Embassy in downtown Saigon.

Less than ten days earlier Major Jim Kean, U.S.M.C. had requested travel orders to Saigon to asses the likelyhood of further disaster following the fall of the ligations at Da Nang and Na Trang when they were abandoned and over run by the communists. Based on the fact that he was the C.O. of Charlie Company and the marine charged with command of the security contingent assigned to the various embassy installations in South Viet Nam, his request had been approved.

Now on the fourth day of his inspection he had been given some unofficial intel by a SOG officer he came across in a bar. The Special Operations Group guys, more so than any other ground units, had their finger on the undulating pulse of the ground war.

The evacuation of non-essential personnel from the theater of operations had seripticiously commenced as soon as the word was queitly passed down, sometime around the middle of March, around St. Patrick's Day, and had been continuing on into April.

It was illegal for the Defence Attache's Office to evacuate non-U.S. citizens, so it was less than two days before all the civilian flights were full and booked weeks into the future.

Based on what the commies did in Hue City, the rape and butchring of civilians, many American citizens refused to leave the country without their indig spouses and friends, and so the DAO started shuttling those folks to Clark AFB in the P.I.

Major Kean's mission that morning was a meeting with Ambassador Graham Martin at the main embassy in Saigon to pass on what he had learned during the inspection of his embassy contingent.

He had sent word via land line yesterday that he had significant intelligence and advised a meeting with Ambassador Martin at his earliest convienence. The Deputy Chief of Mission, Lehmann advised him that a meeting would be set for 11:00 the next day.

Kean glanced at his watch as he drove through the city. It was 10:36.

Within the embassy heirarchy the ambassador is supported by an array of Foreign Service Officers and specialists who perform the full range of mission activities, as well as representatives of many other U.S. agencies, such as USAID and the Departments of Defense, Commerce, Justice and Agriculture. The Deputy Chief of Mission is essentially the number two

Politically Erect

man at the helm.

It was 10:47 as the black Mercedes was recognized and waved through the side gate of the embassy compound.

The elevator was taking too long so Kean decided to take the stairs to the fourth floor. Noticebly out of breath he arrived at the meeting room. He pushed through the door, stood and stared. The room was empty.

Ducking back out into the hall he caught site of the Deputy Chief of Mission casually thumbing through a sheaf of papers as he strolled through the hall.

"Mr. Lehmann, what's going on?"

"How do you mean Major?"

"We spoke on the phone yesterday. You set up a meeting with Ambassador Martin. Today, at eleven?" The Deputy Chief showed no decernible reaction. "The meeting room seems to be empty. Has it been moved?!"

"Oh, oh yeah, your meeting. The Ambassador has a pretty heavy schedule today. I'll see if we can set something up in the next day or so." He casually announced as he pushed past Kean.

"Mr. Lehmann, what part of 'priority' especially during war time, do you not understand?"

"Let's not lose the run of ourselves Major Kean! Yours is not the only office in this embassy!"

"I'm fully aware of that but it is the only office who's job it is to keep everyone else alive when the shit hits the fan!"

Lehmann glanced up and down the narrow corrodor. "Let's step in here." He took Kean by the elbow and guided him back into the conference room. "What's this all important, 'priority' intell you've got that can't wait?"

"This information is not for you to filter through before it gets to the ambassador."

"You want to get info to Ambassador Martin the only way you're going to do that is through me."

"What's the status of the other western embassies?" Kean pushed.

"Follwing 'Operation Babylift', the Austrailians like others, decided jurnalists and students were to be sent out on Quantus flights between the fourth and the seventeenth."

"The embassy?"

"The last Australians from the Embassy, including Ambassador Price, were evacuated by the RAAF on the 25th."

"So despite the fact that the commies are in spitting distance and other emabassies are pulling up stakes and leaving we're here still deciding what we're going to do?!"

"What' this all important intell you have?" Lehmann insisted.

"I'm told Martin went on TV the other day and promised he would be the last one out after he had personally shaken hands with each and every evacuee as they left? What's this guy plan on running for Congress when he gets home? Or does he think this is the end of a football match where both sides just shake hands and walk away buds, no hard feelings?"

"You got something you want to pass on this is your last chance!"

"Fifth SF have an A camp south of Plei Me –"

"I thought all the A camps were abandoned!"

"As I was saying, the intel strongly indicates that the PAVN's are going to attack most likely in force, within the next forty-eight hours, as soon as they can amass enough fire power and get it within range."

"The PAVN's are gonna bomb Saigon?! You're insane!"

Politically Erect

"Not necessarily Saigon first, but certainly startegic targets like maybe the airbase at Tan Son Nhut for instance. They want to raise the flag over Saigon before May nineteenth."

"What the hell's May ninteenth? That suppossed to mean something?"

"It does to the commies. It's Uncle Ho's birthday!"

"How did you come by this 'intel' Major?"

"An SF operative. Met him over in the P.I., in a bar. He had just come from Cambodia."

"Cambodia?! We got nobody in Cambodia!"

"Of course not! That woud be illegal. I believe his intel is acuurate. After all, these are the guys that are actually-"

"A Green Beret in a bar! That's some intel network you got there Major!" Lehmann turned and left.

*

HM2 Cervantes, alias Bulldyke, was gowned, scrubbed, gloved and backing her way through the swinging door to OR2 when what she saw shocked her. The space was completly empty.

"What the fuck?" Just as she questioned herself the marine orderly poked his head in the door.

"Show's been relocated to the fantail! They're waiting on you!"

Having not been briefed on the case Bulldyke wasn't clear about what she was hearing and so, hands still folded at chest height, she backed out of the door and yelled after the marine.

"You assholes better not be fucking with me!"

"Get up to the fantail! The barrier's nearly finished!"

Paddy Kelly

He yelled back.

As she rose on the aircraft elevator along with a pair of Sea Bees hauling several sheets of corragated steel she scanned the expansive, dead quiet flight deck.

Things were clearly not normal.

The Sea Bees quickly wheeled the sheets to the fantail where a ten foot square section of the deck was being cordoned off by a hastily constructed barrier of some sort.

Crossing the flight deck diagonally she looked forward to see the entire deck crew had been herded forward of the flight deck and off to the port side well out of the potential blast area.

"What the hell's going on? What's all this?!" She quizzed the marine guard stationed at the small improvised doorway of the semi-circular barrier.

"A blast barrier, ma'am."

"A BLAST BARRIER?! WHAT THE FU-"

"CERVANTES, IN HERE!" Shelton's voice rang out from behind the eight foot high corragated wall. Cervantes, still maintaining sterility ventured behind the barrier. Inside she found a pair of Mayo trays on roller stands set up besides a draped patient with Lt. Commander Shelton to the right of the gurney which would serve as an operating table. "Come on in here." While the small team of Sea Bees hummed away on the improvised blast shield of corragated metal laid over a wooden frame and she silently stared Shelton filled her in.

"It would appear that the poor unfortunate sergeant Park here did a service to his fellow squad members while on patrol by considerably catching a 60mm mortar shell in his thorax."

"Fuck me!" She involuntarily blurted.

"And it also appears, so far anyway, that his god is on

his side. His vitals are stable, blood loss is low to moderate and he is now approaching the end of the golden hour." She leaned forward and perused the wound.

"Fuck me. Sir." She mumbled.

"He can't be medivaced without exposing a flight crew and corpsman to extreme risk, so the projectile has to be removed here."

"Fuck me!!"

"HM2 Cervantes, you realize I can't order you to be here. You're under no obligation to scrub in on this case." She looked over and saw the bomb fins peaking out above the Korean's collar bone then across the table at Doctor Shelton.

"You married sir?"

"Yes, what's that got to do with anything?"

"If this thing goes south and you don't have the best O.R. Tech in the fleet with you, I'll be left alone to explain to your wife why you were saddled with a seond rate tech, and sir, I've faced angry women before. It ain't no day at the beach!"

A Sea Bee poked his head in around the wall.

"Commander, your barrier's finished sir!" The Sea Bee reported. "Anything else we can do for you sir?"

"Negative Chief. Well done. Get your men to the green zone."

"Sir, I'm gonna detail a volunteer to standby outside here, off to the port side. If you need anything just holla!"

"Roger Chief. Much aoppreciated."

"We'll be forward of the island structure if you need anything else. Good luck sir!"

The four X-rays were tackd up on the interior frame of the barrier for easy reference as was a portable, battery operated light box.

"Judging by the films the two and a half inch diameter shell is about 16 to 18 inches . . ." Cervantes turned to look at the three films hanging behind her. ". . . 400 to 450 mm in length overall. That puts it well above the large intestine so there's no danger of rupture."

"How do you want to extract it sir?"

"I'm going to incise from the axilla down to just above the illiac crest." He explained as he lifted the soldier's arm and laid it above his head to allow access the arm pit. "We're going to cut ribs three, four and five, which should relieve some tension and we can ease it out backwards, back through the entrance wound."

"Sounds like a plan sir."

"The tip is surrounded by soft tissue so as long as we avoid contact with any bone it shouldn't detonate."

"Number ten?" She suggested the blade size and handed him a premounted scalpel.

"Thank you."

Out on the bow of the ship, save for the soft wind, there was a haunting silence. The crew, herded together and meandering about the launch deck area, were caught up in the tension.

"Bitch of it is I heard the poor bastard of a surgeon just signed on. Came out from Clark less than two months ago." One of the crew members commented.

"Hope he don't smoke."

"Why?"

"He gets the shakes while he's cutting and it's all over but the crying."

"I got ten bucks says he gets that thing outta that guy."

"You're on!"

"Count me in." A third sailor chirped in.

"Cough up the cash!"

Politically Erect

"Will you meatheads pipe down!"
"Sorry Master Chief."

*

Twenty minutes after the first incision the unlucky-luckiest Korean in Viet Nam was split partaially open like a Thanksgiving Day Turkey.

"Okay, it feels like it's loosening." Shelton held the projectile just below the fins. "Hold the muscle flap back while I lay his arm back down at his side." Cervantes complied.

With extreme caution Shelton slowly and carefully slid the projectile back out, working it out of the tunneled crater it had made going in.

"Shit!" Cervantes, with her right hand deep in the guy's chest cavity, depressing the lung tissue to help avoid laceration during extraction, had the back of her hand pressed gently against his cardiac sack. With the bomb nearly halfway out she felt his apical pulse slowly but steadily begin to climb. A sign of deepening shock.

"What's wrong?"
"His pulse is going crazy! It's up around one fifty!"
"It's the alteration in thorasic pressure!"
"GUARD COME IN HERE! WE NEED YOU!"
"Yes sir?!" The marine reported but as he entered his eyes were forced to the gapping wound of the split open Korean and his knees appeared in danger of buckling.

"You okay?" Bulldyke quickly asked, moving away from the marine as much as possible.

"Marine if you're going to pass out step back outside the barrier!" The Commander ordered.

"I'm good sir. I just . . . never seen . . ."

"Neither have we! Cervates, five more miligrams of chloral hydrate."

"Corporal, take that syringe off my right tray." She nodded. "Yeah that one. Without touching anything else, remove the needle cover and stick the needle in that little port there, on his IV tube. Yeah that's it. Now slowly inject the rest of what's in that syringe." The marine complied, removed the needle from the port and recapped it.

"Meds are in sir!"

"Pulse?"

"It's slowing."

"He should stabilize after we get this thing all the way out. Keep the lung tissue as clear as you can. How's it look?"

"Cyanosis is dissapating, lung tissue is regaining color!"

"Okay, good. Orderly, step around here besides me with that tray." Again the marine complied and as he came alongside Shelton's operating area Shelton carefully finished withdrawing the bomb and placed it on the towel covered tray to prevent rolling.

"Move immedaiatly to the rail and dump it over the side! Make sure it's clear of any hull fixtures when you jetison it!"

"Aye aye sir!" As soon as the marine began to move they both realized that the metal tray wasn't going to make it as the mortar round jiggled uncontrollably. Shelton lifted it back off the tray.

"Get rid of the tray and take it by hand."

"What, carry it?!"

"Move!" Shelton ordered and the corporal slowly moved out to the edge of the fantail and tossed it out overboard. It detonated as it hit the sea five to six stories below.

Politically Erect

At the muffled sound of the explosion cheers and applause broke out across the flight deck.

"I'd say that was and H.E. round." Shelton exclaimed as he commenced suturing vessels.

TING, TING, TING!

The resonance of the hits rang out across the deck and both Shelton and Cervantes looked up from their work as the unmistakeable sound of high caliber rounds bounced off the ship's hull from some unknown location.

"What the hell was that?" Dr. Shelton asked. The marine quickly scurried back to the barrier.

TING, TING, TING! In answer to his question the 1MC blared to life throughout the carrier.

"NOW HEAR THIS, NOW HEAR THIS! MARINE SECURITY CONTINGENT REPORT TO BATTLE STATIONS ON THE DOUBLE. IGBG ATTACK UNDERWAY. ALL HANDS ARE ADVISED TO STAY AWAY FROM THE RAIL. THE CLOCK STARTS NOW. THAT IS ALL."

Shelton was distracted while Cervantes seemed undisturbed.

"Cervantes, questions!"

"Yes sir?"

"What the hell is an IBGB attack and is it my imagination or did that sailor manning the 1MC seem unduly calm if the ship is under attack?"

"IBGB, Itty BItty Gook Boat attack and it's not really an emergency although it kind of is." It was then, s they went to work looking for secondary damage to the the patient's vicera and closing up that they heard two squads of manines, each hauling an M60 and bandoliers of ammo as they double timed out across the flight deck and took up prone positions along the port side rail.

Cervantes explained as they worked.

Paddy Kelly

"Charlie doesn't have a navy sir, at least one you'd notice. So every once in a while some young buck will get souped up on rice wine and the local version of scag, H or Horse, grab a speedboat and a captured M60 and take a run out to the fleet to try and shoot up one of our ships. Usually the biggest boat which means either us or the Midway. Guess today it's our turn."

From behind the blast barrier they could hear the marines sporadically firing at the small boat as the two NVA aboard zig zagged around the Hancock spritting off rounds when ever one of the marines would pop his head up above deck level to draw fire and allow one of the other squads to walk a line of fire up to the buzzing little speed boat getting slightly closer with each burst. The boat zipped out aft of the carrier and at around the 500 meter mark did a U -turn to come back in for a third pass.

After several minutes of cat and mouse, just as one squad had a solid zero on the stupid but brave little gook boat crew, it was without warning that the little target was replaced with a huge geyser of sea water, debris and pieces of NVA all followed by a low boom.

The 1MC again blared to life. "NOW HEAR THIS, NOW HEAR THIS. SECURITY FORCE SECURE FROM BATTLE STATIONS. THE CLOCK IS NOW STOPPED. OFFICIAL TIME IS SIX MINUTES AND SEVENTEEN SECONDS. THAT IS ALL."

The angry marines pushed up off the deck and looked out across in the direction of the *U.S.S. Johnson*, a neighboring DD off the rear of the port bow. The gun crew on the rear gun mount were waving at the angry marines.

"What clock is he talking about?" Shelton asked.

"Right after an IBGB alert the crew place bets on how long before the Jarheads erase them. The rules state

Politically Erect

they have to go by the official 1MC announcement for the tme."

"Quaint. Hemostat please."

Two and half hours, one IBGB attack and a hell of alot of stress later Sergeant Park of the Korean Marines was patched up and being wheeled back below decks to begin recovery. A very long, long recovery.

As they rode the aircraft elevator back down Shelton leaned in to Cervantes.

"You did good. Pleasure working with you."

"The guys call me Bulldyke, Commander."

"Okay Bulldyke, call me John." As they went their seperate ways Bulldyke smiled and let her mind relax.

"Dear Diary . . ." She mumbled once below decks as she tossd her scrubs into the contaminated linen bin.

Above decks the flight deck crew got the all clear and driftd back to their duty stations as money once again changed hands.

*

Paddy Kelly

**SAVE FUEL;
BURN A VC!**

Politically Erect

CHAPTER EIGHTEEN

Tan Son Nhut Commissary
Monday 14:10, 28 April, 1975
Saigon, Republic of South Viet Nam

The main two story building which housed the Defense Attaché's Office, was situated just beside the air strip at Tan Son Nhut air base. Aside from a pair of mile long runways, a sizeable tarmac and a collection of hangers it sported several small offices for the in and out processing of military personnel, a depot for non-military, administrative supplies and served as the arrival and departure point for all civilians and some military travelers. All this was managed in and around the compact main terminal.

The handful of cooks manning the bijou commissary kitchen were equipped to serve three meals a day to upwards of two hundred staff and travelers.

It was nearly two hours after lunch that Monday afternoon when the two cooks on duty casually worked away preparing the evening meal as the shelf mounted, plastic Emerson radio blared through the chrome shelving and across the boxes of vegtables stacked up on the spotless work tables.

The temperature in Saigon is currently 105 degrees and rising. Now an all time favorite, Bing Crosby with White Christmas.

"What the fuck?! That's the third time that fool's made that same announcement and played that same sorry damn song!" The big cook complained.

"Dope smokin' white boys." His colleague commented as he laid out a second tray of dinner rolls to be baked.

"I'm just wonderin' what calendar that fool got? It ain't Christmas! Those boys at AFN losing they-" A muffled explosion out near the airfield perimeter interrupted his one man bitch session.

"They play some more music when they gets to it." The older one assured.

"What the fuck was that?!"

"I look like I can see through walls?! Go and look!"

*

Out on the Hancock the daily routine in sick bay carried on oblivious to activities ashore. However, Billy noticed something that morning and brought it to a senior corpsman's attention that morning when passing him up on the flight deck just after sick call.

"Hey Chief, is it me or is there an unusual number of civilian indig been showing up to the sickbay in the last week?"

"Not all that unusual since there's no longer a dedicated hospital facility at Ton Son Nut, just the small dispensary."

"Not unusual except for the fact that many of them seemed to be hanging around the ship long after their treatment or course of meds has finished." Billy pointed out. "What's your guess about what's going on around here?" Billy asked.

"Don't know for sure but I agree there's something in the wind. I spoke to a buddy in the radio shack yesterday. He said there's something cooking but whatever it is it's classified."

Politically Erect

"Meaning he's full of shit or-"

"Or it's classified." The chief insisted. "I'll do a little snooping around, meanwhile don't go spreading any scuttlebut!"

"You know me chief!"

"Why do you think I told you to keep it under your hat?" The cheif headed below decks.

Instead of heading back down to sickbay Billy stepped back out on deck and took a bearing from the sun then glanced up to the signal deck of the island structure. He saw the anemometer and observed the wind was definatly picking up speed and the wind vane on top of it was changing direction to come parallel to the flight deck.

Despite the fact the 1MC had not called the pilots to alert, the *U.S.S. Hancock* was turning into the wind.

***

Back in the commissary the big cook pushed the panic bar on the back fire door and opened it to look out across the airfield. What he saw was not a good thing.

Two A-37 fighter aircraft were coming in low and as he watched they flew nearly wingtip to wing tip, leveled off and strafed the two runways, while 200 meters away a company of PAVN's rushed the perimeter fence all firing on full auto.

Mortar rounds began to slowly walk their way perpendicular across the airfield.

"MOTHA-FUCKA!" The big cook yelled into the kitchen.

"What's happening?!"

"It's fuckin' Pearl Harbor out there!"

Paddy Kelly

The Marine security contingent was already responding but were quickly counter attacked by machine gun and eerily accurate mortar fire.

The first two rounds, fired in quick succession took out a C-47 on a far tarmac followed by a nearby Huey.

Gunny Martin quickly took control of the situation and organized his fire teams into interlocking fields of fire with his two M60's at high points facing out across the airfield. Under heavy fire he then double timed it over to his radio man in the doorway of a nearby hanger and gave orders.

The marines return fire was intermittent but accurate and three sappers coming through the fence fell instantly causing the advancing enemy to hesitate and take cover.

"Get a message to Major Kean at the embassy! D.A.O. and airfield under attack. Company sized elements from three directions. Supporting arty. Arty on target! Do it! Send reinforcements on the double. Find me when you get through to him, clear?"

"Roger that Gunny!" The radio man went to work.

Ten minutes later Major Kean was on the line to the Gunny sergeant. "Gunny, Kean here! Give me a SIT REP."

"Company sized element attacking under cover of mortar fire from three sides."

"You heard arty?"

"Negative they opened up with 80mm mortars, one of the guards reported it as arty."

"Anybody hit?"

"Negative sir. They seem to be going for-" A Loach helicopter out on a tarmac exploded with a direct hit.

"-the aircraft." Gunny Martin finished. "Somehow they're zeroed in on the ranges."

"God damned indig maintenance personnel! NVA must have got them to pace off the distances from known

Politically Erect

ground markers that's why the accuracy. You have any operational vehicles?" Sporadic explosions and steady small arms fire could be heard in the background as they spoke.

"Yes sir, a couple of jeeps, and a deuce and a half."

"Can you hold until dark?"

"I think so, yeah."

"Okay good. Don't move the vehicles before-" A sudden, but muffled explosion was heard on the other end of the line and Kean lost contact with the D.A.O.

"SHIT!" Over the still open line Kean could hear a series of loud explosions quickly followed by long bursts of M60 and M16 fire. Finally the line went completely dead.

Kean immediately realized that Tan Son Nhut airbase and the D.A.O. were the primary evac point on all the U.S. E&E plans.

Also not lost on him was that fact that it was less than an hour ago that the change of presidency in Viet Nam had been announced.

****

While the Marine guards began to struggle to keep the crowds outside the embassy walls from getting inside the walls, alone upstairs in the conference room, Major Kean was trying to sell Deputy Chief of Mission Lehmann on the idea that it might already be too late to start planning a plausible evacuation.

"As soon as we know what the situation is with the South Vietnamese government-"

"We already know." Lehmann cut him off.

"What?" Kean was shocked and incensed that there

was still more intel he had not been privy to.

"We already know. There ain't one. President Thieu was told to resign or he and his family would be executed. They've already appointed a 'care taker' government under Huong."

"As a fall guy?"

"No, CIA says he's a Commie sympathizer." Lehmann informed him.

"Then what?"

"The intel boys think that rather than a full surrender he'll attempt to negotiate with the People's Revolutionary Government to form a coalition, then-"

"Please! The PCA congressional committee has a better chance of finding Nixon's eighteen minutes of missing tape!"

"No argument here Major."

"So next guess?" Kean pushed.

"It's generally agreed that in that instance the Ambassador will be handed an ultimatum to withdraw all U.S. personnel within forty-eight hours or face complete annihilation."

"We get the air support we need and I'll have them out in twenty-four." Kean insisted.

There was a knock at door.

"Major, the information you requested earlier." The corporal announced as he handed the sealed message to his boss.

"Excuse me." Kean stepped to the side to read the hand written note.

Two way door to the French embassy ordered by the ambassador will be finished 18:00 tonight.

"Thank you corporal." He dismissed the Marine. "Any reports of what's happening in any of the other western embassies?" Kean baited. "I notice some activity next door."

"The French have brought in some Legionnaires just in case."

"How many?" How many would give Kean a good idea of the difficulties the French anticipated for their small embassy. Lehmann's answer would also hint at how truthful he was being.

"About a hundred."

"There's a hundred already on the grounds since March!" They stared eye-to-eye. "I can't protect you people if I don't know what I have and don't have to work with God damn it!" He tossed the note on the table in front of Lehmann who picked it up. "I only get my Marines out, you and the ambassador buy it or get captured, I get court martialed. A year or two later I get another job but you're still dead."

"Alright, I get it."

"What's with this secret door?"

"They're bringing in three hundred Legionnaires, and when the shit hits the fan the French intend to button down and recognize whatever new government pops up."

"You think if my Marines can't protect the Ambassador the French are going to do any better?"

In an effort to salvage what was left of their professional relationship Lehmann produced a memo from his breast pocket and slid it across the table.

"I didn't want the staff to see this. Martin sent it a few hours ago." Lehmann informed. Kean read it.

Paddy Kelly

28 April, 1975

TO: Henry Kissinger

FROM: Ambassador Graham Martin

While we still have a functioning Republic of Viet Nam, and will for quite a while I think, I see no U.S. policy interests to be served in either leaving in pique or trying to create conditions that would force our departure.

"So on top of saying live on TV he's going to personally stand there and shake hands with each and every evacuee as they board the aircraft he still thinks there's a Republic out there beyond those gates?" There was no reply from Lehmann. "We have a name for that type of behavior. It's called denial!"

"He just can't bring himself to turn his back on these people! To just bail out on them and leave after all the government has promised them!"

"News flash Deputy Lehmann, that ship has sailed! Ambassador Martin is now most likely taking his orders from Kissinger which means Ford and, as far as I'm concerned, this is no longer an administrative matter, it's a matter of survival. And since we're baring our souls you need to know two things: this evacuation is going ahead, now with or without your staff's or Amabssador Martin's okay and if push comes to shove I'll have the Ambassador arrested and forcibly put on the aircraft to get him out of here safely!"

Lehmann fell back into a chair which he nearly missed as he sat down. There was a pause and along with his mental will to continue to resist, he released a deep

Politically Erect

sigh.

"Alright! What do you need?!" He asked.

"With the D.A.O. and the airfield out of commission we need to rework our plans readjusting and conducting the E&E from here." Kean offered to Lehmann.

"Okay, I'll detail the grounds people to cut down trees to clear an LZ." Lehmann offered.

"Not advisable just yet." Kean suggested."There's gonna be more and more civilians gathering at the gates expecting us to get them out as the commies get closer. They see us cutting down trees and lowering the flag and we haven't opened the gates yet they're gonna think it's a panicked withdrawal and are likely to storm the place. My Marines can't hold off the entire city."

"Alright, what then?" Kean realized that with Lehmann's cooperation he would now have no more resistance from the remaining staff.

*

It was just past fifteen hundred when Billy wandered up onto the flight deck to get some air. He was surprised when he looked out across the fleet and saw the increased chopper activity in the airspace above. His curiosity was peaked when two pairs of F-104's streaked across the fleet heading inland.

Whiskey Tango Foxtrot? He mumbled to himself

"Chance, just the man I'm looking for!" It was the Senior Chief approaching him.

"I didn't do it Chief."

"Do what?!"

"Whatever it is that you're gonna accuse me of!"

"Very funny asshole! You wanna go for a helicopter

ride?"

"Might as well Senior Chief can't dance. Where am I going?"

"Grab an M-1 med bag out of supply and hitch a ride on the next Huey heading into the city. Word's been passed there's some civilians and some banged up SVA personnel who might need some patching up on the way in."

"I'm on it Chief." Billy headed for the sick bay supply locker to grab a bag.

"AND DON'T FORGET A STEEL POT! Dumbshit!" The Senior Chief yelled after him to late for Billy to hear.

Fifteen minutes later Billy was inbound to Saigon on a UH-1H with a pair of pilots and a crew cheif who were also on their virgin run.

As a precaution against any stray small arms fire the pilot climbed to 5000 feet as he banked in towards the outskirts of the city. The crew chief passed Billy a head set and they introduced themselves.

The journey was about thirty minutes in from the fleet but if carrying a load, forty to forty-five minutes heading back out.

Air traffic was roughly organized into lanes, right or north of the city for incoming aircraft and the south lane for outgoing aircraft leaving out of the capital and flying east to the sea. The anti-clockwise pattern was decided upon because the NVA were coming from the north and the inbound lane was more likely to take fire. Better to risk near empty aircraft. Addtionally if they took fire coming in they could warn others as they diverted further south. Overall intel of exact enemy locations would be non-existent. At least until the first aircraft was shot down.

Once the Huey cleared the sea the city almost

instantly came into sight. A giant black and white sea of people and vehicles came into view.

"Fuck!" The crew cheif exclaimed. "World's biggest traffic jam!"

"Looks like a Black Friday sale at Macy's!" Billy added.

*

15:01, 28 April, 1975

Major Kean stood with Top Valdez, the NCOIC, working things out on the west balcony of the Chancery building as they scanned the crowded parking lot.

"Once the birds start coming in expect the crowds to rush." Kean advised.

"Aye sir. I'll pass the word."

"Above all we must not open fire unless Marines' lives are in imminent danger!"

"I understand Skipper."

A messenger scurried up to the two as they spoke.

"Sir, Gunny Martin out at the D.A.O. on the line for you."

"Thanks corporal."

"You can take it on the lobby phone." Down in the lobby Kean picked up the phone.

"Major?"

"Gunny, how's it looking?"

"There seems to be a lull here, no doubt they're re-arming and re-loading I expect a full on attack at some point soon. We're gonna need an ammo re-supply if you want us to hold out sir."

"Casualty report?"

"Six wounded, two medivaced out. And sir . . ."
"Yeah Gunny?"
"Two KIA."
"Who?"
"Corporal McMahon and Lance Corporal Judge."
"Shit!"
"They both went down fighting Major."
"Can you get them out?"
"Done sir. I commandeered a civilian vehicle, sent a one man escort and tasked the driver to get the bodies to the medical center in town. I have their personal effects."
"Well done Gunny."
"Sir, they've taken out the vehicles."
"All of them?!"
"The deuce and a half and one of the jeeps."
Kean cursed Lehmann under his breath.
"I make it 15:17 now. I'll have a Chinook and a gunship out to you before nightfall. Are you surrounded?"
"Negative sir. The most feasible avenue of approach for the birds is from the south east. As soon we hear them I'll pop smoke and lay down a blanket of 60 cal for the 46 right behind the commissary. It's our best bet."
"Roger that Gunny. Stay on the secure freq! I'll brief the air ops people to make sure the bird is on your freq."
"Sir, make sure they know it's gonna be a hot LZ!"
Less than an hour later the Marines' taxi, with a Cobra escort circling overhead, was touching down across the road from the main admin building.
Gunny Martin and his thirteen Marines hustled into the CH-46 and the crew chief radioed the pilot all aboard as he raised the ramp.
The Gunny leaned in to the Crew Chief to fill him in.
"All of the civilians are out. The last fixed wing took off around the wreckage of the other aircraft a couple of

hours ago. Nothing's getting in or out of there except choppers and then only with gunships!" Gunny infomed him and he passed the info on to Kean back at the embassy via radio.

Suddenly, as the bird gained altitude and they watched out through the partially retracted tail ramp, the main administration building disintegrated in a series of three explosions and began burning out of control.

"What the hell was that, artillery fire?" The crew chief asked. The Marines smiled.

"About a hundred pounds of C-4." The Gunny informed him.

"We leave anything of value back there?" The crew chief asked as they lifted off and rose over the city.

"Only about a half million in cash!"

By 17:30 that afternoon the destroyed airfield belonged to the PAVN's.

*

A week ago when Kean first arrived in country he found the D.A.O. in a somewhat controlled chaos. In contrast when he arrived at the embassy he found there was a concentrated effort to maintain a 'normal' workday attitude. A concentrated effort that was clearly achieving nothing but paralysis of the entire staff. It was as if there was a bomb of an unknown tonnage in an unknown location waiting to detonate at an unknown time in the near future.

Ambassador Martin had issued strict orders that no preparations for evacuation were to be made while constantly reiterating that the situation would stabilize. As a result Kean observed that a thinly disguised complacency seemed to dominate. A complacency hiding a palatable undercurrent of fear.

Based on the fact that first the Nixon then the Ford administration had, for almost two full years, lied to the South Vietnamese about their unreservedly backing them, the South's fears were totally justified. Even as Da Nang was being over run in the last days of March the best that Ford did was issue a statement of his "Strong support for the South Vietnamese people."

Would Washington leave the embassy staff, or those who couldn't get out by some arbitrary deadline set by D.C. to be abandoned? Precedents had been set. There was nothing but a weak 'official' protest when the two ligations in Da Nang and Na Trang had to be abandoned as they were being over run. Evacuation was left to the SVN forces until it was clear they couldn't handle it and were over run.

Now in the main embassy nobody really seemed to be concentrating on getting any work done, instead people's minds were preoccupied with just what exactly Martin's grand scheme of things was.

Probably all the better that the staff had no clue that there wasn't a plan.

Even Marvin Garrett, the Regional Security Officer for overall security of the embassies and civilian personnel in Viet Nam to include responsibility for all E&E plans, all the security assistants etc . . . had no apparent idea of the reality of the situation or what to do about it.

Understanding that somehow the embassy had reached the point where things were quickly deteriorating, their primary escape plan was being neutralized and there didn't appear to be any Plan B, or at least no one who knew what the hell it was, Kean quickly realized he had to fall back and punt, that is

Politically Erect

invent a plan B.

Having foreseen the attack on the D.A.O. and airfield he had spent adequate time before the 28th working out the best plan with what he had at hand. Wisely ignoring an order from Regional Security Officer Garrett to return to his office and go back to work, Kean took it upon himself to set plans for the defense of the embassy compound and the evacuation. The plans were immediate and well thought out.

Coordinating with Top Sergeant Valdez, his senior enlisted man, he ordered four interlocking and mutually supporting machine gun positions and four squad area assignments. The small auxiliary areas of the main building were essentially indefensible so he wasted little time on them.

The overall plan called for a forced withdrawal into the main embassy building, or Chancery, and to fight floor by floor to the roof and attempt to effect an aerial exfil.

The primary problem was, now with no airfield and that fixed wing cargo craft with their increased capacity were out of the equation, where to land helicopters? The only helo pad was on the roof and that was designed to accommodate only one UH-IH at a time. Fifteen or so people at once.

There were now five to five and a half thousand already milling around the gates as soon as curfew had been lifted that morning.

By-passing Garrett as well as the rest of the civilian staff, Kean got to work instituting his plan immediately. One of the first tasks was to hunt down the senior petty officer of the Seabees and issue a checklist.

"Paint the parking lot with luminous paint to I.D. it as an improvised LZ so they can land after dark."

"What about all the trees sir?"

"They're gonna come down but not until I give the order. I don't want to alert the Ambassador."

"Sir . . . does he really think we can stay here and greet the commies, exchange the flag and all that bullshit?"

"Don't know and don't care but most importantly we're not gonna find out! But that's between you and I, understood?!"

"Roger that Major! Illumination sir? The birds are gonna need lights if we're planning on using the parking lot as an L.Z." The Seabee ponited out.

"I'm working on it. Meanwhile find a hose and wet down the parking lot after the paint dries, keep the dust and debris down when the birds flare in to land."

"We got some paint in the paint locker downstairs."

"Pace off the center area of the parking lot and let me know if we'll get a CH-53 in there or are we restricted to Huey's and Chinooks."

"Anything else Major?"

"Negative Chief, just get back to me when you're guys are done."

"Aye aye sir!"

Ten minutes later the Chief sent a runner to find the Major.

"Sir, Chief says to tell you there's plenty of room for a Jolly Green to land and lift off."

"Tell the chief I got the message. Also go find Top Valdez tell him about the Jolly Green and tell him I need all hands for tree duty."

"Tree duty sir?"

"He'll know what you mean."

"Aye aye sir."

Politically Erect

05:10, 29 April, 1975

Between 10 o'clock and 12 noon vehicles were moved to clear the parking lot, trees were cut down and details were quietly assigned to the Marine security contingent around the perimeter of the embassy.

By about noon, as they wrapped up the parking lot preparations, the crowd outside the compound had swollen to over ten thousand.

With 2,500 evacuees already scattered in and around the compound, Kean was forced to rework his calculations on how many lifts would be required. With no guidance he assumed an order of march. Civilian government personnel first, indig civilians second and Marines last. The senior Marine, himself, absolutely last.

Behind the stacked sand bags of the guard post up on the roof the sound of rotor blades was heard. The three marine guards of the roof top fire team looked up.

"What kind of fool flies an all white Huey in a war zone?" One asked.

"It's an Air America bird!" His team mate informed. They watched as the Huey gently floated down to the center of the parking lot. Kean ran out through the rotor wash to the pilot.

"You folks call for a taxi?" The pilot asked.

"What's happening outside the walls?" Kean inquired.

"Saigon's about to set the Guinness World Book of Records for yard sales."

"So official word's come down?"

"Not sure, we've been on standby since yesterday but as soon as we got word about the D.A.O. we rounded up the cavalry and rode out. What's your status Major?"

"We should have birds laid on from the fleet. But we could use a little help getting ready."

"Stand by one." The pilot manned his mike and made a call. An immediate response was forth coming. "There's Army evac teams floating around, I'll have one to you in the next half hour."

"Much appreciated!"

"You got any Priority evacs you want me to take anyone out?"

"Better to make your regularly scheduled evac points around the city. At least we have a wall and armed guards. The civilians and dependents out there are exposed."

"Roger that sir! Catch you in the O Club sometime!"

"First one's on me!" Kean shut the door and stepped back and the big white bird was up and gone in seconds.

"At least we know the LZ works." It was Top Valdez standing next to Kean.

"Top, gather up all the Mission Warden personnel and find the rest of the Seabees, we're gonna need them!"

"Will do sir."

"And get one of the Marines to find a ladder to get to the helo pad on the roof. Those stairs have no direct access."

"Roger that Major."

A five man Army evac team arrived by Huey a short time later and they went to work arranging evacuees into evac teams assigning numbers and assembly areas to spread them out to avoid cramming around the LZ's.

****

Gliding over the city Billy and the crew chief peered down and watched the crowd which at times appeared

Politically Erect

eerily quiet but always on the edge of a full panic. Thousands of people slowly undulated in all directions unable to see from ground level exactly which way led to freedom.

The pilot chanced it and took the chopper down to 1000 feet for a closer look.

Throughout the city center heavily armed ARVN paratroops manned roadblocks, checked I.D. cards, turning away most vehicles and apparently admitting little or no foot traffic.

Ironically it was in the waning days that Billy had found the war he was looking for.

"Kinght takes queen!" The pilot radioed to the co-pilot who nodded in acknowledgement. The co-pilot leaned back and passed the word to Billy and the crew chief.

"What?" Billy asked.

"Charlie just ramped it up a notch. The Commies' 223rd has cut off Route 4 so there's no more access to the Delta by road."

"What about Cu Chi north of here?" Billy asked.

"Over run by NVA."

"There were three battalions of ARVN's defending that area!" Chance exclaimed.

"Not anymore! The ARVN's are stripping off their uniforms as they flee!" He went on to explain that Binh Duong to the north and Bien Hoa had also been captured.

Saigon was surrounded and John Wayne was not coming with any cavalry. The fact is that the cavalry couldn't come because they had no horses. Their funding had been stopped abruptly and without notice by the U.S. Congress less than a month ago.

Unfortunately for the people of the doomed Republic

of Viet Nam the communists, who also had subscriptions to the *New York Times*, read of the Congressional elimination of funding and had patiently planned their attacks accordingly.

***  ***

Politically Erect

CUBA. THE PHILIPINES. VIET NAM:

THERE IS NO FURY LIKE A VESTED INTEREST MASQUARADING AS A MORAL PRINCIPLE.

Paddy Kelly

CHAPTER NINETEEN

U.S. Embassy, Saigon
14:52 29 April, 1975

A pack of 104's, Tomcats and Loaches acting as scouts constantly prowled the skies over the fleet hunting for suicidal communist flyboys. Sacrificing little speed boats to repel the Western White Dogs was one thing but even the godless commies saw the logic of not sacrificing the few aircraft they now possessed.

"CHOPPERS INCOMING!" A marine on the elevated helo pad ran to the rail and yelled down to the rooftop guard who in turn passed the word down to the embassy's crew and the hundred people lining the stairwell. When word reached the parking lot where Major Kean was walking the perimeter checking on his men, a coordinated cheer went up across the compound.

It was at around 15:00 that the first of several CH53's appeared over the horizon and the onset of *Operation Frequent Wind* commenced for those at the embassy.

Anticipation, relief and joy swept the huge crowd but quickly gave way to shock as the two CH-53's flying in offset tandem, continued on past the embassy and veered off to the northwest.

Typical of the uncoordinated communications that had plagued the last months in Viet Nam, word had not reached the fleet that the D.A.O., the original primary evac point, was in enemy hands.

Kean dashed across the parking lot and rushed up to the radio room in the embassy to establish commo with the fleet and instruct them to reroute the aircraft. But there was yet more confusion. Only after he overcame the static interference and and the unusual volume of radio traffic was he able to make a connection. As if Kean didn't have enough headaches, he was informed that the D.A.O. had originally only scheduled two lifts from their location and so Fleet was only prepared for two sorties of two 53's each. Kean quickly appraised them with an up to date status of the actual numbers of evacuees at hand. So far. Word was passed and panic stations were manned across the decks throughout the fleet.

Under his breath he cursed Ambassador Martin for not having keept up to date commo with the fleet's flag ship, the *U.S.S. Blueridge*.

All of this instantly became a non-issue as soon as the 53's reached Tan Son Nhut about ten minutes after over flying the embassy. Both ships immediately came under heavy enemy fire and realized that the D.A.O. had fallen.

The lead pilot pulled back on his collective, climbed out of small arms range and alerted his wing man. Next he radioed to the fleet who were only able to make sporadic radio contact with Major Kean so were compelled to contact the embassy via land line.

With things finally on coordinted, Kean passed a perimeter alert and ordered the formation of loads of 20 man helo teams lead by a Marine to be formed up and to standby.

By now the embassy compound was surrounded by 10 to 15,000 plus with an additional several thousand inside the wall.

Outside the gates the previously heard sporadic pistol shots had now noticeably increased to a steady staccato occasionally punctuated by rifle fire. However, the direction and distance of the weapons remained indiscernible.

The Marines had prepared for enemy action,

particularly following the fall of Na Trang and Da Nhang, but now it seemed to have morphed into a situation where they were facing walls of civilians who may or may not suddenly start producing hidden fire arms or other weapons. Tensio amongst the troops grew.

After experiencing repetitive instances throughout the war where people previously marked as 'friendly civilians' turned out to be enemy combatants, the entire contingent was on edge and not just from the pending enemy attack. Problem was, there were several thousand 'friendlies' already inside the compound.

Fortunately Kean's foresight had put the entire marine contingent on full alert at the same time he passed the word to his team leaders that the airfield had been over run. Unlike Ambassador Martin's civilian staff the Marine's had no illusions about where the Americans stood.

As the choppers began their runs, by Kean's request, additional forces were being flown in. With three squads of FMF marines in Sparrow Hawk teams, a recon detachment and a five man Helicopter Support Team, the total of the marine security guards were boosted to 156 combatants on the ground giving Kean much more reasonable latitude in operations.

By the onset of curfew the crowds around the embassy walls seemed to be swelling at an exponential rate, consequently two reaction squads were kept on six hour rotation.

As dark was setting in some of the cars which had been moved from the parking lot to clear an LZ for the CH-53's to land, were brought back in and arranged in a large rectangle aligned with the fluorescent paint the Seabees had laid down on the blacktop earlier. Their engines were started up and their headlights turned on to light the improvised LZ.

Politically Erect

The embassy roof, which could only accommodate smaller birds, was equipped with roof floods and so was easily lighted on its own.

As Major Kean was again making the rounds of the perimeter guard he paused to watch the next 53 settling down onto the parking lot. To his surprise Gunny Martin stepped off the chopper as it touched down. They traded salutes as they approached each other.

"Couldn't stay away from the place huh?" Kean spoke first. They stepped outside the rotor wash to speak.

"Thought you might need a hand what with all these civilians plugging up the works!"

"You get the two KIA's remains squared away?"

"Corporal McMahon and Lance Darwin yes sir." He reaffirmed. "They've been turned over to Graves Registration who've confirmed they've been transferred to the *Midway*. They'll be shipped home as soon as next of kin can be located and notified." The Gunny filled him in.

"Top Valdez is overseeing this LZ, why don't you make the rounds to the machine gun nests and the fire teams make sure they're up to snuff? Ammo, water and such. I'm going to find the Ambassador."

"Will do sir."

By 19:30 things seemed to be progressing well. The lifts had settled into a rhythm where-by two birds, one Huey and one Jolly Green Giant, were landing and a load of people was lifting off about every fifteen to twenty minutes. More importantly, with the exception of the few occasional desperados trying to scale the wall, the swollen crowd outside the compound seemed to be behaving. The presence of the South Vietnamese M.P.'s helped. But all good things must come to an end.

First twenty minutes then thirty passed without the arrival of any more choppers. At just past 22:20 a lone 53 appeared and drifted down to the parking lot. As the next load of passengers was being escorted onto the bird Kean appeared and ran around to the cockpit.

"What's the hold-up? Where's the rest of the birds?" He asked the pilot.

"Looks like a reinforced battalion of PAVN's has outflanked us, came down from the north along the coast. They've cut off the harbor and are setting up anti-aircraft defenses. Admiral's ordered the lifts to terminate at 23:00."

"SHIT!" As he swore a Marine came around the other side of the bird and banged on the fuselage and gave the thumbs up. The crew chief confirmed the ship was buttoned up and the pilot closed the window and slowly lifted off.

"What's the word sir?" The Marine scurried over and questioned Kean.

"Find Top Valdez, tell him to start shuffling as many as he can back and up into the building. We need to clear the decks out here as soon as possible!" Kean took off across the parking lot and into the embassy where he found the Ambassador upstairs squirreled away in his office speaking on a satcom line.

"One minute Mr. President." Martin instructed when he spotted the major in the doorway. Kean stood dumbfounded as Martin held the over sized transceiver attached to the large black satellite box on his desk. The fact that the White House now appeared to be calling the shots was a game changer.

"Yes Major?"

"I've just been informed that Fleet has given the order to terminate the airlift in one hour. There are still over a thousand people to get out of here!"

Politically Erect

"Can we not resume in the morning?" Martin, unbeknownst to Kean, had a classified hot line to the White House and had been updating President Ford all along. His question alerted Kean to the fact that Martin was still not exactly up to date on their situation.

"Darkness is not the issue sir. The enemy are closing in. Fast. At 38 persons per 53 and 24 persons in a 46 that's 62 per sortie, that's 15 to 20 more sorties! That's based on my guess of how many people are left! Those pilots can't fly non-stop plus there's refuel time to consider. As it is, it's going to be very close Mr. Ambassador!"

"Thank you Major. I'll send a messenger." Kean made no effort to move. With a glassed-over look in his eyes Martin stared up at the Major.

"Do the best you can." He uttered.

On his way back down to the parking lot Kean paused and peered between the railings into an office. Several senior officials were getting drunk in the conference room.

"Fucking civilians!" He muttered.

Down on the fourth floor the major was pulled aside by the two marines he had tasked earlier with clearing stragglers floor by floor. As he came down the stairs he observed the smashed window of the door to the Cash Liquor Sales Outlet.

"Are all decks clear?" He asked the two lance corporals.

"One through three sir. We're still at it, but . . ." He was cut off by his less patient shipmate.

"Sir, there's a bunch of drunk Koreans demanding priority in line!"

"They wait like everyone else! Deputy Chief Lehmann says they get no priority."

"A couple of them got a belly full of booze and are getting pretty pushy sir!"

"You got a weapon?"

"Yes sir!"

"You train on pugil sticks in basic?"

"Knocked a guy out once sir!" The troop proudly admitted.

"Do what you have to do corporal!" Kean instructed before heading back down stairs.

"Those poor bastards are gonna wake up to the worst hangover of their lives tomorrow morning!" The young corporal observed.

"If Charlie let's them wake up at all! Let's go!" The rest of the floors were clear of stragglers and they headed back up to find Top Valdez for their next task.

*

It was less than 48 hours ago, back in the officer's mess, that both pilots on Billy Chance's Huey had talked about getting to Subic Bay or Guam by the second or third of May, San Diego by the fifth and enjoying the ship's first liberty in nearly two years. Now it looked like they'd be going home ahead of schedule.

By 20:00 it was nearing the crew's sixth sortie of the day as the Huey flared in to land on the deck of the *U.S.S. Midway*. The dozen evacuees and two wounded were off loaded and, as the pilots decided they were okay on fuel for one or two more runs before they needed gas, they were airborne and heading back into the city again in ten minutes.

Five miles off shore out in the fleet, the ongoing action, occasionally but only briefly, paused when a stray IBGB suddenly appeared from the west raking the hull of one of the ships with small caliber fire. Other than providing live fire target practice for the crew he accomplished virtually nothing as the mosquito like disturbance was swatted by a ship board rocket fired from a near-by destroyer escort.

"You see that LCC down there?" The crew chief pointed down as they flew at 2,000 feet. Billy glanced out the starboard hatch and nodded. "That's the *Blueridge*, command ship for the Seventh fleet. Right now those guys down there are running around like one legged bastards in an ass kicking contest!" The crew chief knew exactly what he was talking about. The ship's decks, in less than one hour had turned from routine to an all hands operation on all vessels.

Mindful that fuel would become a priority soon enough but also realizing that they were witnessing history, the pilot slowed his bird and allowed Billy and his crew chief to take in the scene. A line of Hueys marched across the sky, all the way back to shore it almost seemed, while a steady stream of the air taxis lifted off from the various ships and headed back in along the northern air lane of the fleet.

The resourceful crew chief produced a Kodak instamatic and started snapping away.

"Looks like you're doing a magazine shoot!" Chance quipped.

"And in a magazine is exactly where these puppies are going to be! Right next to a big fat royalty check! Folks back home will pay big bucks for these!"

When he had exhausted his last frame of film the chief stowed his camera in his cargo pocket.

The brief show finished, the pilot checked the air space around them, pushed forward on the collective and headed back into shore at 125 knots.

Paddy Kelly

Although evacuation preparations had been underway since late March to institute one of the two or three evac plans, with three more back-ups on the board, the official word to commence the actual evacuation had only come down the pipe around 13:00 on the afternoon of the 29th, taking until about 14:00 to launch the first aircraft.

Guessing, back in March, it would take until dark to complete *Operation Frequent Wind*, the brass decided with the combined resources of fixed wing and rotary aircraft they had available that would easily allow them to be packed and out of Dodge by late that night.

As a famous game show host once said; "Wrong answer, thank you for playing!"

Those estimates were based on having an airfield and open roads neither of which was now the case.

Thanks to Ambassador Martin's piss poor administrative planning, General Westmoreland's underestimating the enemy and Richard Nixon's political shananigan's back home, Kean's taxis had become the last stagecoach out and all that stood beteween freedom and years in a communist 're-education camp'. Or public excecution.

It was well past dusk and less than a quarter of the people the Navy needed to evacuate had made it out.

Curiously the U.S. generals seemed to have overlooked the fact that very few of the local populace, especially the ones who had worked for the Americans for the last decade, were struck with the overwhelming desire to hang around for the commies to show up. You know those guys that became renown for raping, pillaging, plundering and metering out random torture to innocent civilians.

Curious feature of war - brutality.

So far Billy's crew had made two attempted runs to the remnants of the D.A.O., both aborted, three to the embassy and three to a small camp on the outskirts of Tan Son Nhut.

Now they were enroute to a small government supply building where a report came in that armed looters had several government civilian employees trapped on the roof. Possibly with one or more casualties.

As they found the building marked by yellow smoke released by the manager of the small facility, they were prevented from landing when the crowd over ran the parking lot in the rear of the building, the intended DZ.

"FUCK, SHIT PISS FUCK!" The crew chief cursed as they came close enough to make eye contact with the terified government employees. There was no mistaking the abject fear which contorted the faces of the three women and two older men as the out of control crowd crept up the side and back ladders and onto the roof to charge the victims.

The pilot pulled up on the collective to avoid the few crazed dare devils lunging at the skids. "FUCK, SHIT PISS FUCK!" The chief repeated his angry mantra as he produced an M-16 from the fire wall in back of the co-pilot's seat. He called into his head set to hold hover, slapped in a 20 round mag and switched to full auto. Two short bursts between the rioters and their intended prey convinced the rioters to seek revenge elsewhere. He reloaded and, with the weapon at the ready kept lookout as he guided the pilot down to within a few feet of the roof. Billy quickly helped the civilians into the chopper as an ambitious young man appeared over the rampart of the roof with a pistol. He took aim at the open door of the bird seconds before a small hole appeard on his forehead and the back of his skull exploded outwards.

With the employees loaded up the co-pilot smiled and gave the crew a thumbs up as they gained altitude and turned south towards the embassy. The crew cheif restowed the weapon.

"Got it from a jarhead on the last run. Figure if we were going down only fair I take a couple of the bastards with us!" The chief explained.

"Can't argue with that logic!" Billy concurred.

As the bird would now need fuel before the next trip and the crew were scheduled for a thirty minute break. Billy also decided he would finish up this run, sign some red bennies out of the pharmacy to keep awake until morning and then remain on board the Hancock to lend a hand vaccinating and in-processing evacuees as they were brought aboard.

Out in the fleet the rescuer's work woudn't be over until the thousands of civilians were searched for weapons and cleared by the M.P.'s, had been medically examined, innoculated and assigned an evacuation vessel. With most evacuees arriving with little or no I.D. it was impossible to know exactly who was being airlifted aboard and being granted transport to America.

Although the Hancock was the largest vessel in the Gulf at the time it had limited capacity to facilitate large numbers of civilians and so once *Operation Frequent Wind* was declared terminated, the evacuees could be parceled out to the rest of the task force for the ride to their new lives. Whatever those lives were going to be.

Unbeknownst to Billy and the crew as they unloaded their latest cashé of evacuees, they and all the other people risking their lives helping the citizens of the former Republic escape certain death were unaware of the ramifacations and the bigger picture of what they were doing.

State-wide protests from New York City to Los Angeles had erupted against the proposal to resettle America's former allies in the United States as the

Politically Erect

hallowed words engraved on the Statue of Liberty were swept under the rug.

Due largely to inaccurate, prejudicial and some out right slanted reporting by the corpoeate media in the U.S., few people back home knew of the contributions to the war effort these evcuees made.

As Saigon once again slowly crept through the encroaching dusk and came into view the chopper floated in over the city. The street and shop lights added a surrealism that was Biblical in nature.

Crowds slowly but steadily pushed and undulated towards the waterfront as if Moses himself were about to appear and part the South China Sea to allow the people to walk to the U.S. Seventh Fleet anchored off shore.

From that point on tens of thousands of South Vietnamese going to travel, attempting to travel and currently enroute, travelled by water craft of all descriptions, sampans, motor boats and small rubber rafts. With no guarantee of making it the five miles out to the fleet it was going to be a long night for many of the evacuees.

On shore, packed like cattle in a Chicago stockyard, they toted, hauled and dragged bundles of clothes, personal goods and oversized suitcases. Women struggled with children and elderly hobbled along with help from relatives.

"Now I know how the Israelites must'a felt leaving Egypt!" The crew chief, looking down from the side hatch mumbled into his head set.

Downtown several well dressed indig stood off to the sides of the street with open suitcases stuffed with, in lieu of clothing, cash. Some of them appeared to be stashing jewelry in the linings of the cases.

One short-sighted escapee fell to his knees and

screamed, thrown into shock when the rotor wash from another Huey passing low overhead blew nearly all the cash from his case, scattering it along the street.

No one scurried to snatch it up.

Warnings to the chopper pilots came over the radio from Fleet ops who were becoming increasingly obstructed by South Vietnamese pilots buzzing around the larger ships in a last ditch effort to find themselves and their family members some respite of sanctuary aboard one of the nearly four dozen American vessels spread across the Tonkin Golf. The flat tops *Midway* and *Hancock* appeared to be their preferred targets.

As if they had seen one too many NBC Saturday night news broadcasts of the nation-wide racial riots sweeping the U.S., the streets of Saigon mirrored Watts, Atlanta and Newark, New Jersey as the residents not concerned with escaping the oncoming commie hoard looted wildly, rummaging through furniture, clothing and various household goods strewn through the streets. No shop or storefront was safe.

The out dated fluorescent street lamps lent an eerie yellowish-white glow to the whole scene.

Former General now President Minh's caravan was rolling through the streets announcing the government's surrender, advising the people to acquiesce to the impending flood of communist troops.

Billy's UH-1H was currently ten minutes from their objective, the embassy. They had been contacted after launching with their next objective radioed to them enroute.

Talon One, Talon One this is U.S.S. Blueridge, how copy? Over.

"Blueridge Talon One here, good copy. Send traffic."

Talon One what is your status?

"Blueridge we are enroute to objective Echo, over."

Politically Erect

Talon One request you divert and proceed to following coordinates to evac several casualties of the Sierra Victor Alpha and transport to embassy for liaison with their commander. How copy?

"Blueridge, Talon One. You got an estimate on number of casualties to be evac'ed?"

Talon One, that's a negative. Report simply stated 'a couple' That is all. Are you ready to copy coordinates?

"Blueridge Talon One, roger. Send traffic. Over."

Proceed to Juliet 10492 78829. How copy Talon?

"Good copy Blueridge. Talon One enroute. Out."

With the coords copied, the ship headed for their objective a mere two miles away.

Twenty-five minutes later they were once more heading back out to the fleet with their chopper nearly empty. Onboard were Billy the crew chief, the pilot and co-pilot along with the two South Vietnamese Army casualties taken on board from a small camp just north of the now occupied D.A.O. All that was left of the fearless contingent of SVA who didn't run and shed their uniforms but stayed to fight the overwhelming combined NVA and PAVN forces pushing towards Saigon that evening. These two were the last of their battalion still alive.

Using the embassy as a way point they were about one mile out when they spotted two SVA in the middle of a broad intersection of the street. One was attending to the other who appeared to be wounded. As he looked up he waved the chopper in.

The pilot informed the crew they were going in and as they drifted to the side and began to lower altitude a barrage of shots ripped through the rear of the fuselage. They looked down and the two SVA had shedded their jackets and revealed they were NVA. They both opened fire on the Huey.

The chief quickly reacted with his M16 killing one and driving the other off but the ship was damaged.

"86 THIS SHIT!" The pilot yelled into his head set, pulled on the collective and banked left to climb out of small arms range but the ship only responded sluggishly. They managed to climb to 5000 feet but the tail rotor was respoding eraticaly.

"Plan B." The crew chief said to Chance.

"What's Plan B?" Billy asked.

"Get the fuck out'a here and try'n make it o the water!" Pulling on the collective the pilot climbed a bit further and headed east.

"Back to the Hancock?" Billy yelled over to the crew chief.

"Yeah but there's too much traffic on the main air lanes so we'll swing north, north east then drop back down once we're back out over the ocean."

"Sounds good to me!"

The crew chief, sitting across from Billy smiled and gave the thumbs up as he gazed back at the bullet holes peppered along the tail section.

His expression quickly melted to fear as seconds after leveling off the crew chief screamed into his head set.

The trail of the RPG 7 rocket etched aross the sky was more visible than the projectile itself now only a hundred meters out.

"INCOMING PORT SI-!"

The rocket hitting the fueselage was more of a loud thud but the detonation, which took a second or two, was deafening and the loss of control was instantaneous. They had been hit in the aft quarter of the passenger's compartment.

"MAYDAY, MAYDAY, MAYDAY! THIS IS TALON ONE WE'RE HIT! I SAY AGAIN TALON ONE HIT!"

Politically Erect

Under the counter force of the main rotor assembly and loss of the tail rotor the fuselage spun wildly flinging one casualty out the door along with the crew chief who now dangled ten feet below the craft by his monkey harness.

Chance followed close behind but was able to grab the door fame and fight his way back into the aircraft as they decended. Chance instinctivly dove on top of the remaing casualty to pin him to the deck while they autorotated in as the main blades maintained partial but weak lift capability.

Talon one, Talon one this is Blueridge, do you read? Over. Back on board the command ship static filled the airwaves.

Talon one, Talon one this Blueridge, do you read? Over.

After three to four minutes and several attempts at relay calls through other aircraft a call came into the radio shack aboard the *Hancock*.

Mother Goose, Mother Goose this is Talon. We are- The call was interrupted by the sound of small arms fire then cut off. For the next fifteen minutes only static followed.

From a distance, the survivng NVA soldier who helped ambush the helo, had watched the Huey spin down and crash behind a warehouse. He cheered as he observed the small plume of smoke and flames rise up. His victory was hardly noticeable to others as the chaos of the streets continued on into the night.

CVA-19, *U.S.S. Hancock*, pride of The Tonkin Gulf Yacht Club, TF76 on Yankee Station of the U.S. Seventh Fleet, had lost the last chopper of the war.

Paddy Kelly

*

As Major Kean was herding his troops into the lobby, a straggler from the Agricultural office made his way down from the roof to the incinerator room on the top floor. He found his colleague frantically throwing documents into the small burn oven. He poked his head in through the door.

"Jimmy, let's go! Birds are on the roof!" Jimmy frantically kept at his task.

"We're supposed to get all this shit burned before we leave!" He argued.

"That shit should have been burned a long time ago! We have to go now! Taxi's waiting, he's blowin' his horn! You coming or not?"

Jimmy quickly perused the stacks of classified documents on the tables and across the floor, looked over at his mate and mumbled.

"Fuck it! Let's get the hell out'a here!" He declared as he let the thick sheaf of of papers he held slip fom hi hand and scatter across the floor.

They took the steps up to the roof two at a time.

The stack of documents now littering the floor contained hundreds of names of indig South Vietnamese who had worked for or with the U.S. government as well as their former positions and the locations of their extended families.

Hundreds who had not made it to the embassy.

*

As the help lifts continued Major Kean was enroute through the crowded offices and hallways to a land line to take a call from Fleet Command. The significance of

Politically Erect

the fact that Fleet Command appeared to have by-passed the Ambassador was not lost on the Major.

"Major Kean here sir."

"Major Kean, this is Vice Admiral Keller, Deputy Fleet Commander."

"Yes Admiral?"

"From this point forward U.S. military and civilian personnel **only** are to be allowed to board your aircraft! Is that understood Major Kean?"

"Admiral sir, there's still eight, nine hundred people down there including some 300 plus Koreans!" There was a short silence. "This is non-negotiable Major! This is by order of Admiral Weisner but it comes straight from the White House. You have your orders!"

Shit!

"Is that understood Major?"

"Yes sir. Understood."

Kean hung up and looked out to the people sleeping on the floors, at their desks and some on top of one another waiting to be called to the roof.

By one o'clock in the morning some of the car batteries down on the LZ had started to fade threatening the night ops however this became immaterial as the choppers had to refuel after running constant sorties for the better part of thirteen to fourteen hours.

The limited number of birds in the fleet, totalling about 100 in all, combind with the secondary commitments to a few coastal areas, further restricted the ability of pilots to rotate machines in any organized fashion. That is the pilots who had managed twenty to thirty minutes rest between runs and were considered still capapble of competent flight.

Paddy Kelly

All this taken into account, there was still one seemingly insurmountable obstacle at the embassy. Only LZ space to accommodate one CH-53 and one Huey.

There was however one stroke of luck which went their way; by around 03:45 the compound crowd had been reduced to the point where everyone was able to fit inside the embassy building.

Now Kean had another critical decision to make: Keep the 53's coming into the parking lot and hope the crowd doesn't break through the perimeter too soon and storm the place, or squeeze everyone left into the building which would make fighting off the crowd or the enemy, when they did eventually break through the gates, near impossible.

Fortunately, although there was little doubt come day light the walls would be breached, the darkness and quiet also seemed to quiet the outside crowd somewhat.

Making his way to the furthest machine gun outpost in the parking lot Kean continued his command and control role as C.O.

"Corporal, all the remaining civilians are now in the Chancery building so disengage and station yourself and your fire team around the front door. I'm going to pass the word to start bring the perimeter in. When the others arrive set up an arching perimeter with your squad and then I'll start filing the Marines inside."

"Aye aye sir!" The corporal threw his M-60 over his shoulder. "Come on Pruitt!" He ordered his assistant gunner and ammo bearer.

"Where to Biggs?"

"The fucking Alamo brother!" They took off at a dead run for the front of the embassy a hundred and fifty meters away.

Kean rotated through the posts and over the next twenty minutes gradually shrank the perimeter all the way back until all four abbreviated squads were up against the building itself.

A couple of civilians perched in trees outside the walls watched as Kean's Marines conducted their orderly withdrawal. Panic masked their faces and a couple of them yelled out loudly in Vietnamese.

The loud rumbling of the wave of humanity throwing itself against the front gates woke those in the street crowd who were resting or sleeping.

The black wroght iron gates began to heave and the din of the mob grew louder.

It was the point Kean had dreaded but expected.

From just inside the main entrance in the vestibule, through the glass front doors, Kean surveyed the situation. He pushed the door open and stepped back outside. All eyes of the remaining troops were glued to Kean.

"ON MY COMMAND, IN AN ORDERLY FASHION! WEAPONS OUT BOARD! RETREAT INTO THE BUILDING!" Kean stood off to the side of the double doors as his men carried out his command.

Another Huey landed up on the roof.

At the same time people began to appear at the top of the perimeter wall at multiple locations.

"DO NOT FIRE WITHOUT THE ORDER!!" He yelled.

To keep shouting to a minimum he manually directed the men in towards the main entrance of the building and this maneuver quickly filled the foyer.

"File to the stair well and make your way up. DO NOT use the elevators! Head up and make your way to the roof. No elevators!" He instructed as his men slipped into the building. The lead marines started up the seven flights of stairs.

By now it was around half four in the morning and they realized the sun would be breaking soon prompting the thousands outside the wall to become more bold, but the Marines had no desire to create a massacre.

"Is everyone inside?" Kean asked to no one in particular just as three crazed locals ran up and started banging on the reinforced glass of the front doors. One held a death grip on a trombone. Kean and the Seabee chief standing next to him exchanged shrugs. Another brandished two fists full of cash trying to buy his way in.

"Sergeant!" He waved the NCO over as the organized mob in the lobby gradually ebbed up the stairs. "Detail four men to take up our six and have them sweep each floor for stragglers. When finished have them secure all the stairwell doors with whatever they can find. Report to me when they give you the all clear!"

"Yes sir." The sergeant moved out.

Spotting the senior Seabee across the lobby Kean made his way through the fifteen or twenty marines and over to him.

"Chief, do your men have the ability to lock the elevators in place?"

"Roger that sir, we can do that!"

"Lock them n the top floor! Make it happen!"

Just then a loud crash was heard outside the gates. Both men turned to see a giant water tanker being used to bash into the gates which didn't immediately buckle but were defiantly not going to hold for long under the weight of the industrial vehicle. The driver backed the four ton lorry up and shifted into drive for another go.

"Shit!" Kean looked up through the stairwell. The first through the third floor stair cases were clear and the evacuees seemed to be moving at a slow reasonably good pace upwards.

Politically Erect

"We'll get it done Major! Meet you on the roof!" The chief replied as he took off.

Outside the compound the sporadic small arms fire was now continuous as they pushed their way up the narrow stair case. One young Marine turned to an NCO behind him, controlled apprehension laced his words.

"That the Cong outside shootin'?" The young Marine asked as they made their way upstairs.

"If it is they got a helluv'a surprise if they come knocking on this door!" He tapped his 203 grenade launcher and smiled.

"Who's got tear gas?!" Kean, now quickly moving upstairs yelled out.

"Here sir!" A Corporal worked his way back down trough the people with several canisters of CS gas. "Come behind us and wait until the repel team has finished jamming the door. Pop one canister down the stairwell then follow up. Wait on level four until you hear them coming in and pop another then meet us on the roof landing. We need to buy time."

"Roger that Major!"

The two man repel team was just finishing up barricading the front doors with some broken railings, chairs and fire extinguishers they had scrounged, jamming them through the panic bars. But with the large glass panels it was obvious it was a temporary measure to delay the swelling and advancing half mad crowd.

Just as the team ran to the staircase the first glass panel was smashed and the corporal let go the first canister of CS and ran up behind the team. The broken glass acted as a ventilator sucking the pungent gas out into the crowd and temporarily forcing them back.

A long fifteen minutes later Kean's contingent finally made it to the roof where, save for the ten Marines with him, the last of the military personnel, to include the Chief and his Seabees, were just lifting off from the helo pad.

By this time the only thing restricting more people from cramming into the embassy grounds were the some 10,000 people already filling the compound. The rioters had now smashed through the doors, inundated the Chancery building and filling the lobby and stair wells all the way to the third and fourth floors.

More CS drifted down the stairwell and the improvised masks of tee shirts and scarves did little to stop the chocking and vomiting of the lead rioters.

The last ten Marines and Kean took the top steps two at a time until they reached the roof where they would have to wait for a chopper.

Unaware of how long it would take for the exhausted pilots to rest and refuel, they could hear the enraged mob getting louder as it drew closer.

"Top, grab these timbers and shore up the door!"

They popped their last canister of CS and tossed it down the stair well.

The fire door to the roof was a sheet metal skin on an angle iron frame which opened out onto the roof. *Not an ideal barricade*, thought Kean.

"Keep away from the roof's edge. When the chopper arrives jettison your flak gear and helmets before you board! Weight's going to be a consideration! Everybody got that!" They sounded off in the affirmative and gave the thumbs up. "All right, fan out around the door. Then I want two men in each of the southern corners as look outs. Sound off when you see the bird!" Two marines scurried to the closest corners of the building.

Having done all they could the Marines hunkered down and waited. No one spoke as they waited and listened.

Politically Erect

The din of the melee below in the streets suddenly began to fade as each man stared alternately at the metal fire door and then out at the horizon.

Gradually hurried footsteps could be heard ascending the stairs and voices grew louder. Kean stepped over and gave the timber shoring against the door a hard kick to secure it just a little more.

Little by little the screaming of the crowd encased in the stairwell got louder.

Just then hard banging started from behind the door, but it held fast. It was obvious there were more than a few persons attempting to break out into the roof.

"Lock and load!" Kean ordered and only one of the men had to follow the order. The others had never ejected their magazines.

"If they breach the door don't fire until I give the order. Is that clear?" He ordered as he readied his .45.

"Yes sir!" Top Valdez, squatted behind a roof fixture with his .45 also aimed at the steel door. He looked over at a young lance corporal hugging his M16, eyes wide with anticipation.

"Johnson!" Valdez called over catching the kid's attention.

"It's gonna be okay." The corporal smiled back and nodded. "This war story is gonna get yur ugly ass some pussy!"

"I know Top. Least I'll have something to tell my kids!"

Valdez smiled.

"Top!" Kean yelled over. "Detail a couple of men to do a quick scan over the edge and around the perimeter! Make sure no clever asshole is trying to scale the wall!"

Valdez pointed to two men on either side of the penthouse containing the elevator machinery and the four Marines quickly moved out. Rifles at the ready the two teams scurried along behind the three foot ledge peering down the side of the building every ten feet or so.

They double timed it back to where the rest were huddled facing the door and reported all clear to Top Valdez.

After what seemed like an Orwellian hour the interminable wait was over as the slap of helicopter blades was heard in the distance. Like an isolated clan of Meerkats on the desolate plains of the Kalahari virtually the entire remaining Marine contingent popped their heads up over the roof's ledge. A broad smile crept across Kean's face. There was a CH-46 inbound.

The roof door seemed to be holding.

Not quite able to touch down completely and delicately maneuvering so as to avoid rotor contact with the penthouse machinery housing on the roof, the bird came to rest hovering a few feet off the ground with his ramp parallel to the deck.

"Alright gentlemen, maintain weapons accountability, dump your pots and flak gear!"

With his hand on the kid's shoulder as they lined up to climb into the chopper Valdez leaned into the lance corporal and yelled above the rotor wash. "They had to come back! You got any idea how bad it would look on the *Six O'clock News* if they left us here?"

"Yeah! Eleven marines kill ten thousad indig! Not a pretty headline."

Kean was the last Marine to climb up onto the ramp, the crew chief radioed the pilots and the Chinook lifted off with a 180 loop around and tilted towards the sea.

Twisting around to peer out the port hole behind his seat Kean watched as the desperately enraged crowd broke through the fire door and spilled out onto the roof.

Politically Erect

One indig picked up a flak vest and hurled at the climbing chopper.

Major Kean never harbored a doubt about a chopper making it back to the roof top to rescue them. He, as well as every Marine with him however wasn't as confident about the trip back out over the city to the fleet.

Just over an hour later Major Kean, the last man to get off the CH-46 stepped foot onto the deck of the *U.S.S. Okinawa*.

It was approximately 09:30 in the morning.

[*]

Word had been relayed from the fleet to the DAO HQ compound at 14:00 on the 29th of April, 1975 to commence *Operation Frequent Wind* and less than 48 hours later the safe evacuation and escape from the onslaught of the godless Commie hoards was finished.

Operation Ho Chi Min, the forced retreat and evacuation of the white foreign devils who had occupied their country for nearly a century, was complete.

For four years Billy Chance had done everything within his power to catch up to the war. Ironically it was in the waning days of Viet Nam that Billy had found the war he was looking for.

[*]

Paddy Kelly

**ASK NOT WHAT YOUR HEAD CAN DO FOR YOU,
BUT WHAT YOU CAN DO FOR YOUR HEAD.**

Politically Erect

CHAPTER TWENTY

The rain hadn't abated for eight days and the difficulties of negotiating the muddy road were compounded by the current unrelenting, driving rain, which was loud enough to compel the passengers to shout. It might have been the 21st century with eight lane, paved highways somewhere, but in this part of the world, it sure as hell was still the 19th Century.

"They said up near the Myanmer border!"

"Where the fuck is My-na-meer!?"

"Burma, Colonel sir. You call it Burma!"

Despite their state-of-the-art rain gear, and the fact that the vehicle had a canvas roof, the four men in the refurbished 1944 Willy's Jeep were soaked to the bone.

The density of the ancient, tropical forest precluded visibility beyond 50 meters to either side of the pock marked road and, due to the mountainous terrain straight stretches were all but non existent.

"Did the consul say **near** the border or **on** the border, god damn it!"

"Near the border, sir!"

"Are there checkpoints?"

"Not this far out."

"Then how the fuck we gonna know when we're at the border?!" The Colonel held fast to the dashboard as they took a sharp turn.

"If we pass Vientiane Colonel sir, then we are in Laos." The translator/guide offered from the back seat.

"**Then** what'a we do, god-damn it?!"

"We turn around and go back, Colonel sir." The colonel shook his head in dismay.

Paddy Kelly

"This has to be the only god damned place on earth no matter which way you go you kin only see the forest from the trees!" The officer cursed.

On board the jeep ride from hell was a junior liaison officer from the U. S. Embassy, who looked as if he needed his mother's permission to stay out after dark, a full bird Colonel dressed in civvies from the U.S. Army Military Police who had a face like a barnacle on the hull of battleship and their lanky, bespecled translator appointed by the Thai government at the request of the Pentagon through the U. S. embassy. All dressed in civilian attire.

The driver was a pissed off M. P. sergeant who drew the short straw back down in Bangkok.

"Colonel sir, may I suggest we continue on route #2020 then proceed to the Tha Bo District village. Once there I can talk to the district elder. If your man is anywhere in the district he will certainly know."

"Awright, do it." The Colonel spat out the window but the wind blew the wad back into the jeep and onto his trousers.

"SUM-BITCH!" He cursed.

The embassy liaison read from a manila folder as he bounced around the back seat like an over sized pinball.

"Sir, this guy's a deserter, from the Viet Nam War?! That was three and half, four decades ago! How do we know he's not just a KIA?"

"He disappeared thirty–nine years ago, and we're not sure he's not a deserter. We don't even know if he was really in the military, we're still running checks on that."

"What's the point after so many years?"

"The point is Mr. Liaison, that they's a suspected loss of over $100,000 in military medical equipment unaccounted for. In 1975 dollars! Combine that with a suspected dee-serter, aidin' and abettin' the enemy during

Politically Erect

time of war and that amounts to the death penalty, plain and simple. If this soldier is out here, we gonna find him and bring his ass back! That's what I get paid for!"

"Then why the hell am I here?" The liaison miserably protested as they hit another rut and his ass went six inches off the seat.

"To keep the locals off my back! That's what you get paid for."

They rounded a bend and suddenly the terrain opened up into semi-flat lands dominated by row after row of flooded rice paddies sloped up and down the mountains. Off to the left they passed a large hand dug, flooded water basin apparently used to irrigate the fields in the dry season. A few klicks off to the left they spotted a village.

"Sergeant, turn here please." The translator requested.

"Yes sir" They slowed down as they approached the small hamlet and the translator flagged down a colourfully dressed woman with a large laundry basket strapped across her forehead and slung behind her back. The translator had a brief conversation with her and then thanked her.

"Ban Chang Nam. It's the school. The Pay Sot, he stays near the school!" He pointed ahead and to the right.

"Pay Sot?! What the hell is a Pay Sot?!"

"Pay Sot Chuk-on. It means Medicine Man! That's what they call him Colonel sir."

"Medicine Man?! What the fuck is this, a King Kong movie?!"

"That's the name they call him Colonel sir." He apologetically reiterated.

"Let's fuckin' go!" The Colonel ordered.

They drove another hundred meters and on the right they came on the school building nestled amongst a heavy cluster of large palm and Aglaia with Xylia and Durian trees interspersed between them.

"Pull in here." The Colonel directed as they approached a small, shaded drive.

"They tell me his real name is actually Fortune or something like that?" The liaison asked as they dismounted the jeep.

"Chance, William Joseph Chance. Former Special Forces, supposedly."

Half naked, young children ran screaming amok the school grounds playing as several brightly garbed, elderly women laid out baskets of fruit across long narrow tables in the shade of the trees.

"Sergeant, you and the others stand by the jeep. I'll call if I need you."

"Yes sir." The Colonel headed around back of the school while the driver lit up a cigarette.

"You might need a translator sir!"

"I'll call you if I do!"

The school building was a green, corrugated roofed, open plan structure which looked to hold about fifty or sixty kids. Long, hand-made benches served as seats and there were no desks, just individual black slates placed in neat rows along the benches, each with a lump of white chalk on top. A small table in the center front of the space stood in front of a long, tall slate hung on the front wall. Neatly drawn Thai characters decorated one half the board while the other side, showed shaky, smaller characters lower down on the board. Under each word was it's rough English equivalent.

On the opposite side, sitting perpendicular to the school the Colonel found a similarly built, 'L' shaped building albeit closed in with walls lending it a more Western conventional type appearance. A short thick red

Politically Erect

cross painted next to a similar sized, red crescent moon adorned the transom above the door.

He let himself in and was surprised to see several native nurses in starched white uniforms and caps scurrying about the long corridor in and out of a half dozen rooms off to each side. He passed down the corridor towards the short leg of the 'L' with slow deliberation. Being an officer he couldn't help but notice the military neatness and immaculate nature of the place.

Small, hand painted signs in Thai and English denoted the various departments of the jungle dispensary.

How in the hell did a cowardly deserter wind up in a place like this? The Officer pondered.

At the far end of the short leg of the building he found the 'office'.

As in the rest of the compound, indeed the entire hamlet, the door was unlocked so he let himself in and, fancying himself a detective, began to snoop.

It was more of a library than an office. The right hand wall was stacked ceiling to about three feet off the floor with medical books. The wall opposite likewise but with literary classics, non-fiction, history and a complete collection of some paperbacks called *Casca*.

He grunted a sneer of derision as he picked a copy of Mao's *Little Red Book* from the shelf and quickly replaced it least his hand become contaminated.

All the remainder of the wall space was covered with various photos of Thai, Laotian and Burmese award ceremonies featuring an unknown westerner. Ribbons and plaques were stuck here and there where ever they'd fit. The desk on the far side of the room had various stationary and medical files, a singular ocular microscope, from The Fifties guessed the Colonel, a

Merck Manual, a *Physician's Desk Reference* and the little green *Special Forces Medic's Handbook*. Next to this brief collection stood a photograph in a gold frame.

The snap was of two children, both girls. The eight to ten year old in an oversized tee shirt was holding a young infant in pink pyjamas with penguins on the bottoms.

Catty cornered from where the colonel came in was a second entrance to the office to allow direct access from the outside and that door now swung open with a bang. The Colonel jumped at the dishevelled figure, a white man, draped with military canvas bags which stumbled his way through the doorway. The officer quickly replaced the photograph looking the man up and down.

"AHH! A Farang! Huan ma Farang!" The 60-something guy coming in greeted with a big smile and a slight bow. "A white man." He clarified.

"Chance, William Joseph Chance?" Snapped the Colonel.

"Chance!" He repeated. "Now that's a name I have not heard in a very long time!" He smiled at the colonel who showed no reaction. "Not a Star Wars fan huh?"

"What the hell you talking about boy?!"

"We get films in from the capital a couple times a month."

Billy, who had clearly not showered for several days, hesitated then smirked at the visitor. He sat the several medical supply bags on the floor next to the door, removed his Thai army issue jacket and web belt and hung them on a wall rack near the door. A teenaged Thai boy came in behind him lugging a large, portable lab kit which appeared to weigh more then he did.

"Can I offer you a cup of tea, Captain? Coffee's a bit scarce in these parts ever since the French left."

"No, thank you. And it's Colonel, Sergeant."

Politically Erect

"Colonel! I'm impressed!"

"I was a Captain when I first came across your file at C. I. D." He corrected. "I vowed then I'd find you."

"I didn't realize I was lost." As Billy moved to the other side of the room the Colonel eased his hand to the 9mm Beretta slung low on his hip John Wayne style. Billy looked back at him and smirked. *They never change*, he mused as he began to pour some already brewed tea while politely addressing the boy in Thai who set the lab kit on the floor. The boy then carefully opened it and removed a rack of blood samples, asked a question which Billy answered in the affirmative and the boy left with the rack of test tubes.

"Blood samples, for parasites. Hope you don't mind cold tea. We've only the one generator and that's reserved for the surgical suit and main wards." The Colonel didn't reach for the tea.

An exhausted Billy motioned for the officer to have a seat as he set the tea on a small table and moved to plop down behind his rough hewn desk.

"Beautiful grounds you got here, sergeant."

"Not mine Colonel. Belongs to the village."

Through the windows the Colonel noticed the villagers going about their business as the rains began to let up. "Trees were all transplanted in the Fifties. First to keep the Chinese from bombing the school, then the French and finally the Americans. Back then everything north of Route 202 was jungle but the village was considered an open target. After all, what better way to win a war then by killing all the kids, eh? No future fighters." The officer indicated Chance's hiking gear and the medical supplies as he spoke.

"You've been travelling?"

"We rotate weekly medical patrols between the Akha, Lahu and Karen tribes. The Hmong, Mien and Yao are too far out so we can only visit them two, maybe three times a month."

"You don't mind me askin', how you get around these territories, sergeant?"

"There's half a dozen vehicles between the provinces. The elders decreed that anyone who owns a vehicle is obligated to drive me on a rotational basis." The army man glanced down at the tea but made no move to touch it. "We have to keep the roster locked up. Last month alone we caught three different guys tampering with it."

"Nobody wants the shit duty, eh?"

"On the contrary. They wanted to move up the list. They considerate an honor! They feel it upgrades their karma."

The Colonel eyed a young, pretty nurse as she entered with a plate of fruit and nuts.

"You seem to have plenty of help."

"If you wish hot meal one ready in thirty minutes, Pay Sot Chuk." The young, petite nurse informed him.

"Ka khoon klap, Sumalee." Billy thanked her. "The medical personnel, seven nurses, three medics and four orderlies, all came out of Ban Trang Nam school next door."

"Where'd they go to school?"

"Ban Trang. Next door."

"No, I mean to learn Medicine!"

"Come on Colonel, you read my file. I trained them."

"You trained all of them?!"

"Everyone here. Then they train others. Primary mission of Special Forces, to act as a force multiplier. I thought you would have known that, sir."

"I find that hard to believe Chance!" Billy took another sip of his tea and smiled at the Colonel's naivety.

Politically Erect

"My Philosophy prof back in New York used to say, 'The less you know, the more you believe.'" The army officer wasn't amused. "Starting this year I've convinced the provincial governor to convince the King to allow two medical students from Chulalongkorn University down in Bangkok to spend their Summers here training and working."

"Am I supposed to be impressed?"

"You should be, but it's not really important if you aren't." Chance's tone took on a slight, mockingly dramatic air. "No doubt you came up here looking for a traitor, a deserter. A thief. A common criminal who betrayed his country in her time of need! Sorry to disappoint you, Colonel."

"The Army reckons you stole $100,000 of U.S. government medical supplies and equipment from them."

"Ignoring the fact that government contractors jack up their prices to rape the taxpayer of those great United States, then tack on another 20% to grease the palms of the senators who get them those contracts, $100,000 is a little unrealistic colonel. However, accepting your premise that all that gear and medication was stolen, the price of which is about the cost of a surgeon's fee alone for your average boob job in The States, it would be the CIA you'd have to arrest because everything that was used to launch this operation was bought with hard currency on the black market which flourished all over these parts, compliments of The Agency. Or is it the Company? Or the Firm? What'a we calling the spooks these days?"

"Chance, you know why I'm here?"

Paddy Kelly

"Your civvies are no disguise Colonel. I was told the American military police were here long before you drove up. I don't need anyone to draw me a map."

The Colonel sat up, leaned his arms on his knees and looked down at the floor.

"I'm Supposed ta take your ass back to stand trial for desertion. If you're found guilty –"

"Take me back? Take me back to what? The chaos of a country where the system of government dictates that anybody can have anything, as long as they can afford it? A system where the leaders lie, cheat, steal, fuck and kill to move up? Every department of every branch of your government has been rocked by major political scandals and corruption since the war and not a one works like it's supposed to!" Billy took his feet down off the desk and sat up straight.

"Take me back to a system that in the end is about failing to measure up to the government's system regarding race, creed or national origin? These people don't care if I got an A in physics, Statistical Analysis or if I spent half my life in medical school! They care if I can make their pain go away so they can get on with the business of eeking out a subsistance living by farming. Get on with loving their wives and sweethearts, feeding their families and avoiding the next war to come ripping through these hills and mountains."

The colonel remained unimpressed as Billy continued.

"Oh I know what you're gonna say, 'It's like that everywhere!' Well I got a news flash for ya sir; no it's not! And you know what?! Even if it were, America's supposed to be different. But it ain't. It ain't like that everywhere and America ain't different from the Third World countries it so sanctimoniously condemns. Not only that, it's worse because it pretends to be better!"

Politically Erect

"Don't give me any of your sanctimonious -"

"When I was a boy everybody used to say, 'America's different. America's not like other countries. We honor our commitments!' Now everyone says, 'Oh yeah, that happens here. But it happens everywhere else too!' That's the current logic. 'It happens everywhere!' Horseshit! Right is right no matter if nobody does it and wrong is wrong no matter if everybody does it!"

Billy nonchalantly crossed the room and refilled his tea cup then sat by the window, focusing on not getting too worked up.

"In 1971, dicounting the 57,000 American lives lost and the 100,000 crippled for life, the U.S. Navy reported a 97% divorce rate amongst its troops. Less than a year later Tricky Dick announced the war was over. Tens of thousands of broken families, all those damaged kids for nothing! The welfare of millions of people in half a dozen countries was subverted, marginalized and sacrificed so one sweaty-lipped bastard could get re-elected. And what happened when he got re-elected? He turned out to be the biggest lying, thieving bastard of all! You think that clown you got incharge now is any better just becaue he's half black? He a Chicago democrat fer fuck's sake! Daley and his gang taught the Mafia!"

Sensing an increasing intensity in Chance's mood, the Colonel slowly pushed up from his chair and stood.

"Ya know colonel, most guys get Dear John letters while they're away. Mine was different. She fucked a lawyer on the side. Got him to do all the paper work and when I came home on leave the divorce papers were sittin' on my desk, signed sealed and delivered. There was no contest. I was divorced."

Billy stood to confront the army cop.

"So beacause your wife bailed on you, you deserted?"

"Viet Nam was nothing more than a 26 year sneak preview of Afghanistan. We promised these people help and then reneged. Just like you're gonna do over there. Pull out half way to orgasm!" He drained his cup and sat it down on the window sill. "Life's a circle Colonel. So's history. Well, I became sick of riding the merry-go-round! I decided to break the circle. Set my own destiny."

As Chance walked back to his desk the Colonel noticed some commotion outside. Just then the Liaison burst through the ward side door.

"Colonel, we have a problem!" The Colonel, with the Liaison close behind, darted to the office window.

Out side, the dispensary was surrounded on all sides by hundreds of locals, ominously armed with farm implements, machetes and clubs. The lone M.P., his 9mm side arm drawn, was slowly climbing out of the jeep and carefully backing towards the hospital door as the Thai translator scurried around him and darted inside. The Colonel cursed under his breath. In shear panic the young liaison turned to the translator, calling him by name.

"Piyawat! Do something! We're in trouble here!" The translator was already halfway on his way to the other door which led to the wards to seek refuge as he spoke.

"What's this 'we' shit white man? This is your fight!"

Billy, finally calm, sighed and walked to the exit door casually holding it open for his guests.

"You can't just kill us!" The liaison blurted out.

"I don't take lives anymore. Only save them. Besides, I have nothing to do with this. This is their country. You're the intruders here. You want me? Negotiate with them." The officer and the liaison exchanged glances. "Either of you guys speak Thai?" Chance asked. There

Politically Erect

was no reaction. "If you leave now, I'll guarantee your safety."

The liaison dashed through the rear door but stopped just out side and yelled.

"SERGEANT, START THE JEEP!" The confused driver eased back towards the vehicle, weapon still drawn and obeyed. The angry colonel took his time but followed suit.

As he stepped through the doorway his face passed within inches of Billy's who still held open the door.

"You ain't heard the last of this, sergeant Chance!"

"Sir, all I know is as long as I die here, and not over there, I win. And it's Pay Sot Chuk-on, not sergeant."

When the three were in the jeep the Colonel looked back at Chance who stood on the top step of the doorway, his hands folded in front of him in his Thai Special Forces tee shirt, stethoscope folded around his neck. They locked eyes. Neither smiled, neither blinked.

To the occupants of the jeep, surrounded by hostiles, it seemed the seasons moved faster then did that vehicle. All eyes stared straight ahead as they slowly backed through the parting crowd of tightly packed, little brown bodies and sat perfectly still as if a sneeze would be their last act on earth.

Chance watched as the jeep rolled off the small, grassy drive, turned and headed out of the village. He then went back inside, around to his desk, picked a bottle of Irish whiskey off the shelf and poured some into his tea cup. He kicked his feet back up on the desk.

Billy glanced over his shoulder and out the window as the crowd began to dissipate.

"Man's gotta make his mark, even if it's only scribble." He whispered to the empty office. He glanced at his watch. *Time for a quick meal and then rounds.* He told himself. "Opressor liber!" He said as he threw back the drink, replaced the bottle and headed for the kitchen.

A short time later, out on the road south, the M.P. driver was able to put it in third gear and three pairs of eyes which had been fixed on the side mirrors watching the village fade into the distance behind them, relaxed and all breathed a sigh of relief but it was a good twenty minutes before anyone spoke.

"What'a we do now sir?" Asked the shaken sergeant.

"Nothing. There's nothing to do."

"I'll report this to the Ambassador as soon as we're back in Bangkok Colonel!" The liaison bravely touted.

"No you won't."

"Sir?!"

"You'll report it? To what end? You think the Army's gonna send more troops up here and risk an international incident? For one 'suspected' criminal? Ya wanna start another god damned war over here over a delusional medic!"

"We can get Thai troops to take care of it! He's an illegal alien!"

"WE DON'T KNOW THAT FOR SURE! LOOK PRETTY FUCKIN' STUPID IF HE HAS THAI, LAOTIAN OR CAMBODE CITIZENSHIP NOW, WOULDN'T IT?"

"I could find out!" The liaison protested. The colonel ignored him.

As they cleared the open country of the province and reached the wooded area along Route #2020 the formally shaken sergeant regained his macho bravado as well.

"I don't understand sir. He's a war criminal! We can't just let him get away!" The extremely pissed off Colonel turned and addressed the liaison.

"You'll report that it was a false lead. There was no ex Green Beret up here. Are we clear?" The offended

Politically Erect

liaison stared out the window. "Are we green ambassador man?!" The colonel pshed. The liaison gave a weak nod. "And private, as far as you're concerned, this never happened."

"My rank is sergeant sir!" The driver protested.

"Not if I get wind you opened your mouth!" The Colonel lit a cigar, kicked his feet up on the dashboard, slid down in his seat and stared out the open side of the jeep.

Fuck! It's all one big FUBAR anyway! The Colonel rationalized to himself as they drove south.

Sitting at his desk Billy's mind wandered also.

In 1971, back in City University of New York Professor Carroll never mentioned that no matter where the protagonist started from, he never wound up where he thought he was going to. Or that, just as those wily ancient Greeks intended, the journey was never real.

Only this journey wasn't metaphorical. It was real and Billy Chance found out the hard way, as is usually the case, war doesn't decide who wins or loses.

It only decides who's left.

*

THE END

EPILOGUE

The politicians who answered the call of duty to serve their country in time of war, Kennedy, Kerry, McCain etc . . . all seemed to wind up politically fucked one way or the other.

Those who turned yellow, 'Tailgunner' Joe McCarthy, George W., who bailed on his Air National Guard contract when it looked as if his unit might be activated, 'Slick Willie' Clinton who ran to England to go to school to avoid joining up and was too stupid to know you're supposed to inhale when you smoke dope, all came out on top of the heap. The shit heap that is Washington D.C.

Moral of the story? If you're gonna go into American politics, wait until there's a war, you never have to wait long, then take advantage by signing up and not going. You'll make senator at least. Run away and you'll have a shot at President.

All the people who evaded military service but rose to the halls of power did little, once they got there, in the way of significantly improving the American health care system.

There is however one crevice of humanity in American medicine where the AMA haven't sunk its talons into - the U.S. Navy Hospital Corps. True also for the other branches.

To be treated at a Naval Medical facility, from hangnail to cancer, you show up, show your I.D. card and get treated. This includes your exam, diagnosis, treatment and follow-up.

Without exception the members of the U.S.N. Hospital Corps, the only enlisted corps in the entire United States military, are trained to treat and stabilize any emergency trauma situation until evacuation to a competent medical facility can be provided.

Politically Erect

I personally find solacae in the fact that any casualty that was breathing when I arrived at a scene, whether it was when I was with the Navy, the Corps or Special Forces, was still breathing after I treated them and got them on the evac chopper, boat or ambulanece.

I put that down solely to our training. We were trained to keep the patient alive until they could be transported to a competent medical facilty when still others who were the best in the world at getting them through the worst of it, back on their feet and into society as soon as possible took over.

It is for this reason alone that it is common to find personnel of all ranks at ease taking instructions from U.S. Navy enlisted medical personnel. I, as an HM2 and later as a sergeant, have personally treated admirals and generals.

Consequently both the enlisted and commissioned population have come to hold a special trust in the U.S. Navy's Hospital Corpsmen.

*

Paddy Kelly

Also by Paddy Kelly

Operation Underworld

The American Way

Don't Eat to Live. Live to Eat!
(A Book of Recipes)

American Rhetoric

There's An App For That!

There's An App For That Too!

Kelly's Full House

Politically Erect

Ghost Story
(A play)

Synopsis, purchsing or option information
available on line at:
paddykellywriter.com or at
paddy.incanto@gmail.com

Politically Erect